THE FATHERS OF THE CHURCH

A NEW TRANSLATION

VOLUME 57

THE FATHERS OF THE CHURCH

A NEW TRANSLATION

THE HOMILIES OF SAINT JEROME

Volume 2
(Homilies 60-96)

Translated by
SISTER MARIE LIGUORI EWALD, I.H.M.

Marygrove College
Detroit, Michigan

THE CATHOLIC UNIVERSITY OF AMERICA PRESS
Washington, D. C. 20017

NIHIL OBSTAT:

REVEREND JOHN C. SELNER, S.S.
Censor Librorum

IMPRIMATUR:

✠PATRICK A. O'BOYLE
Archbishop of Washington

November 18, 1965

The *nihil obstat* and *imprimatur* are official declarations that a book or pamphlet is free of doctrinal or moral error. No implication is contained therein that those who have granted the *nihil obstat* and *imprimatur* agree with the contents, opinions, or statements expressed.

Library of Congress Catalog Card No.: 64-13360

To

SISTER M. HONORA

CONTENTS

Page

VARIOUS HOMILIES

INTRODUCTION

IN THIS VOLUME of the *Homilies of Saint Jerome*, there are fifteen homilies of a second series on the Psalms, Homilies 60-74; ten homilies on St. Mark's Gospel, Homilies 75-84; and twelve homilies touching on a variety of topics, Homilies 85-96. In general, as in Volume 1, Morin's text has been followed as reproduced in the *Corpus Christianorum, series latina*, 78: *S. Hieronymi Presbyteri tractatus sive homiliae in Psalmos, in Marci Evangelium aliaque varia argumenta.*

The editors of the *Corpus* have added two homilies, one delivered on the Feast of the Epiphany from the Gospel of our Lord's baptism and on Psalm 28, edited by B. Capelle; the other on the First Sunday of Lent, edited by I. Fraipont. In the present volume, they are Homilies 89 and 90.

Dom Germain Morin, as noted in the Introduction[1] of Volume 1 of this translation, discovered fourteen homilies, providing a second series on the Psalms, in four Italian Codices dating from the tenth and fifteenth centuries. He examined with great care their probable identity with, or relationship to, the lost homilies of St. Jerome catalogued in *De viris illustribus*: 'on the Psalms, from the tenth to the sixteenth, seven homilies.'[2] There is more work to be done and many problems to be resolved, however, before this identification can be established with certitude. The chief obstacle is that of chronology. The *De viris illustribus* was written in all probability in 392-393, whereas the homilies appear to have been written in 402,

1 Volume 1 (Vol. 48, this series) contains 59 Homilies on Psalms 1-149; also a general introduction to all of the material contained in that and the present volume.

2 *De viris illustribus* 135, PL 23.758 (956).

the date determined by the study of Dom Morin. Other scholars, as U. Moricca, A. Penna, G. Grützmacher, give 394 and 413 as the earliest and latest dates, respectively, for all the homilies.

There is question also whether the Septuagint or the Hebrew Psalter was in the hands of Jerome when he wrote or preached the homilies on Psalms 10 and 15. They seem, in fact, to have been written rather than delivered, for he speaks of readers rather than hearers. They differ from the regular series of sermons in their greater erudition, more sophisticated language, many Greek expressions, and variations from the *Hexapla.* The closing doxology so characteristic of the other sermons is missing in them. They are much longer, and Jerome speaks of certain details as if he had already explained them. On the whole, they give evidence, too, of greater care in preparation.

In the translation that follows, scriptural quotations have been taken or adapted from the Confraternity of Christian Doctrine version wherever possible; in all other instances, from the Challoner-Rheims translation. Cross references to Jerome's other writings are from Migne, *Patrologia Latina,* and to facilitate their location, section numbers follow the column number. A select bibliography on the Homilies will be found in Volume 1 (Vol. 48, this series). The indices appended to this volume cover the material of Volume 48, that is, Volume 1 of Jerome's *Homilies on the Psalms.*

HOMILIES ON THE PSALMS

(60-74)

HOMILY 60

ON PSALM 10(11)

WE HAVE GIVEN AMPLE TREATMENT above to the import of the phrase *'in finem,'*[1] which Symmachus translates 'epiníkion' [song of victory]; and Aquila and the Sixth Version,[2] 'tôi nikopoiôi' [for causing victory]. Now, let us go back to the proper order of Psalm 10. Its number symbolizes both the beginning and the end; it is the number around which all reckoning revolves; the number to which we also owe the decalogue, the first Law. Then, too, the just servant in the Gospel, because he had doubled the Lord's money, received authority over towns corresponding to this number. And to mention something even more striking, Jesus, the name of the Savior, begins with a letter that is the sign for this number, and with it begins, also, the ineffable Tetragrammaton of the Hebrews, written with letters, IOTH [YOD], 'IOTH HE WAU HE.' From its decades, moreover, the number one hundred evolves, and again, one thousand derives from ten times one hundred.[3] As far as human calculation is able to proceed, this number always is the beginning and the end in line with the significance of: 'I am the Alpha and the Omega, the beginning and the end.'[4]

'In the Lord I take refuge; how can you say to me, "Flee to the mountain like a sparrow!" '[5] They who eat the raw meat

1 Cf. Ps. 10(11).1.
2 *'sexta editio,'* the reference is to 'Sixth Version' in Origen's *Hexapla*.
3 Cf. *Commentary on Amos* 5.3, PL 25.1038(283).
4 Apoc. 21.6.
5 Cf. Ps. 10(11).1.

of the lamb[6] and follow the letter that kills[7] insist that it is David who is speaking at the time when he fled from Saul and had to hide in the desert wastes of Juda. They claim that what David is saying is: Even though Saul and his whole army prevent me from dwelling in my own country; and like a wanderer and vagabond, I flutter hither and thither like a bird or run about like a beast, nevertheless, God is my refuge and under His protection I have no fear of your snares. As a matter of fact, if one were to confine himself solely to the opening verses of the psalm, this explanation is not unworthy of consideration, but beginning with the words: 'For they have destroyed all that you have accomplished,'[8] down to the end of the psalm, there is no congruence with their exposition.

Now, the spiritual man who 'judges all things, and he himself is judged by no man'[9] discerns, on the basis of a twofold interpretation, that it was our Lord and Savior who uttered this psalm. Either He spoke to the angels who were ministering to Him,[10] or He addressed opposing forces, the devils that tried to frighten Him with their mockery. If it was to the angels, then the tenor is: Why do you urge Me to return to heaven, to renounce the earthly and the lowly and dwell in My mountains because of the snares of the devil and his whole army that you see aroused against Me? Would you have Me put on the wings of My Godhead, abandon the ways of man, and live untroubled in the heavenly regions, when it was for this purpose that I came: to overcome My boasting adversaries by relying upon the Lord, that is, upon My divinity? If, however, He is directing these words to the opposing powers, then we must understand them thus: In vain do you think to terrify Me with your voices and your throng marshalled against Me, since for this reason I have come, to give battle and to prevail in battle—as the title of this psalm according to Aquila and

6 Cf. Homily 91 on Exodus, The Vigil of Easter, p. 238.
7 Cf. 2 Cor. 3.6.
8 Cf. Ps. 10(11).3.
9 1 Cor. 2.15.
10 Matt. 4.11.

Symmachus indicates. Another exegete (since there is nothing in this psalm particularly incompatible with the character of a just man) will support the saintly choice of those who refer the psalm to Christ, but would also claim that one may interpret the entire sequel in the name of the prophet, that is, in the name of a just man.

'In the Lord I take refuge; how can you say to me, "Flee to the mountains like a sparrow!" ' Shrewd adversary; he tempted the Lord Savior in the desert, and now wants the faithful, every one of them, to depart from the land of Juda and to dwell in a wilderness barren of virtues, that there he might crush them more easily.[11] Even the counsel itself is crafty. It is not an exhortation to assume the wings of a dove, a gentle, simple, and domestic bird—one, they say, entirely lacking in gall—which was offered in the temple in behalf of the Lord; but the wings of a sparrow, a chattering, roving bird, one that is a stranger to its mate after hatching its young—notwithstanding that Aquila and Symmachus have usually translated 'bird' in the place of sparrow. The mountains, moreover, we may identify as those to which Scripture refers in another place: 'Draw you near to the everlasting mountains';[12] and in the second of the gradual psalms: 'I lift up my eyes toward the mountains, whence help shall come to me.'[13] They are the mountains, too, in which we must take refuge after the abomination of desolation shall stand in the holy place.[14]

'For, see, the wicked bend the bow; they have prepared their arrow in the quiver; to shoot in the dark at the upright of heart.'[15] Instead of this, the Hebrew has: 'See how the sinful bend the bow; they place the arrow on the string to shoot in the dark at the upright of heart.' That is why, He says, you want Me to flee to the mountains, because sinners or rebels have ready burning arrows that must be repelled with the

11 Cf. *Commentarioli in ps.* 10.2.
12 Mich. 2.9, LXX.
13 Ps. 120.1.
14 Cf. Matt. 24.15.
15 Cf. Ps. 10(11).2.

shield of faith. In their quivers, they carry darts to shoot at the just, not in the daytime, not in the glimmering night when the moon comfortingly tempers the darkness, but when the night is deep and the darkness groping—'psēlaphētòn skótos.' Know that I am not heeding your counsel for the very reason that adversaries are prepared for battle. It is not so much their desire to harm Me whom they cannot vanquish, as it is to wound My faithful; and since it was for their safety that I came from heaven, I must not leave them orphans. See; it is just as you say: they have their arrow poised on the string ready and determined to capture My youth—sons in their puberty—My young men, with the sweet allurements of pleasures, for the devil's power, all of it, is in the loins.[16] Indeed, that is why when Jacob wrestled with Me, I caused his 'glaphurón' to dry up and wither.[17] Because, then, they are aiming to shoot in the darkness at the upright of heart, let My just man speak up and say: 'A lamp to my feet is your word, a light to my path.'[18] Moreover, I am standing in the battle line, alert and girt for battle; I am not overlooking the struggle that has begun, especially since you say that they have strung their bows, that they have arrows ready in their quivers, that they are waiting in the darkness to wound My saints; but they have not, as yet, been able to shoot. They have bent the bow; they have filled the quiver; they are ready to discharge their arrows in the darkness at the true of heart. Since they are so well prepared, I shall place Myself between them and intercept their arrows, so that by My pain My servants may not feel pain, that by My wounds they may be healed, that by My suffering they may not suffer, and may say: 'O Lord, you surround us with the shield of your good will.'[19]

There is, however, another possible explanation for this

16 Cf. Job 40.16; cf. Letter 22.11, PL 22.401(96); 7.3, PL 22.340(19); 130.10, PL 22.1116(987); *Commentary on Ezechiel* 16.4, PL 25.126(145); *on Jeremia* 1.17, PL 24.686(842).

17 Cf. Gen. 32.32.

18 Ps. 118.105; cf. *Commentarioli in ps.* 10.3.

19 Cf. Ps. 5.13.

passage, namely, that heretics, or demons through the teachings of heretics, have bent the bow of their blasphemy and contrive to beguile My just with every sort of subtlety. They are skilled bowmen who, under cover of their own darkness, which they recognize as the divine mysteries concealed from them, are eager to strike at the unoffending hearts of the just. It is necessary, therefore, for Me and My saints to migrate to the lofty pinnacles of Holy Writ, where, according to the Gospel: 'If someone strike thee on the right cheek, turn to him the other also.'[20] It does not say turn to him the left, but the other, that is, the other right cheek, because the just man has nothing in him that is left-handed.[21] If he shall confound you, the Gospel says, in one Testament, vanquish him with the other Testament and fulfill the word written in another psalm: 'Deep calls unto deep in the roar of your cataracts,'[22] so that the two Testaments fortify each other, and in so doing break the heretics' net by the counter evidence of another right hand, by transmigration to the mountains, and by deep calling unto deep.

'For they have destroyed all that you have accomplished.'[23] Here, they are still speaking as above, either to some just man, or to the Lord, and are saying: That is exactly why You must return to heaven, because powerful adversaries are ready to fight, and they are tearing down whatever You build up. Every day they are undermining Your commandments and the law written in the hearts of the faithful, and by their suasion are subverting irresolute hearts.

'What can the just man do?' This versicle admits of various interpretations. It may pertain, certainly, to the just man in the following manner. To those who are striving to efface God's laws, the just man has done nothing deserving of destruc-

---

20 Matt. 5.39.

21 Cf. Homily 20 on Ps. 90, p. 161; 48 on Ps. 136, p. 359 (Vol. 48, this series).

22 Ps. 41.8; cf. Homily 10 on Ps. 76, p. 74; 92 on Ps. 41, to the Neophytes, p. 246.

23 Cf. Ps. 10(11).3.

tion, and vainly suffers their treachery; or to those opposing and attempting to destroy the commandments of God, the just man does one thing only: he prays for the help of Him who dwells in His holy temple, whose throne is in heaven, whose eyes behold the helpless man that He may rescue him from the traps that they have set. In reference to God, the interpretation goes this way: Even though adversaries are all ready for conflict and are lying in ambush like a lion in its den, hiding in secret places to slay the innocent and destroy the temple of God, nevertheless, the Lord dwells in His holy temple, and He is never without temple or throne, because for those that fall, others arise. Whereupon in the following verse, it is written: 'The Lord is in his holy temple; the Lord's throne is in heaven.'

Let us follow the usual practice of Holy Writ and take *sedem*, the throne of God, for His kingdom,[24] as, for example, in the passage: 'God will give him the throne of David his father';[25] and in another: 'By righteousness the throne of government is established';[26] and again: 'When a righteous king sits on the throne.'[27] The Lord is in His holy temple; the Lord's throne is in heaven. Before Solomon was to build the earthly temple, the prophet knew of the Lord's spiritual temple and of His throne in heaven.

While you are meditating on that saying found elsewhere in Scripture: 'The heavens are my throne,'[28] consider that, inasmuch as the Lord's throne is in heaven, heaven surrounds it, and the throne of the Lord is in part of heaven; inasmuch as His throne is heaven, all heaven becomes His throne. Then, when you employ the anagogical sense [anagōgē], the Lord, dwelling in His holy temple, i.e., in the soul of one who believes in Him, dwells either in part of that soul or in the whole. Since we are still imperfect beings and there is in us

24 Cf. Homily 14 on Ps. 81, pp. 102-103.
25 Luke 1.32.
26 Prov. 16.12, LXX.
27 Prov. 20.8, LXX.
28 Isa. 66.1.

something of good and something of evil, God dwells only in part of our soul, that is, in heaven; but when we have been consummated and are perfect, then we change wholly and entirely into the dwelling place of God, and we become heaven, His throne. The temple of God, in the proper sense, is, however, our Lord and Savior, who says: 'I am in the Father and the Father in me';[29] or it is the human nature that had been assumed by the Savior; or, in general, it is the Church; or, in particular, any one of the saints.

'His eyes behold the poor man, his eyelids search mankind.'[30] Against the opinion of those who accept the wrath and fury of God unqualified, we propose the eyelids and the eyes of the Lord, for if they accept the former 'anthrōpopathōs' [anthropopathically], then, they must also accept the latter, the same way. If, however, it is absurd to posit eyelids and eyes in the omnipotent Lord, then, by the same token, it is necessary for them to seek the spiritual sense of wrath and of fury. Surely, it is most inept not to apprehend the former and the latter in the same way, either spiritually or carnally.

In this passage, therefore, it is essential to conclude that the just man does not fear the attack of adversaries because he has God for his Helper, who surveys the universe and does not permit His poor man to be deceived by their frauds or wounded by their darts. 'The poor man'—him of whom it says above: 'On you the unfortunate man depends.'[31] At the same time, it is to be observed that God is opening His eyes in bringing manifest justice to the support of the humble man, for even if he is alone and poor, God's solicitous glance is always upon him. Where He is Judge and they who are being judged are the sons of men (for they do not deserve to be called sons of God), there He does not look with His eyes, but searches with His eyelids, half closing His eyes and, in a certain measure, hiding and not wanting to know what He

29 John 14.10.
30 Cf. Ps. 10(11).4.
31 Cf. Ps. 9B(10).14, (Hebr. 10.14).

knows, for: 'If you, O Lord, mark iniquities, Lord, who can stand?'[32] Varro claims that eyelids take their name, *palpebrae*, from the fact that they move and quiver, *palpitant*, and, therefore, are derived 'onomatopoiôs [onomatopoetically].

'The Lord tries the just and the wicked; but he that loves iniquity hates his own soul.'[33] For this verse, the Hebrew has a better reading: 'The Lord proves the just, but the wicked and the lover of iniquity His soul hates,' so that when it is joined to the preceding verses, the full meaning becomes: In vain do foes prepare to discharge arrows in the dark at the upright of heart, for the Lord is a just judge and nothing can be concealed from Him; consequently, He proves His just by trying them, and the wicked He hates. His soul abhors the wicked who love iniquity; in other words, He hates them with all His heart and all His soul; but we must understand soul in the same way that we do His eyes and eyelids, as in Scripture: 'New moon and sabbath, and the other festivals, these my soul detests.'[34]

Furthermore, the meaning of the Hebrew verse is quite different from that of the Septuagint: 'The Lord tries the just and the wicked'; He is judge of both just and wicked; and the wicked are to be condemned because, by loving iniquity, they detest their own soul. To a certain extent, there is interwoven here the conclusion of a syllogism, for even if one denies that he detests his own soul, nevertheless, because he loves wrongdoing, he proves beyond doubt that he despises his soul. As Solomon says in Proverbs: 'He who rejects admonition despises his own soul.'[35] If, moreover, the man who loves iniquity despises his own soul, then, the man who loves justice loves his soul—this, in agreement with the Proverb: 'He who possesses wisdom loves himself.'[36] Besides, the Savior says: 'He it is who

32 Ps. 129.3.
33 Cf. Ps. 10(11).5.
34 Cf. Isa. 1.13, 14.
35 Prov. 15.32.
36 Cf. Prov. 19.8.

loves me, who keeps my commandments';[37] He is, indeed, Justice.

By no means, however, does the Septuagint translation, 'the Lord tries the just and the wicked,' contradict in any way what is written in the first Psalm: 'Therefore in judgment the wicked shall not stand.'[38] In the same way that there is variety among the just, so also is there diversity among the wicked; and even as the just will possess different mansions, so the wicked, confirmed in malice and iniquity and rebelling against the Lord with all their soul, have no chance before God's judgment; but other men who are sinners and sometimes confused with the malicious do have a chance because their wrongdoing is of a lesser degree.

'He rains upon the wicked snares.'[39] Without any doubt, it is the Lord who contrives snares for sinners themselves, in order to entrap those who abuse their freedom and to compel them to tread the right path[40] under His bridle, thereby making it possible for them to advance through Him who says: 'I am the way.'[41] Wherefore, in Jeremia,[42] the Lord sends fishermen and hunters to spread nets for the lost fish tossed about in whirlpools, and to hunt down unto salvation the beasts that rove through mountains and hills. This and the following versicles do not promise punishment to sinners, as many believe, but rather give them promise of healing.

'Fiery coals and brimstone; a burning blast is their allotted cup.' It is said to Babylon: 'Seeing you have coals of fire, sit upon them, and they will give you relief.'[43] Brimstone enkindles into flame these fiery coals; then a sudden blast of wind snatches up the flames in a whirl and fans them into a heat that consumes, according to the prophecy of Ezechiel,[44]

---

37 Cf. John 14.21.
38 Ps. 1.5; cf. *Against the Pelagians* 1.28, PL 23.545(724).
39 Cf. Ps. 10(11).6.
40 Cf. Homily 6 on Ps. 66, p. 45.
41 John 14.6.
42 Cf. Jer. 16.16.
43 Cf. Isa. 47.14, 15, LXX.
44 Cf. Ezech. 22.18-24.

any dross, any silver, bronze and tin, iron and lead, in our gold. Isaia has a parallel thought: 'The Lord washes away the filth of the sons and daughters of Sion, and purges the blood from her midst with a blast of searing judgment';[45] and Malachia: 'Lo the Lord comes like the refiner's fire, or like the fuller's lye. He will sit refining His people like gold or like silver.'[46]

The cup of sinners is full of fiery coals, brimstone, and burning blasts: 'A cup full of spiced and foaming wine' from which 'all the wicked of the earth shall drink.'[47] In my judgment, it was from this cup of fire and brimstone that Sodom had drunk, and Ezechiel prophesied, therefore: 'Sodom shall return to her former state.'[48] In the Gospel, we read: 'More tolerable for the land of Sodom.'[49] 'The Lord will not punish twice for the same thing.'[50]

There is also Lazarus, who had vindicated his sins in his lifetime and had drunk of the Lord's fury; in the bosom of Abraham, he drank the cup of which it is written: 'The cup of salvation I will take up, and I will call upon the name of the Lord.'[51] Jerusalem, likewise, had drunk the cup of punishment unto her healing; hence, it is said to her: 'Arise, arise, O Jerusalem, you who drank the cup of his destruction, the cup of his wrath.'[52] Jeremia received this same cup of foaming wine from the hand of the Lord in order to give it to Jerusalem to drink, and to all the nations round about; and upon drinking of it, they are convulsed and fall to the ground and, with broken pride, lie prostrate unto repentance.[53]

'For the Lord is just, he loves just deeds; his countenance

45 Cf. Isa. 4.4.
46 Cf. Mal. 3.2, 3.
47 Cf. Ps. 74.9.
48 Cf. Ezech. 16.55.
49 Cf. Matt. 10.15.
50 Cf. Nah. 1.9, LXX; cf. Letter 68.1, PL 22.652(410).
51 Ps. 115 (116B).13(4).
52 Cf. Isa. 51.17.
53 Cf. Jer. 25.15-26.

beholds righteousness.'[54] For this verse, the Hebrew has: 'For the Lord is just, and loves justice, their faces shall behold righteousness.' The Lord, it says, is just for the reasons stated above: He abandons the just man to trials and temptations in the present life, not to punish, but to test him; but His soul abhors the man of violence, the friend of vices. Truly, it is one thing to sin under the compulsion of the flesh, and another to transgress because of attachment to sin. That is why the Lord's soul detests men whose hearts are wed to sin. Because He rains snares upon sinners and gives them to drink the cup of torment which they deserve, God is just and loves just deeds.

Even as there is one true God, and as there are many who are called gods by participation in Him, and as there is one begotten Son of God, but others are called sons by adoption; so also there is one true Justice—as it is written in the introduction of the Book of Proverbs—[55]but the Lord loves the many acts of righteousness that are pronounced just because of their participation in true Justice. Where, moreover, the Psalm says: 'His countenance beholds righteousness'—that is, the righteousness of God—so that the meaning is, He judges deeds that are just, the Hebrew agrees with: They who will be judged—the just as well as the wicked sinners—will behold the justice of God, and their faces will contemplate the Lord's righteousness, and they will say: 'You are just, O Lord, and your ordinance is right.'[56]

54 Cf. Ps. 10(11).7.
55 Cf. Prov. 1.3, LXX.
56 Ps. 118(119).137.

HOMILY 61

ON PSALM 15(16)

MONUMENTAL INSCRIPTION FOR DAVID.'[1] In place of this superscription, the Fifth Version (in Origen's *Hexapla*) retains the Hebrew, 'MACHTHAM David,' which Aquila has rendered 'of David, humble and simple,' and Symmachus, 'of David, humble and chaste.' Again, in Psalms 55 to 59, Aquila's version of Hebrew 'MACHTHAM' becomes 'David, humble and perfect.' From these various translations, we conclude that one word connotes three qualities, simple, chaste, and perfect, always, however, with each of these attributes combined with 'humility.' In the Hebrew, therefore, one word is composed from the union of two, so that in much the same way, for example, that our 'omnipotent' includes two words in one, the Hebrew combination MACHTHAM has in the syllable MACH only one meaning, humility, and in the following THAM each of the three attributes just mentioned.

Now, unless I am mistaken, there are six psalms inscribed with this title: the fifteenth, fifty-fifth, fifty-sixth, fifty-seventh, fifty-eighth, and fifty-ninth. Each of them refers to the divine dispensation and the Passion of our Lord and Savior. Although, too, the psalms differ mutually in their titles by the addition, subtraction, or variation of other elements, they all agree in one phrase, 'a monumental inscription,' which now appears by itself at the beginning of Psalm 15. In the other five, certain historical facts are placed first in order to make the

1 Cf. Ps. 15(16).1; cf. *Commentarioli in ps.* 15.1.

prophecy of our Lord Savior evident, not only in word, but also in deed. I think that six psalms embody this mystery and are designated by such a title because it was on the sixth day of the world that the crucified Savior, dying and rising for us, left us, as it were, this monument of His victory. His intention was that we engrave upon our souls these psalms, marked with His inscription, that we bear in our hearts the words of God, and that we be ever mindful of the death of the Lord. As Jacob erected a pillar over Rachel's grave, and the memorial remains to this day,[2] even so may we perpetuate in our heart the inscription and the memory of His Passion.

Nor let anyone think that the Lord's warning in the Law: 'Nor shall you set up for yourself a pillar, which things the Lord, your God, detests,'[3] opposes our exposition. On the contrary, with the singular number of pillar, He has combined the neuter plural of the relative pronoun, saying: 'which things the Lord, your God detests'; in other words, 'you shall not perform works of the sort that shall remain forever unto your condemnation.' These are, indeed, the things that your Lord God hates. If, perhaps through our neglect, it should happen that the enemy who sows weeds[4] erect such pillars in the Land of Promise, the 'dioratikoí,' the prophet-teachers, to be sure, will command the children of Israel to pull them down, smash them to pieces, and abolish[5] them from the land flowing with milk and honey. It was just such a monument that Absalom erected for himself in vain, and it remains to this day[6] a reproach and witness to parricide. This is also the kind of pillar the wife of Lot[7] became when she insisted upon looking behind instead of ahead.

The question naturally arises why the Septuagint is different from the Hebrew and the other versions. There are many

2 Cf. Gen. 35.20; cf. Letter 108.10, PL 22.884(698).
3 Cf. Deut.16.21,LXX.
4 Cf. Matt. 13.24-30.
5 Cf. Num. 33.52; cf. *Commentary on Isaia* 30.10, PL 24.343(407).
6 Cf. Josephus, *Antiquities* 7.10.3.
7 Cf. Gen. 19.26.

passages in Scripture where the answer may be found, but it is especially well demonstrated in the title of the ninth psalm. The Hebrew there is LAMANASSE ALMVTH LABEN, which Symmachus construes, 'the triumph of the Son, a youth,' but the Fifth Version, 'the triumph of the Son in the flowering of young manhood.' The Septuagint translators, not wanting to reveal openly the Passion and Resurrection of the Savior to the king, Ptolemy,[8] and to the pagans, rendered it, 'Unto the end; on the mysteries of the Son,'[9] and indicated by the very title that they were deliberately concealing certain secrets they chose not to translate. So in this psalm, because humility, simplicity, stainlessness, and perfection cannot be ascribed to man (for there is no one who would dare to distinguish himself by such attributes), but the Son of God, they deliberately substituted 'stēlographía,' that is, 'an event worthy of a memorial inscription.' They wanted us to comprehend that there was one thing veiled in the title and another revealed in the word. Monuments are also placed over the tombs of brave heroes as a memorial of pristine courage, and over the graves of those who have died for their country; moreover, inscribed memorials are set up wherever there are trophies of victories and where public laws are set forth. In the light of all this, exposition in the name of the Lord Savior becomes less difficult.

'Keep me, O Lord, for in you I take refuge; I say to the Lord, "My God are you, for you have no need of my goods." '[10] If an apostle were to expound this psalm, great would be his authority; if two, it would be greater still. Now truly (a fact recorded of no other psalm), we find in the Acts of the Apostles that Peter, with Christ's apostles—Matthias had already taken the place of Judas—interprets this psalm and, lifting up his voice, says, after many other things: 'Brethren,

8 Cf. Homily 4 on Ps. 9, p. 36; cf. *Preface to Hebrew Questions on Genesis*, PL 23.985(303-04); *Commentarioli in ps.* 9.1; cf. *Commentary on Isaia* 2.20, PL 24.56(44); on *Jeremia* 17.1, PL 24.786(956-957).

9 Cf. Ps. 9A.1.

10 Cf. Ps. 9A.1, 2.

let me say to you freely of the patriarch David that he both died and was buried, and his tomb is with us to this very day. Therefore, since he was a prophet and knew that God "had sworn to him with an oath that of the fruit of his loins one should sit upon this throne," he, foreseeing it, spoke of the Resurrection of the Christ. For neither was he abandoned to hell, nor did his flesh see coruption. This Jesus God has raised up, and we are all witnesses of it.'[11] Since, therefore, all the apostles share equally in referring this psalm to the Lord Savior, we who want to be Christians[12] surely must follow their judgment; nor is it any wonder that He who was equal to God and humbled Himself, taking the nature of a slave,[13] should speak now with the words of a slave. That, then, is the reason why the title of the psalm describes Him as humble, simple, stainless, and perfect; He who was in need of help from no one, so humbled Himself that He besought the Lord for us, for the Church which is His own Body.

Great humility, indeed, it is for God to beg for mankind, for the Lord to pray for slaves, the Saint to pray for sinners. Not only does He declare that He Himself is clothed, given drink, visited in the person of His slaves, but also when they plead and obtain an answer to their prayer, He confesses that He it was who prayed, and it is His prayers that have been heard. When, therefore, He assumed a human body, He saw the opposing power; He saw, too, the army of the devil drawn up in wedge formation against Him. That is why He says: Keep Me safe, Lord, for unless You protect My Body, the Church that trusts in You, her guardians keep watch in vain.

The words that follow, moreover: 'I say to the Lord, "My God are you" ' extend to the apostles, to the disciples, and to us, if we but merit to be disciples, and make known what He has said to the Lord of the universe. What, then, does He say He has said to the Lord? 'My Lord are you,' or, You who are

11 Acts 2.29-32.
12 Cf. Homily 11 on Ps. 77, p. 80.
13 Cf. Phil. 2.6, 7.

Lord of all, are more especially My Lord; You have become the Lord of Mine. He was, naturally, Lord of all, even in the Old Testament, since He had created the universe; but He specifically became Lord of the faithful when He said: 'I am the God of Abraham, and the God of Isaac, and the God of Jacob.'[14] Just as You are their God, so now You are in particular My God[15] because You deign to be the Lord of My faithful servants. He adds the reason why He is His Lord: 'For you have no need of My goods.' God, the omnipotent, does not need man's goods, nor do our virtuous acts contribute to the perfection of God, since increment is impossible to Him, but whatever we produce by toil and bring forth in labor, that He exacts and takes from us in order to give back to us what He has received.[16]

The servant in the Gospel, [17] for example, whose one gold piece had earned ten, received not only what he had made, but also another gold piece that the other servant had not been able to multiply. Again, there are the words to Job: 'Is it any profit to the Lord, if you should keep a straight course?'[18] No other lords, no matter how powerful they may be, can say to their servants, 'We do not need your work,' since, indeed, they exploit their servants' labor. God, alone, truly is Lord, who requires service of His servants only that He may have occasion to bestow more gifts upon them. Along with this, we learn the lesson that if the Savior pleads in our behalf (certainly, He pleaded for the apostles in the Gospel, and permitted them to sleep, although, at first, He had constrained them to keep watch), surely, we ought all the more to pray for ourselves, because however fast we may run, without Him we cannot arrive at the goal. Such an interpretation follows the translation of Symmachus and the Fifth Version: 'Apart from you I have no good,' and corresponds with the thought: 'Un-

14 Matt. 22.32.
15 Cf. Homily 7 on Ps. 67, p. 56.
16 Cf. Homily 34 on Ps. 107, pp. 245-246.
17 Cf. Luke 19.13-27.
18 Cf. Job 22.3, LXX.

less the Lord build the house, they labor in vain who build it. Unless the Lord guard the city, in vain does the guard keep vigil.'[19]

'For the holy ones who are in his land, how wonderfully has he accomplished all his desires in them!'[20] For this, the Hebrew text has: 'For the holy ones who are on earth, and for my exalted ones, all my desire is in them.' My faithful servants, O Father, are in need of the good things which You do not need, My saints for whom I have wonderfully accomplished all My desires. Wonderfully, moreover, have I accomplished all My desires, not outside them, but within them; so that while each one is reforming and realizing who he was before and now has begun to be, My wonderful desires are being accomplished in them to the extent that, if they depart from Egypt and cross the desert, they shall be able to enter the Land of Promise, which is the entrance to the land of the living. Nor is there any contradiction between the fact that wonderful things are said to have been accomplished only in the land of God, and the fact that wondrous things did take place in the plain of Tanis,[21] that is, in Egypt.

There is a great difference, surely, between the miracles performed by Moses and those of Jesus. In the former, there is flight from Egypt; in the latter, entrance into Judea; there, escape is sought from the royal Pharao; here, faithful servants gather together; there, frogs, gnats, ashes, hailstorms, and darkness are accepted as miraculous signs; here, the sun and the moon obey a command; there, a pillar of cloud and of fire go before the people of God; here, the Savior Himself appears in the way, grasping a sword and attesting that He will fight for His own army. Do you see, then, how much greater are all the miracles that took place in the Land of Promise than those that occurred in Egypt or in the desert? We may even understand the land of God to be the Church: to the saints within

19 Ps. 126.1; cf. *Against the Pelagians* 3.1, PL 22.595(781).
20 Cf. Ps. 15(16).3.
21 Cf. Ps. 77.12.

it, all the desires of God are seen to be wonderful; to people outside, nothing seems wonderful that is even truly marvelous by its very nature. May we be in the land of God, and may we be transformed into the image of the Savior, and may He accomplish wonderfully in us all His desires.

'Their infirmities were multiplied; afterwards they made haste.'[22] Whose infirmities were multiplied? Those of the saints, of course, mentioned above in the land of the Lord. When they were foolish, incredulous, erring, slaves to desires and pleasures of all sorts, stirring up trouble in greed and envy, they multiplied their weaknesses; when they were baptized and sanctified; when, converted to repentance, they abandoned their sins of the past; then, they made haste. I have read in the Letter of Barnabas[23] (if you accept evidence from that source) that God chose as apostles men lawless beyond all sin. It follows that, if they were more wretched than any sinner, their infirmities were, indeed, multiplied; but see how quickly afterwards their weakness vanished. The Lord says to Peter and his brother Andrew: 'Come, follow me,'[24] and the same to James and John who left their father, their boats, and their nets. Matthew[25] arises from the tax collector's place, and immediately he is an apostle; Zacchaeus[26] comes down from a tree and is a saint. Paul, while persecuting the Church, suddenly believes, is baptized,[27] teaches, submits to persecutions, and is beheaded. What is swifter than this conversion?

Before the Gentiles were converted to the Lord and heard through Isaia: 'Drink this first, do it quickly,'[28] they suffered every kind of infirmity, whether in the 'hardships' of Symmachus' translation, or whether, more aptly, in the 'idols' of Theodotion and the Fifth Version. Although the cults of

---

22 Cf. Ps. 15(16).4.
23 Cf. Ep. Bar. 5.9; cf. *Against the Pelagians* 3.2, PL 23.598(783).
24 Matt. 4.18-22; cf. Letter 14.6, PL 22.350(32); 38.5, PL 22.465(175).
25 Cf. Matt. 9.9; cf. Letter 118.4, PL 22.963(795).
26 Cf. Luke 19.2-10.
27 Cf. *Commentary on Ezechiel* 1.3, PL 25.18(5).
28 Isa. 9.1, LXX.

idolatry had multiplied, at the first sound of the apostle's voice, the Gentiles believed and turned to the Lord. In fact, Aquila's translation, 'diaponēmata,' also signifies image, for certainly the Hebrew text says ASABOTH, the same word employed in the verse: 'The idols of the Gentiles are silver and gold.'[29]

In moving forward where it says 'proikisaménōn'—in the Septuagint, 'they made haste'—it seems to me that there is a sublime instruction. After the apostles or the Gentiles embraced the faith of Christ, and the Lord forgave them their sins (that is the implication in 'proikisaménōn,' because 'proíkia' means their sins were pardoned freely), their 'diaponēmata' [sorrows] increased as they realized in what deep waters they were and from what kind of abyss they were liberated, as it is written in Ecclesiastes: 'He who stores up knowledge stores up grief.'[30] Paul puts it: 'I am not worthy to be called an apostle, because I persecuted the Church of God.'[31] It is possible, however, to construe this thought a little differently as, 'strength is made perfect in weakness';[32] when the apostle is weaker, then he is stronger. We, too, if it is our desire to reach the Lord quickly, must multiply our infirmities, so that made weak in the flesh, we may become strong in the spirit.[33]

'I will not gather together their meetings for blood offerings.'[34] Obviously, it is the Savior who is speaking. Who else could say, 'I will not gather together their assemblies for blood offerings'? Understand 'their,' moreover, with reference to the Gentiles or the apostles. If it means of the Gentiles, then the sense here will be: Even if they be guilty of blood and have perpetrated many crimes, because they hastened to Me after their sorrows, their meetings shall be pure and unbloody. If 'their' refers to the apostles, then the meaning will be: By no means shall they offer victims to Me as in the Old Testament,

29 Cf. Ps. 113B(115).4(12).
30 Cf. Eccles. 1.18.
31 1 Cor. 15.9.
32 2 Cor. 12.9.
33 Cf. 2 Cor. 12.10; cf. Letter 39.2, PL 22.467 (179).
34 Cf. Ps. 15(16).4.

but their offering shall be the pure, sacred rite of the New Testament.

It is well, at least, to mention an older interpretation: 'The bloodthirsty and the deceitful the Lord abhors';[35] the watchman will be responsible for the wicked man's death[36] if he is unwilling to warn him of the coming wrath of God, and God will destroy him who has scandalized[37] one of the least brethren; those whose hands are full of blood positively cannot gather together in the assemblies of the Lord until they have been washed clean 'by the blast of searing judgment.'[38] The gatherings of the Lord we may consider the churches in the present world or, what I think is better, the different mansions in the heavenly abode of the Father which the sinner, bespotted with blood, shall not be able to enter.

'Nor will I take their names upon my lips.' Because the saints, whose sorrows have been multiplied and whose assemblies for blood offerings have ceased, have come to Me in haste, I shall not call them any more by their earlier names, but by new ones. After I have cleansed them in My baptismal font, I shall not call them as formerly, the sons of men, but sons of God. Or He may be saying: I shall change their names, and from Simon I shall make Peter, because upon this rock My Church has been established; from the sons of Zebedee, I shall make sons of thunder, for to them I am going to entrust the sublime mysteries of My Gospel. Not only their names were changed, however, but also Abraham's and Sara's; nor is it fitting that their names[39] should remain unchanged whose way of life has been completely transformed. Still another writer interprets the words, 'Nor will I take their names upon my lips,' as: I shall not call them by name indifferently, as it were in passing, but I shall cherish them deep in My heart

35 Ps. 5.7.
36 Cf. Ezech. 33.6, 7.
37 Cf. Matt. 18.6; Mark 9.41; Luke 17.1, 2.
38 Cf. Isa. 4.4.
39 Cf. *Commentary on Daniel* 1.7, PL 25.495-496(624); *on Philemon* 1-4, PL 26.639(746).

and keep them within My soul. Just as it is said to an incredulous people: 'This people honors me with their lips alone, though their hearts are far from me,'[40] so, on the contrary, the Lord not only names His saints with His lips, but holds them fast in the intimate affections of His soul.

'O Lord, my allotted portion and my cup, you it is who will restore my inheritance to me.'[41] In Holy Writ, our Savior is called both High Priest and King; High Priest, in the passage: 'You are a priest forever, according to the order of Melchisedec';[42] King, where it says: 'I have been set up as king by him on Sion, his holy mountain.'[43] Since He is priest, the Lord is His portion, for it is written in the Law: 'To the Levites you shall not give any heritage in the land of the Israelites, for I am their portion, says the Lord.'[44] That is why the Levites did not receive from Jesus a portion in the land of Juda, but were scattered throughout the tribes and thereby fulfilled the prophecy: 'I will disperse them in Jacob, I will scatter them in Israel.'[45] If the Levites had no portion except the Lord, how much more, indeed, does He, who is High Priest and dares to say: 'The Father dwelling in me, it is he who does His works,'[46] have the Father for His special and proper portion. As king, however, it is said to Him: 'Ask of me and I will give you the nations for an inheritance and the ends of the earth for your possession.'[47]

Notice how carefully defined each statement is. Of the Father, it says: You are My allotted portion. 'You are,' not 'You have been,' for the Son has always dwelt in the Father and the Father in the Son; of the Gentiles: 'You will restore my inheritance to me,' for they ceased to be the heritage of the

40 Cf. Isa. 29.13.
41 Cf. Ps. 15(16).5; cf. Letter 52.5, PL 22.531(259).
42 Ps. 109.4.
43 Cf. Ps. 2.6.
44 Cf. Num. 18.20, 24.
45 Gen. 49.7.
46 John 14.10.
47 Ps. 2.8.

Lord when their weaknesses multiplied and they assembled in their meetings for blood offerings. I grant there are some authors who think that the latter part of the verse is also to be referred to the Father so that the import is: Because I emptied Myself, taking the nature of a slave[48] and from My divine majesty descended to earth, restore My inheritance to Me; that is to say, do You, in whom I have always been, glorify Me with the glory that I always had with You before the world existed.[49] You will not give Me any new possession, but You will restore My inheritance, manifestly the divinity and the nature of God, which I seem not to have possessed because I had assumed the human nature of man. Again, where it says, 'my cup,' everyone knows that in Scripture, 'cup' is sometimes a symbol of the desire for refreshment and of joy as: 'Your cup that refreshes you, how good it is,'[50] and: 'The cup of salvation I will take up, and I will call upon the name of the Lord.'[51] Just as the Savior is, then, our food and drink (truly, we eat His flesh and drink His blood), so the Father is the food and drink of that human nature that the Savior assumed; with God the Father, He has one common godhead.

'For me the measuring lines have fallen on pleasant sites; fair to me indeed is my inheritance.' By virtue of this one people, I have possessed the inheritance of the whole world; and not of just any people, but of the strong only. That is the force of the phrase, 'on pleasant sites,' that is rendered in Greek by 'on the strong' in agreement with the usage in the text: 'O Lord, my strength, my fortress, my deliverer,'[52] and with: 'My strength and my courage is the Lord.'[53] If one is, therefore, fair and strong, he is of the Lord's inheritance. Because Theophilus, for example, that friend or lover of God, was the kind of person who sought to have the Gospel written

48 Cf. Phil. 2.7.
49 Cf. John 17.5.
50 Cf. Ps. 22.5.
51 Ps. 115(116B).13(4).
52 Cf. Ps. 17.3.
53 Ps. 117.14.

for him, he is called 'krátistos,' fair or strong, which the Latin equates quite simply with 'most excellent Theophilus.'[54]

In the next place, a line is used in measuring fields and in dividing off the land whenever possessions are being distributed or the census is being taken for the land tax, as, for instance, in the Book of Jesus, son of Nave. The angel who is to build Jerusalem appears to the prophet,[55] holding a measuring line in his hand to measure, first, in accordance with plan and design, the length and width of the city; afterwards, to construct it in conformity with the measurements. In the canticle in Deuteronomy, also, we read: 'while the Lord's own portion was Jacob, His hereditary share was Israel';[56] and in the second Book of Kings, where David defeated the Moabites, Scripture records the measuring out of two separate lines for life and two for death.[57] The significance of setting aside some Moabites for life and others for death is made clear by the story of Orpha and Ruth: Orpha, who turned back to idolatry and her ancient country, was destined for death; Ruth, following her mother-in-law, whose name means 'pleasant,'[58] says: 'Your people shall be my people, and your God my God.'[59]

If it is our desire, therefore, to be of the Lord's inheritance and portion, let us be brave and strong; let us attest: I can do all things in Him, Christ, who strengthens me.[60] Let there be nothing weak in us, nothing inconstant, nothing unworthy of an heir, for Christ glories in His saints and says: Fair to Me, indeed, is My inheritance. Would you like proof that the Savior's inheritance has, indeed, been fair? Consider Peter, look at Paul, and at all the apostles and saints—inasmuch as throughout the whole world there have been faithful believers—and you will appreciate Christ's inheritance and how fair

54 Luke 1.3.
55 Cf. Zach. 2.5-9.
56 Cf. Deut. 32.9.
57 Cf. 2 Kings 8.2, LXX.
58 Cf. Letter 54.17, PL 22.559(293); cf. *On Hebrew Names*, PL 23. 856(51), (Lagarde 34.7), '*Noemi pulchra.*'
59 Ruth 1.16.
60 Cf. Phil. 4.13.

[*praeclara*] it is. Aquila's translation of this versicle is, 'Very beautiful [*speciosissima*] to me indeed, is my inheritance,' which accords with the Canticle of Canticles in: 'You are beautiful, my beloved, and there is no blemish in you';[61] and again: 'Ah, you are beautiful, my beloved, ah, you are beautiful: your eyes are doves!'[62] You who are beautiful and strong, because you resemble Him of whom it is sung: 'In your beauty and your splendor,'[63] will hear from your Spouse: 'Forget your people and your father's house. So shall the king desire your beauty.'[64]

'I bless the Lord who gives me understanding; even in the night my reins exhort me.'[65] He who says a little later on: 'My body, too, abides in confidence; because you will not abandon my soul to the nether world, nor will you suffer your faithful one to undergo corruption,' now also says appropriately: 'I will bless the Lord who gives me understanding; even in the night my reins exhort me.' How does He who is Wisdom receive understanding? 'Jesus advanced in wisdom and age and grace before God and men';[66] meaning not so much that the Son was instructed by the Father, as that His human nature was instructed by His own divinity;[67] wherefore there is the seer's prophecy of Him who blossomed from the root of Jesse 'The spirit of the Lord shall rest upon him: a spirit of wisdom and of understanding.'[68]

To refute the insane Arian heresy, however, Aquila and Theodotion have furnished a better translation in, 'I shall bless the Lord my counselor'; so that it was not a question of the Father giving the Son wisdom and understanding that He did not have before, but of the union of the Father's counsel

61 Cant. 4.7.
62 Cant. 1.15.
63 Cf. Ps. 44.4.
64 Ps. 44(45).11, 12.
65 Cf. Ps. 15(16).7.
66 Luke 2.52; cf. *Commentarioli in ps.* 15.7.
67 Cf. *Commentarioli in ps.* 15.7.
68 Isa. 11.2.

with the Son's thought. In Proverbs,[69] for instance, wisdom says that she was counselor to God when she was rejoicing in the world that had been formed, and was delighted every day; hence, Wisdom itself, in assuming a human body, in dying and rising from the dead, manifests that He was not without the Father's counsel, but totally in accord with Scripture: 'To do your will, O my God, is my delight.'[70]

Then, too, in the following part of the verse: 'Even in the night my reins exhort me,' we must understand 'reins' in the sense of inmost thoughts and deepest desire, which is proper scriptural idiom (idíōma).[71] As far as I am able to recall, not in any one of the philosophers nor of the rhetoricians, not in the poets nor among the physicians themselves, for that matter, from whom we expect knowledge of the nature of bodies, have I ever been aware of having found 'reins' employed for perception and profound thought. It is the practice of Scripture, nevertheless, when intending to reveal something secret, hidden, or mysterious, to say: 'O searcher of heart and reins, O God';[72] so since the heart is secret, the more secret regions of the heart are the reins. In Wisdom, too, a book attributed to the fame of Solomon, we find: 'God is witness of his reins, and the sure observer of his heart and the listener to his tongue';[73] and again, in the Book of the Patriarchs[74]—granted it is reckoned among the uncanonical—I have come upon the statement that, just as gall was made for anger, the reins were made for cunning and shrewdness. 'Panourgía,' cunning, may be taken either in a good sense or bad; in a good, according to Proverbs: 'That resourcefulness may be imparted to the simple, to the young man knowledge and discretion';[75] in a bad sense, as in the Letter of the Apostle: 'But I fear lest, as the

69 Cf. Prov. 8.12, 13.
70 Ps. 39.9.
71 Cf. Letter 85.5, PL 22.754(535).
72 Cf. Ps. 7.10.
73 Cf. Wisd. 1.6.
74 Cf. *Testam. XII Patriarcharum* 8.2, PG 2.1108A.
75 Prov. 1.4.

serpent seduced Eve by his guile, so your minds may be corrupted and fall from a single devotion to Christ.'[76]

What the Lord is saying, therefore, is this: My knowledge, deepest thought, and the inmost desire of My heart was with Me, not only in My heavenly mansions, but also when I dwelt in the night of this world and in darkness; it remained in Me as man, and it instructed Me, and never left Me, so that whatever the weakness of the flesh was unable to achieve, divine thought and power accomplished. Or it may be understood in this way: My reins instructed me, and I possessed the interior wisdom of divinity, by which I was schooled not to yield to human frailty in the imminent passion and terror of the cross. Who else[77] (for the life of the Savior is exemplary) may claim that, not only when awake, but even when asleep, he has been without any sin and has remained pure from any lustful phantasm? The saints, therefore, who desire to be like their Lord and Master, keep constant guard over their hearts lest they be overcome, not only while awake, but even in sleep, not only during the day, but even during the night. It is important to note, also, that the psalmist said: 'even in the night my reins exhort me,' in order to show that before it became night, or before the Savior Himself began to dwell in the night, He had always been tutored by His own wisdom.

There is another interpretation as well, for divine Scripture is ever comparing the powers of God to human faculties. In the same way that it says He has feet, eyes, ears, hands, and other such members, so reins must be understood in the sense of seeds. Just as the germs of mankind and the elements of the human body have been buried in a seed, similarly the first stirrings of our judgment and the first impulses of our thinking have their reins, so that before we can perform any act or utter any word, our silent reasoning holds it within its own operation and deliberates upon it. It follows, then, that our Lord and Savior, whom every day the Word of God was in-

76 2 Cor. 11.3.

77 Cf. Letter 133.3, PL 22.1152(1031).

structing, could not commit sin either in His deeds and discourse, in His thought, or in the initial stimuli of His thoughts (in Greek, 'propatheíai').[78] This does not mean that there are two persons in Christ, but that the one and the same Son of man and Son of God now prays as man, now answers the prayer as Lord.

'I saw the Lord ever before me; with him at my right hand I shall not be disturbed.'[79] In the place of the Latin reading *providebam* and the Greek 'prooróměn,' the Hebrew has a better expression, SEBETHI, which we are able to render in Latin by *proponebam*, 'I set.' Accordingly, the translation is: I set the Lord ever before me at my right hand, and no enemy stratagem was able to upset me. Consider here that it is always in our power to set the Lord before us. The man who resembles the Savior in his integrity places God at his right side and says, He is at my right hand to keep me steadfast. The just man places the Lord at his right hand because he keeps his eyes on Him whom he follows, but the sinner casts the word of the Lord behind him and, in so doing, causes the Lord to be on his left side. Then, as soon as the devil spies the Lord at the sinner's left side, he removes immediately to the right side and takes possession of the Lord's place, and fulfills that which is written of Judas: 'Let the devil stand at his right hand.'[80] Why this utterance is in the form of a prayer rather than a statement of fact is irrelevant to our purpose. As I was saying, for the Lord Savior, or through the Lord Savior for His saints, God is always standing at the right side. The just man has, in fact, no left side, and in whatever direction he turns: 'The angel of the Lord encamps round about those who fear him, and delivers them.'[81]

Would you like evidence that the just man has no left side?[82] When Moses lifted up both his hands to the heavens in the

78 Cf. *Commentary on Ezechiel* 18.1, 2, PL 25.168(200).
79 Cf. Ps. 15(16).8.
80 Cf. Ps. 108.6.
81 Ps. 33.8.
82 Cf. Homily 20 on Ps. 90, p. 161.

figure of the cross, Scripture does not say that Aaron was at his right and Hur at his left, but that Aaron stayed up his hands on this side, Hur on that.[83] In the Book of Judges,[84] too, there is Aod, that champion, whose equal use of both hands is another great mystery, who used to carry a dagger on his thigh and had slashed all lustful desires. He it was who had plunged his dagger into an exceedingly gross and stupid enemy; hence, is characterized as being 'amphoterodéksios,' that is, as having two right hands, a versatility that we can describe in Latin as *ambidexter*, ambidextrous.

Someone may object: If the just man should not have a left hand, how may wisdom be represented as having both a right and a left? The careful reader will easily perceive how great a difference there is between the right and the left side of wisdom when he has taken note of what she is reported to hold in her right hand and in her left, for Scripture says: 'Long life is in her right hand, in her left are riches and honor.'[85] You see eternity and everlasting life in wisdom's right hand; but the perishable and fleeting things of time, creatures that are gone the very instant we think we have them in our grasp—riches and honor—are in her left, consistent with the fact that, on the day of judgment, some will stand on the right and others on the left: sheep, naturally, and saints on His right, but goats and sinners on His left.[86]

Perhaps now the inquiring reader will raise this objection: How may we claim that God is standing at the right hand of the just man and the devil at the left hand of the sinner, when one may read what it says of our Lord and Savior in Zacharia: 'While Satan stood at his right hand to accuse him'?[87] Let our opponent read on and see what follows, namely, that when the devil was standing at our Savior's right hand, Jesus was clad in filthy garments. It is logical that He who had taken upon

83 Cf. Exod. 17.12, LXX.
84 Cf. Judges 3.15-22.
85 Prov. 3.16.
86 Cf. Matt. 25.33.
87 Zach. 3.1; cf. *Against Jovinian* 2.4, PL 23.302(328).

Himself our sins and was wearing our transgressions had the devil on His right, not because of Himself, but because of the soiled garments.

At the same time, the reader should examine carefully that it does not say: The devil was standing triumphantly as a victor, but that he was at a halt in the contest and was being held in the battle line and in uncertainty—no, indeed, he was not victor, since he had not yet begun to fight. As for the words, 'to accuse him,' the devil was His adversary, just as we said, because Jesus was clothed in garments that were filthy with our sins; but after Satan heard the command, 'May the Lord who has chosen Jerusalem rebuke you!'[88] he stood no longer on the right, but retired behind Him and crawled under His feet. Without delay, Jesus the High Priest dons the long garment and is clothed in shining raiment, and in harmony with kingly authority—with the hands of Zorobabel[89] —lays the foundations of the Church and erects the spiritual Jerusalem.

'Therefore my heart is glad and my tongue rejoices.'[90] 'Therefore' indicates that this versicle must be linked to the preceding, so that He is saying that the cause of His joy or exultation was the fact that God was always before His eyes, and that, with God always at His right side, He was never disturbed. The sequence of development then becomes: There is gladness in My heart and rejoicing on My lips as I sing a hymn of praise to the Father in thanksgiving for the salvation of mankind, for while I was enduring and sustaining the death of the cross, the Lord was ever at My right side.

This passage, by the way, is proof against the judgment of those who maintain that the members of the body mentioned in Scripture must be taken always in their corporeal sense.[91] Let them but answer this question: How does the tongue

88 Zach. 3.2; cf. Homily 35 on Ps. 108, p. 258.

89 Cf. Zach. 4.8-10.

90 Cf. Ps. 15(16).9.

91 Cf. Homily 22 on Ps. 93, p. 177; *Commentary on Ephesians* 4.5, 6, PL 26.528(610).

rejoice by itself or how is the tongue able to possess a proper joy as if it had feelings and understanding? Besides, it does not say a tongue rejoices, but my tongue rejoices. The tongue, therefore, the same as any other member of the body, is evidently capable of all human performance, in keeping with that saying of Solomon: 'Death and life are in the power of the tongue.'[92]

Furthermore, in place of the reading: My tongue has rejoiced, that is found in the Acts of the Apostles[93] and in the version that is in general circulation, we ought to observe that in the other translations, as well as in the Septuagint,[94] the word 'tongue' does not appear, but in its stead, 'glory,' which in Hebrew is CHABOD, whereas the Hebrew word for tongue is LASON. I suppose because the orator's glory lies in the praise of his speech, just as the glory of the physician is in the exercise of the art of medicine, and of the athlete in fortitude, and in the rest of the arts glory consists in fulfilling their end, the tongue, by means of which one expresses what he feels, has been employed for the concept of glory. Otherwise, tongue must be understood as referring to the glory of that nature which Christ assumed, of whom it is said in another place in Scripture: 'My glory, you lift up my head';[95] or the apostles are to be understood as His glory because they glorified Him throughout the world, just as we say the glory of the shepherd is a full flock; of the teacher, learned students; and of the general, brave armies. Because, however, John says: 'We saw his glory—glory as of the only-begotten of the Father—full of grace and of truth';[96] and in another place, we find: 'Awake, O my glory; awake,'[97] let it be our opinion that the reference is to the glory of the Savior which the apostles perceived in the humility of His flesh, and with more penetrating

92 Prov. 18.21.
93 Cf. Acts 2.24-32.
94 Cf. LXX; Ps. 16.9.
95 Ps. 3.4.
96 John 1.14.
97 Cf. Ps. 56.9.

eyes beheld, not merely what appeared, but what was hidden away in the body.

'My body, too, abides in confidence; because you will not abandon my soul to the nether world, nor will you suffer your faithful one to undergo corruption.' It is superfluous to attempt an explanation of what the apostles have already explained.[98] We shall comment, therefore, only on minor points that they have passed over as less significant, such as the psalmist's reason for saying: 'My body, too, abides in confidence,' which means that the Savior will descend to the dead with the confidence that He will rise again directly. He did not say, will abide, or, will rest, as we read in the Latin manuscripts, but 'kataskēnṓsei,' that is, 'will travel about in a foreign place.' The tenor is, therefore, that He will delay there a very short time and will look upon the kingdom of the dead in passing, nor will His soul be abandoned to the nether world: 'I have the power to lay down my life, and I have the power to take it up again.'[99] The Father will not suffer Him to undergo corruption. Incidentally, the use of the word *videre* [see] for *pati* [undergo] is quite in accordance with scriptural idiom (idíōma), as, for instance, in: 'What man shall live, and not see death?'[100] There is a similar idiom in: 'For our sakes he made him to be sin who knew nothing of sin.'[101]

By the way, notice that the Lord has both a body and a soul, a body that was laid in the sepulchre and a soul that descended to the nether world; and as the body without the soul was a perfect body, so also the soul without the body was a perfect soul and deprived of no function natural to the human soul that is without sin. This is in refutation of a new heresy,[102] for there are some who, from the fact that the Lord entered through closed doors, adduce proof that a different body arose

---

98 Cf. Acts 2.24-32; 13.34-37.
99 Cf. John 10.18.
100 Ps. 88.49.
101 2 Cor. 5.21; cf. *Commentary on Ecclesiastes* 8.5, PL 23.1129(451).
102 Cf. Homily 35 on Ps. 108, p. 268; 88 on the Lord's Nativity, p. 227.

from that which died. Let these heretics hear what the Lord Himself recounts in this verse: 'My body, too, abides in confidence.' Most certainly, after the Savior suffered and died, that body was laid in the tomb that had been alive; that same body, therefore, that had been lying lifeless and dead in the tomb rose from the dead. If, moreover, that same body arose from the dead in the Lord, how do some come to the conclusion that, though it was wonderful and spiritual, it was not a human body? We are not saying that we deny the body of Christ assumed that glory that we believe we also are going to receive as saints, for then, indeed, this corruptible body will put on incorruption, and this mortal body will put on immortality.[103] Just as before the Lord suffered His Passion, when He was transformed and glorified on the mountain, He certainly had the same body that He had had down below, although of a different glory,[104] so also after the Resurrection, His body was of the same nature as it had been before the Passion, but of a higher state of glory and in more majestic appearance, in fulfillment of the words of Paul: 'So that henceforth we know no one according to the flesh. And even though we have known Christ according to the flesh, yet now we know him so no longer.'[105]

I cannot refrain here from quoting the apostle's: 'Oh, the depth of the riches of the wisdom and of the knowledge of God! How incomprehensible are his judgments and how unsearchable his ways!'[106] God the Son, God the Word, as long as He was in heaven and men did not sin to a degree that brought Him down to them, He was dwelling, not composite but simple, with the angels, thrones, dominations, and all the heavenly powers. When He came down to men, however, who are obviously composed of body and soul, He assumed our

103 Cf. 1 Cor. 15.53; cf. Letter 75.2, PL 22.686(453); *Against John of Jerusalem* 26, PL 23.395(434); 29, PL 23.397(436).
104 Cf. *Commentary on Jona* 2.7, PL 25.1136(411).
105 2 Cor. 5.16; cf. Homily 26 on Ps. 98, p. 210.
106 Rom. 11.33.

composite nature, lest composite man be unable to bear the simplicity of God. Furthermore, because in the kingdom of the dead, souls were detained without bodies—souls that are simple by their nature—only His soul, not His soul and body, not the God-Word[107] descended into hell; so that, as every place without exception had need of Him, He was perceived also by the inhabitants of that region.

I know that many, because the Church is the body of Christ and we are members, distinguish anagogically (by 'anagōgḗ') the less perfect men as the body of Christ, from the more perfect, the soul; or, those who follow the historical sense of Scripture, without doubt, constitute the body, and those who rise to spiritual discernment are the soul.

'You have made known to me the ways to life, you will fill me with joy in your presence, the delights at your right hand forever.'[108] Because His body did not see corruption and His soul was not left in hell, after the Resurrection, ascending in triumph to heaven, He says in the person of the risen man: 'You have shown me the ways to life: I have learned how men are to be delivered from death, by what plan they are to attain life everlasting.' Consider, too, that He who is the Way and the Life said that He had learned the ways to life; He had learned in what way men would follow Him who said He is

107 Annotation in Codex O: 'This passage appears foreign to Catholic belief, since it has been accepted (*cum fide*) on faith, that the Word of God descended into hell simultaneously with the soul of Christ.' Morin comments: Jerome is, indeed, a great scholar and one excelling in doctrine; but he was a man and not infallible. It seems to me that in this passage his error is accidental rather than substantial, in his wording rather than in his meaning. Cf. Theophilus of Alexandria, Easter Letter of the year 402 (98.7) translated by Jerome: 'It is not credible that His body descended to hell, or that the *prudentia carnis* which is called the soul, appeared in the nether world; but it is credible that His body was laid in the sepulchre and neither of His body and the *sapientia carnis* nor of His divinity did He say, "You will not abandon my soul to the nether world," but actually of the soul of our human nature, in order to teach that a perfect and rational and intelligent and sensible soul had descended to the nether world.'

108 Cf. Ps. 15(16).11.

the Way and the Life. I think, too, that just as He Himself is Truth and in saying to the Jews: 'If you abide in my word, you shall know the truth, and the truth shall make you free,'[109] speaks as if of another truth; so, likewise, although He Himself is Life, He speaks as of another life, and although He Himself is the Way, He says that other ways have been shown to Him, or, as in the Hebrew, 'the way.' In other words, He is saying that the body He had received—and in His body, the entire human race—rejoiced that the divinity of the Son was made known to it. That is why He rejoices, He says, and has the fullness of joy with the Father (meaning, of course, 'in Your presence,' in the same sense as the text: 'You gladdened him with the joy of your presence'[110]), and His delight is full and perfect and His happiness ineffable because He sits at the right hand of the Father and fulfills the Scripture: 'The Lord said to my Lord: "Sit at my right hand till I make your enemies your footstool." '[111] The Son sits at the right hand of the Father who reigns in majesty; and because He beheld His first martyr, Stephen, contending against the Jews, He rose from His throne and stood at the right hand of the Father as if He were Himself engaging in the combat for His martyr.

This is His delight, this His happiness unto the end of the divine decree, or unto victory—for instead of 'forever,' Aquila and Theodotion and all the other versions, with the exception of Symmachus and the Septuagint, have used 'unto victory,' because the Lord suffered and rose from the dead and entered heaven as victor in order to establish man at the right hand of the Lord. It is also important to observe that where we read: 'You will fill me with joy,' Theodotion said 'seven joys,' and 'In your presence the delights at your right hand for the Victor'; and Aquila and Symmachus have rendered: 'Fullness of joys with your presence,' or 'in your presence.'

Is someone asking why Theodotion said 'seven' instead of

109 Cf. John 8.31, 32.
110 Ps. 20.7.
111 Ps. 109.1.

'fullness'? The answer is obvious to anyone who has even a slight knowledge of Hebrew. The word, SABA, as we have already indicated in the book on *Hebrew Questions*,[112] has four different meanings: fullness, satiety, oath, and seven. Because of this ambiguity, Theodotion, knowing that the various gifts of the Spirit are in God, thought that the translation appropriate to the passage ought to be 'seven' rather than 'fullness,' 'satiety,' or 'an oath.' This is in order to show that the Spirit of wisdom and understanding, the Spirit of counsel and fortitude, the Spirit of knowledge and piety, the Spirit of the fear of the Lord are with God—truly, seven complete joys for Him who has merited forever the delights at the right hand of the Lord, though not for others. Certain authors, I might say, surmise that it is for this reason that philosophers mention seven heavens and name seven wandering stars. Furthermore, where we read:' The delights at your right hand forever,' Symmachus says: 'Virtue at your right hand unto eternity,' showing that He who is the fullness of virtue will abide perpetually in the presence of God.

112 Cf. *Hebrew Questions on Genesis* 21.30, PL 23.1018(337); 26.32, 33, PL 23.1030(348); 41.29, PL 23.1048(366); cf. *Commentary on Isaia* 54.1, PL 24.515(626).

HOMILY 62

ON PSALM 82(83)

GOD, WHO IS LIKE YOU?'[1] No one is like You. 'Be not silent, O God, and be not still!' It is a man of the Church who is speaking, a man from within whom there flows rivers of living water.[2] He beholds a mighty harvest, but few laborers; throngs of believers, but few teachers to instruct them; many heretics, many adversaries, but few warriors to fight for Christ. 'Be not silent, O God, and be not still!' Why this plea?

'Behold, your enemies raise a tumult.' Now the heretics speak and the churchmen hold their peace; they raise an uproar, but we keep silence; they blaspheme, and we are not enraged. 'Behold, your enemies raise a tumult.' Well said, 'they raise a tumult,' for their speech is not ordered and constructive, but only a noise, confused and disruptive. 'They who hate you lift up their heads.' Vast is the multitude of heretics and scant the number of those who believe in You.

'Against your people they plot craftily'; they say they intend to ravish Your Church. 'They conspire against your saints';[3] day after day, they think of nothing save how to trip up and ensnare Your men of the Church.

'They say, "Come, let us destroy their nation." ' I see a new point for consideration here. So vast is the number of heretics and so great their diversity in dogma, that, though among themselves they differ greatly in opinions and doc-

1 Cf. Ps. 82(83).2.
2 Cf. John 7.38.
3 Cf. Ps. 82(83).4.

trines, in their hatred of us, they are of one accord. Just as Herod and Pilate, for example, who were enemies, made their peace in persecuting Christ, and were more formidable in their amity than their enmity, so the heretics, impiously at variance, league together for still greater impiety.

'Against your covenant they are allied.'[4] You have spoken to us through the prophets, and they through Mani, Marcion, Arius, and Valentinus. 'The tents of Edom and the Ismaelites.' Once we have abandoned the meaner historical sense and have committed ourselves to a high mode of interpretation, the allegorical, the fact is simply that the Jews are addressing the other nations contending against them, but be that as it may, whatever has come to pass has happened for us in type. Israel was attacked; her victory was of profit to us. Let us consider, therefore, who the enemies are that are fighting against the Church. 'The tents of Edom.' The translation of Edom is 'the earthly.' The word 'tents' is well expressed, for the Edomites have no firm foundations, no houses, only tents, dwelling places never fixed, but always impermanent.[5] 'Of Edom and the Ismaelites.' The meaning of Ismaelites is quasi-listeners.[6] Neatly put, 'quasi-listeners'; they do not heed God, but pass Him by.

'Moab and the Agarenes, Gebal and Ammon.' Individual names carry their own mystical meanings, for there are as many mysteries here as there are words. The name 'Moab' means 'from the father': they are not in the Father, but from the Father, because they have deserted their first Father. 'The Agarenes' symbolize proselytes and strangers. They who formerly were citizens afterwards became aliens; they are no longer of the household but strangers, strangers, indeed, who are attacking their Father's house. 'Gebal' means a barren valley. The enemies of the Church are not from the moun-

4 Cf. Ps. 82(83).6.
5 Cf. Homily 15 on Ps. 82, p. 112.
6 *Ibid.*, p. 112-113; *Hebrew Questions on Genesis* 16.11, PL 23.1012 (330); *Hebrew Names*, PL 23.824(12), (Lagarde 7).

tains, but from the valley; their wisdom is not from above, but from below; they are not of heaven, but wholly of earth. Scripture specifies a vacant valley because there is a valley that is not vacant. The humble man, who sacrifices all he has for the sake of Christ, is a valley and a field that is not barren, but fruitful. 'Ammon and Amalec.' 'Ammon' certainly implies a deceitful people; hence, refers to heretics, for they are not followers of Him who says: 'I am the truth,'[7] but of him who is the prince of lies. 'Amalec' is interpreted 'licking': they suffer nothing to be left to the Church, but lick away its entire foundation. They do not feed on the words of Scripture, but lick the ground like a snake.

'Strangers with the inhabitants of Tyre.'[8] Where we have *alienigenae* [foreigners], the Hebrew text has PHILISTIM, which is interpreted, a cup of poison, for heretics are all drunk from the cup of Babylon, of which Jeremia says: 'The golden cup of Babylon which made the whole earth drunk.'[9] Note: 'the golden cup of Babylon.' Babylon connotes confusion: 'a cup truly golden,' the teachings of philosophers and the eloquence of orators. Who, indeed, has not been misled by the philosophers? Who has not been seduced by the orators of this world? Theirs is a golden cup, the splendor of eloquence on the outside, but within full of poison that they could never conceal except under the gleam of gold. You taste the sweetness of their eloquence, to be sure, and do not suspect the fatal poison. 'Strangers with the inhabitants of Tyre.' Tyre stands for 'narrowness.' Truly, there is no room there, not the wide open heart of Christ, as the Apostle says to the Corinthians: 'In us there is no lack of room for you, but in your heart there is no room for us.'[10]

'The Assyrian, too, is leagued with them.'[11] The others pre-

---

7 John 14.6.
8 Cf. Ps. 82(83).8.
9 Cf. Jer. 51.7; cf. Homily 11 on Ps. 77, p. 86.
10 2 Cor. 6.12.
11 Cf. Ps. 82(83).9.

cede, but this one follows. Let us see who this follower is. Assur, certainly, typifies the devil, for there is no doubt of his malice nor his vengeance, as it is written in Psalm 8: 'to destroy the hostile and the vengeful.'[12] It is he who causes us to sin, and it is he who arraigns us for punishment. 'The Assyrian, too, is leagued with them.' The devil is their prince, their commander; not the just king, Josias, is their ruler, but the Assyrian. 'They are the forces of the sons of Lot.' Lot means 'turning away,'–from God is understood–just as the Jews did, for all heretics are one with the Jews in blasphemies.

There are many things to be said, but the hour prevents, for it takes time to review each name individually. Who, indeed, could readily discuss: 'Deal with them as with Madian; as with Sisara and Jabin at the torrent of Cison. Who perished at Endor; they became dung on the ground. Make their nobles like Oreb and Zeb; all their chiefs like Zebee and Salmana, who said, "Let us take for ourselves the dwelling place of God." '[13] They imagined themselves men of the Church, claiming it for their own.

'O my God, make them like a wheel.'[14] May there be no stability in them; may they be always unsettled, so that they have no fixed position, but are ever on the move, rolling back and forth. Just as a wheel is not of itself fixed and firm, so, likewise, heretics are not firmly settled in their doctrines and opinions, but are always changing them.[15] 'Like chaff before the wind.' The psalmist petitions eleven penalties against them because they denied the creed of the eleven apostles. The trained reader may object: 'How can you divide one verse into two? Besides you are doing violence to the Scripture. You say there are eleven apostles, when we know that the Lord Savior had twelve apostles.' We say eleven, because Judas, the traitor, who had been the twelfth, had with-

12 Cf. Ps. 8.3.
13 Cf. Letter 106.53, PL 22.856(663).
14 Cf. Ps. 82(83).14; cf. *Commentarioli in ps.* 82.14.
15 Cf. Homily 2 on Ps. 5, p. 21; 54 on Ps. 143, p. 386.

drawn from their number. 'O my God, make them like a wheel.' Here, you have strike number one; count carefully the rest that follow. 'Like chaff before the wind,' is number two; 'As a fire raging in a forest,' is the third; 'As a flame setting the mountains ablaze,' the fourth; 'So pursue them with your tempest,' the fifth; 'Rout them with your storm,' the sixth; 'Darken their faces with disgrace,' the seventh; 'That men may seek your name, O Lord,' the eighth; 'Let them be shamed and put to rout forever,' the ninth; 'Let them be confounded and perish,' the tenth; 'Knowing that you alone are the Lord,' the eleventh. 'You alone the Most High over all the earth.'

Up to only a certain point is there wrath; after that the words bespeak clemency. 'Rout them with your storm.' Note that in the sixth punishment, the psalmist did not say kill, but rout them, in order that they may return to You. 'Darken their faces with disgrace,' not with vengeance, lest cut off by death they should be unable to return to the Lord. 'Darken their faces with disgrace,' not punishments. Why should you not destroy them? The inspired words give the answer: 'That men may seek your name, O Lord.' If they seek, they shall find; they who have been misled by heretics shall return to the Lord; this is the seventh. 'Let them be confounded and perish.' He who is shamed in sins comes close to the sinless: behold the eighth.

The skilled reader may protest: 'let them perish' is a contradiction to the interpretation that you have just made. How, in fact, will they perish who are confounded unto salvation? Let them perish as heretics, says the psalmist, and let them be saved as men of the Church. This is just as if you were to say, let this adulterer perish, not because you hope the man who is unchaste will perish, but that adultery will be detroyed in him; again, when the adulterer is saved, he is saved not as adulterer, but as the just and chaste. That you may know, furthermore, that our interpretation is correct, the

Holy Spirit Himself speaks: 'Let them be confounded and perish.' In what manner perish? 'That men may seek your name, O Lord.' Let them perish in error; in truth, let them be saved. 'You alone are the Most High over all the earth.' Not the gatherings of heretics, not the evil spirits and innumerable days of Valentinus, not Basilides who claims there are 365 gods,[16] not the numberless multitude of false gods, but You alone are the Most High over all the earth. To whom be glory forever and ever. Amen.

16 Cf. *Against the Luciferians* 23, PL 23.186-187(197); *Commentary on Amos* 3.9, 10, PL 25.1018(257); *on Galatians* 1.4, PL 26.339-340(378).

HOMILY 63

ON PSALM 83(84)

SOMETIME AGO WHEN WE WERE discussing the eightieth psalm,[1] we recalled that the title of the eighth, eightieth, and eighty-third—this one—is marked by the words *pro torcularibus,* for the wine presses.[2] We said, then, that *torcularia* were like granaries in which the fruits of the earth are stored. Now for what the psalmist has to say.

'How lovely is your dwelling place, O Lord of hosts!' This, then, is the storehouse in which spiritual grain is to be treasured. 'Make friends for yourselves with the mammon of wickedness so that they may receive you into everlasting dwellings.'[3] 'How lovely is your dwelling place, O Lord of hosts!' 'How lovely is your dwelling place,' through which man transfers his residence from earth to heaven. 'My soul yearns and pines for the courts of the Lord.' Fruitful and happy the mind and heart that day and night are filled with longing for the dwelling place of the Lord! When death comes to the sinner, his thought is not on that dwelling place, but on punishments; he does not meditate upon the kingdom of heaven, but is in dread of the flames of hell.[4] 'My soul yearns and pines for the courts of the Lord!' See how much love, how much yearning pierces the soul of the saint in the courts of the Lord! Excellently did the psalmist say: I con-

1 Cf. Homily 13 on Ps. 80, p. 93, 95; cf. *Commentary on Ezechiel* 45.13, 14, PL 25.452(566); *on Isaia* 63.3-6, PL 24.612(748).

2 Cf. Ps. 83(84).1.

3 Cf. Luke 16.9; cf. Homily 13 on Ps. 80, p. 96; cf. Letter 54.12, PL 22.556(289); 71.4, PL 22.671(433).

4 Cf. Homily 41 on Ps. 119, p. 311.

template the entrance, and what the house is like within, I do not know.

'My heart and my flesh cry out for the living God.' Listen, O heretic, to what the psalmist is saying. 'How lovely is your dwelling place, O Lord of hosts!' He is speaking of the kingdom of heaven. 'In my Father's house there are many mansions,'[5] says the Lord in the Gospel. 'My soul yearns and pines for the courts of the house of the Lord,' the courts in which the saints will dwell for all eternity and for which the psalmist longs. 'My heart and my flesh.' You notice that the soul and the body both share in longing for the kingdom of heaven. If it is true that the body disintegrates, vanishes into air, and does not rise again, as the heretics think,[6] how does the flesh of the prophet long for the kingdom of heaven? 'My heart and my flesh'; because they have suffered and labored equally, equally do they await reward. If their toil is in common, why not recompense in common? I beg of you to listen with indulgence to what I am about to say. The body in the present world labors more than the soul, for the soul commands, the flesh serves. The toil of the server is one thing, the delights of the commander another. The soul yearns for the Lord. The flesh fasts; it is the body that lies down on the ground in the cold, is imprisoned, scourged in martyrdom, slain, cursed, treated harshly. The soul, too, suffers, but suffering does not reach it except through the body.

Someone may interpose, however: What, then, does the apostle mean when he says: 'flesh and blood can obtain no part in the kingdom of God'?[7] Do you want to know what he means? Listen to the Lord speaking in Genesis: 'My spirit shall not remain in man forever, since he is flesh.'[8] Why so? You made the flesh, Lord, and do You accuse and condemn it?

5 John 14.2.
6 Cf. *Against John of Jerusalem* 23-24, PL 23.390-391(429).
7 1 Cor. 15.50; cf. Homily 54 on Ps. 143, p. 381; cf. *Against Jovinian* 1.37, PL 23.275(298).
8 Gen. 6.3.

What God really is saying is: My spirit shall not remain in men like these, for they do not live according to the spirit, but according to the vices and the pleasures of the flesh. Let the apostle bear witness: 'They who are carnal cannot please God.'[9] If all who are carnal cannot please God, how, then, does Paul himself, who is speaking, please God? How do Peter and the other apostles and saints, whom we cannot deny were carnal, please Him? Just as the same apostle says further on: 'You, however, are not carnal, but spiritual.'[10] They were carnal; why, then, does he say: 'You are not carnal'? Because you do not live according to the flesh, for 'our citizenship is in heaven.'[11] We who in this world 'are exiled from the Lord'[12] walk about on earth, it is true, but we are hastening on our way to heaven, for here we do not have a lasting place, but we are wayfarers and pilgrims, like all our fathers.[13]

'Even the sparrow finds a home, and the swallow a nest in which she puts her young.' This is as the Lord says in the Gospel: 'The foxes have dens, and the birds of the air have nests';[14] even the sparrow finds a home. The prophet drew a comparison here from daily life. Since he had said: How lovely is your dwelling place for which my soul pines, and my flesh yearns for the kingdom of heaven, now he says metaphorically: The birds are free and fly about through the air at will; nevertheless, they remember their nests, and return to them. If, therefore, sparrows seek their nests, why should not the human soul seek the dwelling place prepared for it by the Lord?

'Your altars, O Lord of hosts.' How is one to comprehend: 'Even the sparrow finds a home, and the swallow a nest in which she puts her young: Your altars, O Lord of hosts'?

9 Rom. 8.8.
10 Rom. 8.9; cf. *Against John of Jerusalem* 28, PL 23.397(436).
11 Phil. 3.20; cf. Letter 60.3, PL 22.591(333).
12 2 Cor. 5.6; cf. Letter 39.3, PL 22.468(180); 108.1, PL 22.878(690).
13 Cf. Ps. 38.13.
14 Matt. 8.20.

What logical connection is there between these versicles? They depend upon what goes before: 'My soul yearns and pines for the courts of the Lord: Your altars, O Lord of hosts.' In the Apocalypse, John saw the altar of the Lord under which were the souls of the just: 'I saw under the altar of the Lord the souls of those who had been slain for the word of God, and for the witness that they bore to Jesus.'[15] They were under the altar of God because they had been immolated in martyrdom for Christ; the victim of the Lord Savior was deserving to be in heaven under the altar.

'Happy they who dwell in your house!' that is, in the Church, whether the Church of the present or 'the Church of the firstborn.'[16] 'Continually they praise you.' Note the duty of the martyrs in heaven and of the angels. What they are doing in heaven, we accordingly imitate upon earth.[17] When we are called to chant the psalms, therefore, and are careless in our service, we are making light of God's praises.

'Happy the man whose strength you are!'[18] It is ours to take up a task; it is God's to come to our assistance.[19] 'In his heart he has disposed to ascend by steps.'[20] Every day he meditates on how he may ascend, not descend. The sinner, however, sets his heart not on ascent, but upon descent. On that account, Jacob saw angels ascending and descending. 'In his heart he has disposed to ascend by steps'; he plans his good works, but he leaves the outcome entirely to God. It is ours to resolve, His to carry through.

Let us consider where he has set his ascent: 'In the valley of tears, in the place that he has appointed.'[21] We have read in

15 Cf. Apoc. 6.9.
16 Heb. 12.23.
17 Cf. Homily 40 on Ps. 115, pp. 298-299.
18 Cf. Ps. 83(84).6.
19 Cf. *Against the Pelagians* 3.1, PL 23.596(781); 1.5, PL 23.523(700); Letter 130.12, PL 22.1117(989); cf. Homily 2 on Ps. 5, pp. 17, 20; 34 on Ps. 107, p. 252; 61 on Ps. 15, p. 29; 68 on Ps. 90, p. 82.
20 Cf. Ps. 83(84).6.
21 Cf. Ps. 83(84).7.

the Book of Judges[22] that when the angel came and preached repentance to the people saying: 'You have abandoned the Lord, and the Lord shall abandon you,' the Israelites wept aloud when they heard the threat; and that place was called the Valley of Tears. We have called attention to ancient history in order to avoid heresy.[23] The valley of tears, moreover, we may understand allegorically as this world, for we are not on the mountain,[24] that is, in the kingdom of heaven, but in the valley, in the darknesses of this world; through a fault, we have been cast out of Paradise with Adam into a lowly vale of tears[25] where there is repentance and weeping. 'In the valley of tears, in the place that he has appointed.' What did the prophet mean? God made this world an arena that here we may strive against the devil, against sin, in order to receive our crown in heaven.[26] Why did He ordain a contest? Could not He save us without the struggle? He gave us, as it were, a Master of contests; He gave us a stadium in which to carry on our wrestling against vices, so that afterwards He may crown us meritoriously, not as those who sleep, but as those who labor.[27] What follows?

'He who gave the law will give a blessing.'[28] That is why He gave a place for the contest: that He who had given us the rules of the contest might afterwards give us a blessing. 'They go from strength to strength.' You perceive how appropriate the meaning: 'They go from strength to strength'; they fight here that, hereafter, there they may receive a crown. They advance from strength to strength. He did not say they go from weakness to strength,[29] for unless they are strong here, they will not be stronger hereafter. Someone, however, may

22 Cf. Judges 2.1-5.
23 Cf. Homily 19 on Ps. 89, p. 147.
24 Cf. Homily 16 on Ps. 83, pp. 122-123.
25 Cf. Letter 22.10, PL 22.400(95).
26 Cf. *Commentarioli in ps.* 83.7.
27 Cf. Homily 12 on Ps. 78, p. 90; 34 on Ps. 107, p. 252; 68 on Ps. 90, p. 82.
28 Cf. Ps. 83(84).7.
29 Cf. Homily 16 on Ps. 83, pp. 123-124.

object: God is merciful. Yes, but watch what follows: 'Mercy and truth the Lord loves.'[30] He is, indeed, merciful, but He is [also] true. When you hear He is merciful, you must not be indifferent to the 'and true' that follows.[31] On the other hand, when you shall hear that God is truth, do not despair; do not think that God is only severe, for mercy tempers truth: 'For a cup is in the Lord's hand, full of spiced and foaming wine, and he pours out from it this into that,'[32] that is to say, He has tempered in due proportion truth with mercy and mercy with truth. 'They shall see the God of gods in Sion.' When they have gone from strength to strength, then, they shall see the God of gods in Sion. To whom be glory forever and ever. Amen.

30 Cf. Ps. 83(84).12.
31 Cf. Homily 39 on Ps. 114, p. 288.
32 Cf. Ps. 74.9.

HOMILY 64

ON PSALM 84(85)

Unto the end.[1] A psalm of the sons of Core.' The meaning of the name Core is Calvary, the place of the Lord's Passion. We are all sons of Core, we who believe in His Resurrection. What are we saying, therefore, in this song that we sing in unison?

'You have blessed, O Lord, your land.'[2] This is better expressed by the Greek 'Eudokēsas kúrie,' that is, 'You have favored, O Lord, your land'; this was Your pleasure; this seemed good to You; this You decreed in order to fulfill through Your mercy what the following verses record: 'You have turned away the captivity of Jacob. You have forgiven the guilt of your people; you have covered all their sins.'[3] We may also interpret the Latin in this sense: 'You have blessed, O Lord, your land'; the land which previously had been cursed, has been blessed by Your coming. The land that before had heard the judgment: 'Thorns and thistles you shall bring forth,'[4] now is called, as in the Canticle of Canticles: 'the flower of the field, and the lily of the valley.'[5] The land that before brought forth thorns, hears in Isaia the blessing: 'a shoot shall sprout from the stump of Jesse, and from his roots a bud shall blossom.'[6] 'You have turned away the captivity of Jacob.' The Lord has come, therefore, to proclaim

1 Cf. Ps. 84(85).1.
2 Cf. Ps. 84(85).2.
3 Cf. Ps. 84(85).2, 3.
4 Cf. Gen. 3.18.
5 Cf. Cant. 2.1; cf. Letter 22.19, PL 22.406(102); 75.1, PL 22.686(452).
6 Isa. 11.1.

pardon to captives. There is a parallel to this in another passage of Scripture: 'He led captivity captive,'[7] that is, we, who in former times had been captured by the devil unto perdition, now are led away by the Savior unto salvation.

'You have forgiven the guilt of your people.' This we believe has been fulfilled in baptism. 'You have covered all their sins.' This is fulfilled in penance, as the thirty-first psalm says: 'Happy is he whose fault is taken away, whose sin is covered.'[8] In baptism, our guilt is taken away; in repentance, however, sins that have been committed are 'covered'; they are not wiped out, but are forgiven.[9] Let us consider carefully the force of these words. Truly, with the coming of the Lord Savior, all our guilt is wholly removed by baptism. When we were living without the Law, we were sinning without of Law;[10] sin of this kind is called 'anomía' in Greek, in other words, 'without the Law,' sin. After baptism, however, in no wise is it called 'anomía,' but sin is called sin, for sin is not imputed except to him who knows he is committing it.[11] Where there is transgression of God's command, there is sin.

Would you like to know how sins are covered by virtues?[12] Yesterday I was wanton; today I am chaste; chastity covers lust. Yesterday I was imprudent; today I am prudent; I repent of my mistake; prudence covers imprudence. Yesterday I was plundering the possessions of others; today I am giving away my own; almsgiving covers up greed. Happy the man whose sins are forgiven in baptism; second to baptism, however, penance is like a plank after shipwreck.[13] The penitent, too, may, therefore, be called happy. Granted, he is rescued with

7 Cf. Eph. 4.8.

8 Ps. 31.1.

9 Cf. Ambrose *'De paenitentia'* 2.5,35, PL 16.506A (424). Primasius *'Comment. in Apocal.'* PL 68.820C.

10 Cf. Rom. 2.12; 7.7-12.

11 Cf. *Commentary on Osee* 8.13, 14, PL 25.889(89).

12 Cf. Homily 17 on Ps. 84, p. 129.

13 Cf. Homily 23 on Ps. 95, p. 184; cf. Letter 122.4, PL 22.1046(899); 130.9, PL 22.1115(986); 84.6, PL 22.748(528).

peril, but since he is rescued by his regret for sin, he is to be called happy.

'You have withdrawn all your wrath; you have revoked your burning anger.' See how powerful repentance for sin is; it prevents the threatening wrath of God. 'Restore us, O God, of our deliverances.'[14] The psalmist did not say 'of our deliverance'; because we have committed many sins, we are in need of many salvations. 'Will you be ever angry with us, prolonging your anger to all generations?' Your anger has effected our salvation; You were angry with Your former people that you might be merciful to our people. 'Will you not instead give us life; and shall not your people rejoice in you? Show us, O Lord, your kindness, and grant us your salvation.' Where the Latin text has 'salvation,' the Hebrew has 'Jesus';[15] hence, in Hebrew, it goes thus: Show us, O Lord, Your kindness, and grant us Your salvation; unless first You shall have been merciful to mankind, Your Jesus shall not be given to us.

'I will hear what the Lord God proclaims in me.'[16] The prophet is praying for the people and speaks while God is speaking in him: 'I will listen to what the Lord God is proclaiming in me.' You perceive that God does not speak in the ears, but in the heart, as Zacharia says: 'The angel who spoke in me answered me.'[17] The angel is understood to be our Lord who is proclaiming the will of the Father and who, in Isaia, is called the Angel of the Great Counsel.[18] I will listen to the voice of the Lord God within me; I shall attend with the ear of my heart that I may hear what the Lord God speaks in me.

'For he proclaims peace to his people, and to his faithful

14 Cf. Ps. 84(85).5.
15 Cf. Homily 6 on Ps. 66, p. 44; 12 on Ps. 78, p. 90; 25 on Ps. 97, p. 199; 40 on Ps. 115, p. 296.
16 Cf. Ps. 84(85). 9.
17 Cf. Zach. 1.9.
18 Isa. 9.6, LXX.

ones, and to those who turn to him from their hearts.'[19] I note here a threefold classification: His people, His loyal servants, and those who come back to Him in hope. He proclaims peace to His people, not to the Jews of whom in Osee He says: 'You are not my people,'[20] but to all the Christians who have believed in Him. All soever, indeed, who are in the Church, are called in common the Lord's people, but the first among them and the spiritually proficient are called God's faithful, as for example, Paul addresses his letters to the churches and to the saints who are there. The third class is next: 'To those who turn to him from their hearts.' Those who had been deceived by the devil, after repenting of their deeds, put their hope in virtuous acts, for when they sinned they lost heart, I mean the wisdom of heart, that they receive back upon conversion. Take heed, Montanus; take heed, Novation; take heed, Maximilla, and the rest of the Cataphrygians who declare that penance is of no avail. The Lord speaks to His people, to all Christians, in fact, and to His saints who are the foremost faithful in the Church, and to those who come back to Him wholeheartedly—those who do penance. Happy, indeed, is the man whom no sin has ever stained, whom no sin has ever wounded; nevertheless, it is a second happiness to be restored to health by the healing of the wound.

'Near indeed is his salvation to those who fear him.' Note that they who fear the Lord have Him nearby, for fear is not yet perfection: 'but perfect love casts out fear.'[21] We who love the Lord do not have Him near us, but in us: 'I will dwell and move among them, I will be their God and they shall be my people.'[22] 'Glory dwelling in our land.' This is the land of which it says in another place of Holy Writ: 'The earth

19 Cf. Ps. 84(85).9.
20 Osee 1.9.
21 1 John 4.18.
22 2 Cor. 6.16.

has yielded its fruits.'[23] The fruit of our earth is the Bread of Life, who was born for us at Bethlehem.[24] Bethlehem, in fact, means house of bread, and this is the Bread that came forth in Bethlehem, that coming down from heaven, was made for us; the Bread into whose mystery angels desire [to look].[25]

'Truth shall spring out of the earth, and justice shall look down from heaven.' Truth of the promise has sprung out of the earth, and the sun of justice has looked down from heaven, that His light might shine abundantly upon men who have been constituted in darkness and in the shadow of death.

'Kindness and truth shall meet; justice and peace shall kiss.' 'Kindness and truth shall meet.' I see two attributes that, by coming together, are made one. Justice and peace have kissed. All this becomes one in the mystery of the Lord Savior, the Son of man and of God who is our truth, kindness, peace, justice, in whom the justice of the first people and the mercy of the second people are joined together into one peace. The apostle says, in fact: 'He himself is our peace, he it is who has made both one.'[26] This is the mystery for which the Church longs and cries out in the Canticle of Canticles: 'Let him kiss me with kisses of his mouth.'[27] This is the kiss of which Paul the Apostle says: 'Greet one another with a holy kiss.'[28]

'The Lord himself will give his benefits.' The reason for these kisses is for the Lord to bestow His benefits. 'Our land shall yield its increase.' We now see the fulfillment of the promise that was made then. Our land yields its harvest when it is cultivated by the plow of justice, when by fasts, abstinence, and the other virtues, its ancient vices are uprooted that it may yield a hundredfold the grain of the Gospel seed which it has received. Because Peter and the other apostles have cultivated their land with labors of all sorts, they truth-

23 Ps. 66.7.
24 Cf. Letter 58.3, PL 22.581(321); 147.4, PL 22.1199(1088).
25 Cf. 1 Peter 1.12.
26 Eph. 2.14.
27 Cant. 1.1.
28 Rom. 16.16; 1 Cor. 16.20; 2 Cor. 13.12; 1 Thess. 5.26.

fully can say: Our land has yielded its increase. Martyrs, too, when they are being slaughtered, when they are being crucified, are yielding the harvest of their land.

There are ever so many things we could say, but the time forces our sermon to its conclusion. Let us pray the Lord together, that both my sermon and your listening to it may be converted into good works:[29] 'for it is not they who hear that are just in the sight of God, but they who do.'[30] He who speaks or listens and does not do what he says or hears, listens or speaks unto his own condemnation. What does the Gospel say? 'If you were blind, you would not have sin.'[31] Let us alter this a bit: If you were deaf, and did not hear, you would not have sin. Because it is, in truth, sinful to speak and to hear without good works, let us beseech the Lord to walk with us, that He be our companion in the perils of this life; and that walking in our hearts pure of sin, He may delight always to dwell in us. To whom be glory forever and ever. Amen.

29 Cf. Homily 21 on Ps. 91, p. 173.
30 Cf. Rom. 2.13.
31 John 9.41.

HOMILY 65

ON PSALM 87(88)

RIGHT AT THE OUTSET, we encounter a difficulty in the very title of the psalm, and even though we have not yet entered the port of exegesis, nevertheless, many dark problems press down upon us. 'A song: a psalm of the sons of Core unto the end, for Mahalath in antiphonal response to understanding of Heman the Ezrahite.'[1] You see that practically every word of itself poses a question. 'A song: a psalm,' no great obstacles here. 'The sons of Core,' the sons of Caath of the family of Levi. 'Unto the end.' Note carefully: 'unto the end'; not in the beginning, not in the middle, but 'unto the end' the promise is made; not in the beginning to the patriarchs, not in the middle to the prophets, but at the end to the apostles and to us is promised the joy of the song. 'For Mahalath.' MAHALATH is a Hebrew word which means chorus. Now 'chorus' is the term used when many sing together in unison and may be compared to the cithara which with many separate chords produces one sound.[2] Then, that you may be sure that MAHALATH signifies chorus, there follows at once the expletive, 'in antiphonal response,' indicating that, as the prophet sings, the entire multitude responds in the praise of God. It is the mystery of the Church that is being prefigured, the Church gathered together from many nations so that, from separate places and from diverse regions and customs, one choir may sound forth the praise of God.

1 Cf. Ps. 87(88).1.
2 Cf. Homily 59 on Ps. 149, p. 424.

'Understanding of Heman the Ezrahite.' Heman was one of the choir-masters, like Asaph and the rest of them. The epithet, 'Ezrahite,' is interpreted, 'having obtained the help of the Lord[3] (since the meaning of the name Ezra is 'helper') and implies, having cooperated with the help of the Lord; hence, this choir that sings in praise has been sustained by the help of God. Let us run through the versicles one by one, and, since we are pressed for time, let us restrict ourselves to brief observations as we go along.

'O Lord, the God of my salvation.'[4] This psalm is sung in the name of the Savior, really, in the humanity which He deigned to assume. Whatever is expressive of lowliness, therefore, is being set forth by the human person, because it is for the benefit of human salvation. 'By day I cry out, at night I clamor in your presence.' Even though I cry out at night, nevertheless, the consciousness of fortitude is light for Me.

'Let my prayer come before you.' 'Father, into thy hands I commend my spirit';[5] let My prayer reach Your presence. 'Incline your ear to my call for help.' Where are the 'anthrōpomorphîtai' [anthropomorphites] who think that God has a body with members?[6] 'Incline your ear,' O God. It is the voice of the Son speaking to the Father in our name. 'Incline your ear.' It is a mark of great weakness if, when you want to hear, it is necessary to incline your head in order to attend more closely to what is being said. Just think, then, how inappropriate it is to say that the Father cannot hear the Son unless He inclines His head. Scripture speaks in terms of our human frailty that we may the more easily understand.

'My soul is surfeited with troubles.' I am bearing the sins of many; therefore, I am suffering for all. My soul is overflowing with sorrows; I am bearing evil burdens in order to

3 Cf. *Hebrew Names,* PL 23.871(71), (Lagarde 48); cf. *Commentarioli in ps.* 87.1.
4 Cf. Ps. 87(88).2.
5 Luke 23.46.
6 Cf. Homily 22 on Ps. 93, p. 177.

lay them down upon the cross. 'My life draws near to the nether world.' Well said, 'draws near,' for He was not detained in hell, but drew nigh to the nether world for our sake. Another psalm says, in fact, in the name of the Lord: 'Because you will not abandon my soul to the nether world, nor will you suffer your faithful one to undergo corruption.'[7]

'I am numbered with those who go down into the pit.' My slayers thought that because with the rest of mankind I went down into the prison of the Lower World, I was to be retained in the pit of hell. They did not know that I had gone down in order to draw up with Me those who were being detained there. 'I am like a man without help, I am free among the dead.'[8] He did not say, I am without help, but I am like one without help, because He had a helper, the Father. 'I am free among the dead.' Other men are held in the nether world by the bonds of sin: 'There is no man without sin, not if his life were of one day.'[9] We are all bound in sin; hence, whoever goes down into the Lower World is held there by the law of the Lower World. 'In the meshes of his own sin, he will be held fast.'[10] By nature, I was free; I became like to a sinner on account of the sins of men.

'Like the slain who lie in the grave.' Well said, 'like the slain'; He had no wound, but received a wound for the salvation of men, as Isaia says: 'It was our wounds that he bore, our sufferings that he endured.'[11]

'You have plunged me into the bottom of the pit.' I descended into the very depths of hell in order to release all mankind from the chains of hell. 'Into the dark abyss and into the shadow of death.'[12] He did not say into death, but into the shadow of death. Death had not been inflicted upon Me by

7 Ps. 15.10.
8 Cf. Ps. 87(88).5, 6.
9 Cf. Job 14.4, 5, LXX.
10 Prov. 5.22.
11 Cf. Isa. 53.4.
12 Cf. Ps. 87(88).7.

the Jews, but only the shadow of death, for it was My will to descend for the salvation of mankind. I, who am Light, went down into hell, therefore, to liberate souls from that abyss of darkness.

'Upon me your wrath lies heavy,' all Your wrath has fallen upon Me that it might withdraw from others. 'With all your billows you overwhelm me'; the whole tempest rages down upon Me that in the world there may be tranquility.

'You have taken my friends away from me.' In the Passion of the cross, even My apostles fled Me; so completely did they shun Me that Peter himself said: 'I do not know this man.'[13] You notice how we are hurrying along, making very brief comments rather than attempting explanations, since time prohibits. 'They look upon me as an abomination':[14] the Jews, of course, who cry out: 'Crucify him! Crucify him! We have no king but Caesar.'[15]

'I am imprisoned, and I do not escape.'[16] What did He mean by saying: 'I am imprisoned, and I do not escape'? The Jews betrayed Me; nevertheless, in My compassionate mercy, I did not abandon them, but loved them. I was delivered over by them to Pilate, and I did not escape from them but prayed on the cross: 'Father, forgive them, for they do not know what they are doing.'[17] Let us express this another way. 'I am imprisoned, and I do not escape.' When they sought to throw Him down headlong from the brow of the hill, He passed through their midst in safety.[18] This is, therefore, what He is saying: Am I not able, even now when I am imprisoned, to escape the snares of men and the perils of death by the power of My divinity? Since I had come to suffer, it was My whole will to suffer. That I was imprisoned was My will, and that

13 Mark 14.71.
14 Cf. Ps. 87(88).9.
15 Cf. John 19.15.
16 Cf. Ps. 87(88).9.
17 Luke 23.34.
18 Luke 4.29, 30.

I did not escape was My will. Let us give still another explanation. I was imprisoned as man, and I did not depart from the majesty of My divinity. Still another: I was imprisoned by men, and I did not leave the bosom of the Father. And again: I was imprisoned as man on earth, and as God I had not withdrawn from heaven. 'My eyes have grown dim through affliction.' I, who was sound by the power of My divine majesty, became infirm for the sins of men.

'I call upon you, O Lord,'[19] not only with My voice, but with My heart: that is certainly the way we should call upon the Father. 'Into our hearts, crying, "Abba, Father." '[20] 'All day long to you I stretch out my hands.'[21] It is this testimony from Scripture that the apostle employed in the name of the Savior in his Letter to the Romans.[22]

You see,[23] therefore, that we are not forcing the psalm, but are following the authority of the apostle. If he used the testimony of one versicle in the name of the Lord, why may we not choose to expound the entire psalm in His name? Even if we wished to interpret it otherwise, the clear judgment of the apostle would invalidate our attempt. If we should attempt to explain the entire psalm, obviously, we would be the cause of our own delay, for now the hour bids us approach the Body of the Savior, the true Lamb, with pure and chaste conscience in the unity of peace, that worthily we may partake of the heavenly Bread, through Christ Jesus our Lord. To whom be glory forever and ever. Amen.

'Will you work wonders for the dead?'[24] Not for the living-dead, but for Me who lives in You. 'Or will physicians raise to life?'[25] Not the spices of physicians, but You, Father, will

19 Cf. Ps. 87(88).10.
20 Gal. 4.6.
21 Cf. Ps. 87(88).10.
22 Cf. Rom. 10.21.
23 This section of the homily is found only in the Florentine MS.
24 From here to the end of the homily, the Latin original is based on MSS MOV.
25 Cf. Ps. 87(88).11; cf. *Commentarioli in ps.* 87.11.

raise Me back to life; and not they, but I, shall give thanks in the people.

'Do they declare your kindness in the grave?' Not he will praise You who is buried in the riches of the world, and not he who lives in the death of sin.

'Are your wonders made known in the darkness, or your justice in the land of oblivion? But I, O Lord, cry out to you; with my morning prayer I wait upon you': because in the morning, You will glorify Me by raising Me up from the dead.

'Why, O Lord, do you reject my prayer,'[26] that this chalice does not pass from me?

'I am afflicted and in agony from my youth,' from the time of the Incarnation. 'I am exalted'[27] on the cross; 'I am humbled'[28] in the grave.

'Your furies have swept over me.' They have passed, they have not persisted.

'They encompass me like water all the day': the Jews in the waves of persecutions. 'On all sides they close in upon me': the Pharisees with the priests; Pilate with the rulers and the people.

'Companion and neighbor you have taken away from me: and my friends because of my misery.'[29] In the shame of the Passion, even the apostles kept aloof from Me.

26 Cf. Ps. 87(88).15.
27 Cf. Ps. 87(88).16.
28 *Ibid.*
29 Cf. Ps. 87(88).19.

HOMILY 66

ON PSALM 88(89)

PSALM 88 HAS FOR ITS TITLE: 'Of understanding for Ethan the Ezrahite.'[1] Whenever the word 'understanding' appears in the title, it introduces a psalm full of mysteries and obscurities. The name 'Ethan' means brave or strong;[2] Ezrahite means helped, or, having obtained help. I mention these facts because we are treading upon history. Rightly, then, is 'understanding' premised that this brave, or strong, man may obtain help from the Lord to penetrate the mysteries that follow. Ezrahite he is, whether he took his name from a locality or was of the family of Merari. Read Numbers and Leviticus for full information. 'Of understanding for Ethan.' 'Of understanding'[3] is prefaced to challenge the reader's knowledge and experience. If the psalm were merely a record of history without any mystical meaning, why would it be necessary to alert the discerning powers of the reader in the title?[4] So Ethan, as we said, is he who is brave, or strong. Ezrahite, however, whether 'helped,' or 'having obtained help,' is intellectually quickened to understand what is going to be said, for, among other things, in the psalms, it says: 'The Lord has sworn to David his servant: Forever will I confirm your posterity.'[5] The Jews maintain that the Lord promised with an oath that they would

1 Cf. Ps. 88(89).1.
2 Cf. *Hebrew Names*, PL 23.865(62), (Lagarde 41).
3 Cf. *Commentarioli in ps*. 88.1.
4 Cf. Letter 65.4, PL 22.625(376).
5 Cf. Ps. 88(89).4, 5.

never be without a leader or ruler from David's posterity, and that now their patriarchs[6] are, likewise, saying: Behold, down to this day the Lord still keeps His oath to us. If, then, they are right in their thinking, why do we see them subjected to the power of Rome and obeying the orders of the emperors? In actual truth, it is to us that the promise of Christ is being made mystically. 'I will establish your throne for all generations.' Has God lied, therefore, because He promised with an oath and has not kept His promise (although certainly His promise must be immutable), since, down to this day, we see that the promise does not endure in the posterity of the Jews? Here is where understanding is necessary. Justly, then, does that brave, or strong, man have understanding as an indispensable support[7] that he may be able to direct his thoughts to the mysteries of the psalm. Let us turn back, therefore, to the beginning.

'The mercies of the Lord I will sing forever.'[8] The prophet did not say mercy, but mercies. If sin were one, then compassionate kindness was one act; but since sins are many, many also are the merciful favors of God.[9] Your mercies, O Lord, 'I will sing forever.' Because I have obtained mercy forever, I must sing forever, for the cause of my praise is eternal. He who sings sends away grief, sends away fear, and rises to joy, for he has obtained mercy. This, then, is what the prophet is saying: Because my sins have been forgiven through the loving kindness of God, on that account I shall sing of His mercies. What he means by forever is this: because You have taken pity on me, not just for a short time, but everlastingly, I shall, in turn, praise You everlastingly, never ceasing, for You have delivered me for all eternity.

'To generation and generation my mouth shall proclaim

---

6 Cf. *Commentary on Isaia* 3.4, PL 24.64(54); *Galatians* 1.1, PL 26.335(373).
7 Cf. *Commentarioli in ps.* 88.1.
8 Cf. Ps. 88(89).2.
9 Cf. Homily 64 on Ps. 84, p. 52; 17 on Ps. 84, p. 129.

your truth.'[10] O the magnificent sequence of the psalm! The psalmist did not begin first with truth and afterwards arrive at mercy, but he obtained mercy first, and thus arrived at truth when he had received pardon for sins. Indeed, at first, when I was a sinner, I did not dare to approach truth; but when I obtained mercy, then, fearlessly, with a brave heart, I proclaimed it. When he said, 'to generation and generation,' he spoke well, for he did not say to generations and generations, but to generation and generation. He was not calling to mind many generations, but only two, one in the circumcised and the other in the Gentiles; to one, Peter is sent, to the other, Paul.[11] What I forgot to mention in the beginning, I shall bring in now, that the psalm at this point must be identified with the person of the Lord Savior. 'To generation and generation, my mouth shall proclaim truth.' He who first spoke through patriarchs and prophets, afterwards spoke in His own person,[12] as the Canticle of Canticles says: 'Let him kiss me with kisses of his mouth.'[13] He is saying, therefore: now, in My own person, I speak of Him of whom I spoke through the prophets; hence, Him whom the world could not hear in His thundering, may it hear, at least, in His crying.[14]

'For you have said, "My kindness shall be established forever." '[15] I, who then spoke in the Old Testament by the patriarchs and prophets, now am Myself speaking, for I have not come to make void the commandments of mercy that the Law had established, but to build upon their foundation. The Lord Himself says in the Gospel: 'I have not come to destroy the Law but to fulfill [it].'[16] What, then, does Moses say? 'Give ear, O heavens, while I speak; let the earth hearken

10 Cf. Ps. 88(89).2.
11 Cf. Homily 12 on Ps. 78, p. 92.
12 Cf. Heb. 1.1, 2.
13 Cant. 1.1.
14 Cf. Letter 82.1, PL 22.736 (513); Homily 88 on the Nativity, p. 227.
15 Cf. Ps. 88(89).3.
16 Cf. Matt. 5.17.

to the words of my mouth.'[17] Jeremia uses the expression: 'This the Lord says,' and so do the rest of the prophets, for what they utter is the Lord's and not their own; that which the Lord proclaims by their mouths, He speaks as through an instrument.[18]

What is the message, then, when the prophet says, 'shall be established' [*aedificabitur*], as if a mansion or a city were to be built? Let us see where else in Scripture there is anything like this. Let us search in Genesis for the connotation of the word *aedificatione*. 'God took a rib from the side of Adam and made it into a woman.'[19] Here, Scripture said, *aedificavit*. The concept of building, as we have said before, is wont to denote the construction of a great house; consequently, Adam's rib fashioned into a woman signifies, by apostolic authority,[20] Christ and the Church, and that is why Scripture said He formed [*aedificavit*] a woman from the rib. We have heard about the first Adam; let us come now to the second Adam and see how the Church is made [*aedificetur*] from His side. The side of the Lord Savior as He hung on the cross is pierced with a lance and from it there comes forth blood and water. Would you like to know how the Church is built up from water and blood? First, through the baptism of water, sins are forgiven; then, the blood of martyrs crowns the edifice.[21] Since it is evident that the Church is established by the kindness of God, it follows logically that: 'in heaven you have confirmed your faithfulness,' implies that on earth You confirm Your kindness, in heaven, Your faithfulness.

Listen, heretic: in heaven, God's faithfulness is confirmed. If souls have fallen down from heaven because of sins they had committed,[22] how is faithfulness confirmed in heaven? If every

17 Deut. 32.1.
18 Cf. *Commentary on Jeremia* 23.23, 24, PL 24.826(1004).
19 Cf. Gen 2.22.
20 Eph. 5.32; cf. Letter 123.12, PL 22.1053(908); *Against Jovinian* 1.16, PL 23.246(265).
21 Cf. Letter 69.6, PL 22.660(420).
22 Cf. Homily 88 on the Nativity, p. 223; Letter 75.1, PL 22.686 (452).

day souls fall headlong to earth, how does the Lord in the Lord's Prayer teach: 'Thy will be done on earth, as it is in heaven'?[23] On the authority of the Lord and Savior, we ask, therefore, what kind of sin is it that can be committed in heaven by a soul without a body and can also be committed by a soul on earth with a body; and how can the soul bound now by the confinement of the body preserve on earth the justice that it was unable to preserve in heaven when it was free? Here is something novel: in heaven, the soul sinned and was thrust down to earth so that it may find on earth what it had lost in heaven! When the soul was not in the body, it committed sin; how is it possible that it may merit God more easily when it is in the body, for: 'the flesh lusts against the spirit and the spirit against the flesh'?[24]

'I have made a covenant with my chosen one.' Would you know how, even to this day, the Lord makes His covenant? Let us live good lives and we shall merit to be partners of the elect in the covenant of the Lord. 'I have sworn to David my servant.' What has the Lord sworn to David? 'Forever will I confirm your posterity.' Come to our assistance, O Apostle, and throw light upon this versicle. What does the apostle say? 'He does not say in offsprings, but in offspring, who is Christ.'[25] John says in the Apocalypse: 'He who has the key of David, he who opens and no one shuts, and who shuts and no one opens.'[26] This is the key held in the Law by the scribes and Pharisees whom the Lord warns in the Gospel: 'Woe to you lawyers! who hold the key of the kingdom of heaven.'[27] O you Pharisees, who hold the keys of the kingdom and do not believe in Christ who is the gate of the kingdom and the door, to you, indeed, the promise is made, but to us it is granted;[28] you have the flesh, but we have the spirit; nay

23 Matt. 6.10.
24 Gal. 5.17.
25 Cf. Gal. 3.16.
26 Apoc. 3.7.
27 Cf. Luke 11.52.
28 Cf. Homily 5 on Ps. 14, p. 42.

rather, because you deny the spirit, you have lost the flesh with the spirit.

'I will establish your throne unto generation and generation.'[29] Upon two generations, the throne of God is set up, as we have said before, upon the circumcised, naturally, and upon the Gentiles.

'The heavens proclaim your wonders, O Lord.' This thought echoes a verse in the eighteenth psalm: 'The heavens declare the glory of God.'[30] With mystical perception, the prophet calls the apostles heaven. If to the sinner it is said: 'Dust you are and unto dust you shall return,'[31] why may it not be said to the saint or to the just: Heaven you are and unto heaven you shall return? For the saints, as well as the apostles: 'citizenship is in heaven.'[32] Further: 'The heavens proclaim your wonders,' anticipates the repentance to be preached by the apostles which we have accepted in the acknowledgment of our Lord Jesus Christ. If, therefore, we obey their admonitions and follow their example, we, too, may be called 'heaven,' for we shall be imitating those whose citizenship is there. The prophet says, moreover, in another psalm: 'I am but a wayfarer on earth, and a pilgrim like all my fathers,'[33] and this in Judea, his own country. How, then, does he call himself a pilgrim? Because the saints in the present world are but pilgrims on earth with no desire for material possessions; their property, all of it, is in heaven where they have their mansions in a city of which 'the architect and the builder is God.'[34] The prophet, who is not of this world, says he is a pilgrim here and is hastening, with all the ardor of his soul, to his country, Paradise, the kingdom of heaven.

You, O heretic, because I said that Paradise is the homeland of the saints, do not say that I claim that souls existed

29 Cf. Ps. 88(89).5.
30 Ps. 18.2.
31 Gen. 3.19; cf. Homily 46 on Ps. 133, p. 350.
32 Phil. 3.20; cf. Letter 58.2, PL 22.580(320).
33 Cf. Ps. 38.13.
34 Heb. 11.10.

before they came down hither into bodies.[35] I do not say that, but I speak in conformity with the apostle who affirms that, in the transgression of Adam, we have all, through sin, been cast out of Paradise.[36] The apostle teaches that, even in us who were to come later, Adam had fallen. In Christ, therefore, in the heavenly Adam, we believe that we who, through the sin of the first Adam, have fallen from Paradise, now through the justice of the second Adam, are to return to Paradise. 'The heavens proclaim your wonders, O Lord.' What wonders? You have made heaven? You established the earth? You gathered together the waters into one place? What might is this of God, for whom to have spoken is to have created?

These are the mighty deeds, these are the wonders of God: that God became man, was hidden in the womb of a virgin; was born and lay in a manger; that He who healed the wounds of men was wounded by them, struck with blows, crucified; that He who is immortal suffered death and bore patiently so much unjust punishment, lest men be unable to endure retribution for their sins. The sun could not look upon its Lord hanging on the cross, but hid itself lest it share in the sacrilege of the Jews. The earth quakes, rocks are rent apart, all creation is thrown into confusion, because its Creator is slain. The curtain of the temple is torn, for that which had been veiled in Judea is unveiled to all the nations; the curtain is torn and the mysteries of the Law are revealed to the faithful,[37] but to unbelievers, they are hidden to this very day. When Moses, the Old Testament, is read aloud by the Jews on every sabbath, according to the testimony of the apostle: 'the veil covers their hearts.'[38] They read the Law, true enough, but they do not understand because their eyes

35 Cf. Homily 19 on Ps. 89, p. 147; 12 on Ps. 78, pp. 90-91.
36 Cf. Rom. 5.12-14.
37 Cf. *Commentary on Matthew* 27.51, PL 26.221(236); Letter 120.8.2, PL 22.992(831).
38 2 Cor. 3.15.

have grown so dim that they cannot see.[39] They are, indeed, like those of whom Scripture says: 'They have eyes but see not; they have ears but hear not.'[40]

'Who in the clouds can rank with the Lord?'[41] The clouds are the prophets and the apostles who water the arid hearts of men with the showers of their teachings. 'Who is like the Lord among the sons of God? All the saints are called by title and designation the sons of God because they are sons by adoption, but the Son of God, our Lord Jesus Christ only, is Son properly by nature. Of Him the psalmist asks: Who in the clouds or among the sons of God is like the Lord? Who of the angels or saints is to equal the Creator in glory or power, since He Himself gives glory to all, that the praise of Him may be eternal whom every creature fears with a mighty fear and before whom all tremble, whom the cherubim and seraphim and the four living creatures[42] praise together in unceasing chorus, whom the dominations and principalities adore, whom all the earth worships? To whom be glory and empire forever and ever. Amen.

'God who is glorified in the council of the holy ones.'[43] The Paraclete, assuredly, who was to be adored in the assembly of the apostles, is proclaimed equal to the Father and to the Son. 'He is great and awesome beyond all round about him'; they who, by a life of innocence, merit to draw near Him.

'O Lord, God of hosts, who is like you?' in power and in strength. 'Mighty are you, O Lord, and your truth surrounds you.'[44] Truth Himself says: 'Father, I will that where I am, they also may be with me.'[45]

---

39 Cf. Ps. 68.24.
40 Ps. 113B.5, 6.
41 Cf. Ps. 88(89).7.
42 Cf. Apoc. 5.14.
43 Cf. Ps. 88(89).8. Up to this verse in the homily, the Latin text is taken from the Florentine MS. From this point, the Latin text is a series of short notes taken from MSS MOV, which have been incorporated into the *Breviarium,* mixed with other material.
44 Cf. Ps. 88(89).9.
45 Cf. John 17.24.

'You rule over the surging of the sea; you still the swelling of its waves,' the temptations that assail your faithful servants.

'You have crushed the proud one with a mortal blow,'[46] the devil who was mortally wounded by the nails of Your cross. 'North and the sea you created.'[47] By the north is understood the Antichrist of whom the Lord says to Jeremia: 'From the north evil will spread out over all who will dwell in the land.'[48]

'Thabor and Hermon rejoice at your name.' The interpretation of Hermon is *anathema;* Thabor, 'the light coming,' or 'may the light come.' By 'light,' the Old Testament is understood. He who reveals *anathema,* that is, perdition, proclaims the New Testament, in which we are commanded to anathematize sins when the Lord says: 'Unless you repent, you will all perish in the same manner.'[49] 'In the light of your countenance, O Lord, they walk,' in the illumination, surely, of the Holy Spirit. 'At your name,' that is, Christian.

'You are the splendor of their strength and by your favor our horn is exalted.' Even as Your commandments have been a favor to them, Your gracious pleasure, in You their strength is exalted.

'To the Lord belongs assumption,'[50] of a human body, of course; 'and to the Holy One of Israel, our king,' our Lord Jesus Christ Himself, who is king forever.

From here on, the prophet again speaks to the Father: 'Once you spoke in a vision to your sons,'[51] to Your faithful servants, Your prophets, and Your elect; 'and you said, "I have given my help to a mighty one; from my people I have raised

---

46 Cf. Ps. 88(89).11; cf. *Commentarioli in ps.* 88.5.
47 Cf. Ps. 88(89).13.
48 Cf. Jer. 1.14.
49 Luke 13.3.
50 Cf. Ps. 88(89).19.
51 Cf. Ps. 88 (89).20; cf. *Commentarioli in ps.* 88.20; Letter 106.57, PL 22.857(665).

up a chosen man," '[52] Christ the Lord, who is called the elect of the people, because He assumed a human body.

'I have found David, my servant': I chose to assume a body from his posterity. As to the words, 'My servant,' the apostle explains: 'He did not consider being equal to God a thing to be clung to, but emptied himself, taking the nature of a slave.'[53] 'With my holy oil I have anointed him,' with joy and holiness.

'That my hand may be always with him, and that my arm may make him strong,' in the body He had assumed.

'No enemy shall deceive him,' the devil, obviously; 'nor shall the wicked afflict him,' Judas the traitor.

'I will crush his foes before him,' the Jews, surely, who, frequently confounded by the Lord, dispersed from His presence as though struck at with swords. 'Those who hate him, I will put to flight':[54] evil demons who so many times fled from His presence at His command.

'My faithfulness and my kindness shall be with him, and through my name shall his horn be exalted. I will set his hand upon the sea, his right hand upon the rivers,' upon the princes and powers of this world.

'He shall say of me, "You are my father," and I will make him the firstborn, highest of the kings of the earth.' The Lord Jesus: 'the first born from the dead,'[55] as the apostle says, was made highest,[56] ascending into heaven and subjecting to Himself all the kingdoms of the world.

'Forever I will maintain my kindness toward him, and my covenant with him stands firm.' His kindness He preserves perpetually in the Church which He has redeemed through the covenant of His commandments.

'I will make his posterity endure forever and his throne as the days of heaven.' This refers to the assembly of the faith-

52 Cf. Ps. 88(89).20; cf. *Commentarioli in ps.* 88.21.
53 Phil. 2.6, 7.
54 Cf. Ps. 88(89).24.
55 Col. 1.18.
56 Cf. Heb. 7.26.

ful, the Church in which God abides seated, as it were, on a throne.

'If his sons forsake my law' . . . 'the promise of my lips I will not alter.' Deserters of the law, forgetters of judgments, violators of the decrees of righteousness, and transgressors of the commandments are to be punished with a rod, that is, with God's discipline, and divine mercy will not be withdrawn. The truth is being revealed that no one is to be excluded from the Church without the hope of coming back, for just as divine severity terrifies with manifest justice, so even does paternal love restore with a tempering clemency.

'Once, by my holy one, have I sworn,'[57] by that Man, the Lord. 'I will not be false to David,' for by no falsehood is God deceived. 'His posterity shall continue forever,' namely, the people He has won.

'His throne shall be like the sun before me,' signifies that the Church will abide in the brightness of the glory that is to come, 'like the moon, which remains forever'[58] in the fullness of light. 'A faithful witness in the sky': Christ, the Lord Himself, who bore faithful witness in the world to God the Father, was lifted up into heaven.

From here on, it is the voice of the apostles addressing the Father: 'Yet you have rejected and spurned and been enraged at your Christ,'[59] by giving Him over to His enemies.

'You have renounced the covenant with your servant,' through which You had promised us we would reign with Him, 'and defiled his sanctuary in the dust.'[60] You had promised that You would not suffer Your faithful one to undergo corruption,[61] and now He is hidden in a grave.

'You have broken down all his walls,' the words of the Law and the prophets in which we were being detained.

---

57 Cf. Ps. 88(89).36.
58 Cf. *Commentarioli in ps.* 88.38.
59 Cf. *Commentarioli in ps.* 88.39; cf. Ps. 88(89).39.
60 Cf. Ps. 88(89).40.
61 Cf. Ps. 15.10.

'All who pass by the way have plundered him.' They, indeed, passed Him by who said: 'I am the way, and the truth, and the life,'[62] when they divided His garments and dug into His body with the nails and the spear. 'He is made the reproach of his neighbors,' of the Jews and the chief priests.

'You have exalted the right hand of his foes,' when You laid Him low in death: 'you have gladdened all his enemies,' Pilate, the Gentiles, and the Jews.

'You have turned back his sharp sword,' when the word of His preaching did not profit the Jews; 'and have not sustained him in battle,' surely, in the severe suffering of the Passion; 'and hurled his throne to the ground,' that is, the souls of His faithful servants who were thrown into confusion by His death.

'You have shortened the days of his youth; you have covered him with shame,' the shame of death. The apostles said this, not knowing that He was to rise again from the dead. They made comments such as these as if they were reproaching the Father, because they did not know that He was returning from the nether world. The Church, speaking after them, says: 'How long, O God, will you be angry? Will your wrath burn like fire?'[63] How long will You be angry, that You do not call Him back from the dead?

'Remember, O Lord, how frail my life is.'[64] There is nothing to my life except in Him whose return from the Lower World I await. 'In vain have you created all the children of men,'[65] for if You did not create them in vain, but, truly, with the hope of the resurrection, must You not all the more raise up Your own Son from the dead?

'What man shall live, and not see death, but deliver himself from the power of the nether world?' I know that no flesh shall escape death, and no man preserve his soul from hell;

62 John 14.6.
63 Cf. Ps. 88(89).47.
64 Cf. Ps. 88(89).48.
65 *Ibid.*

but I have learned that God was hiding, concealed under the covering of the flesh, for death and hell did not detain Him.

'Where are your ancient favors, O Lord, which you pledged to David by your faithfulness,' if He is not restored to life?

'Remember, O Lord, the insults to your servants' who are awaiting You, 'which I bear from many nations'[66] that I have gathered together, as it were in My bosom, into one house of faith.

'With which your enemies have reviled, O Lord,' the Jews, Sadducees, and Pharisees. 'With which they have reviled your Christ on his way,'[67] when on His way from them, He was saying to the Gentiles: 'Behold, your house is left to you desolate.'[68]

'Blessed be the Lord forever. Amen, and amen!'[69]

66 Cf. Ps. 88(89).51.
67 Cf. Ps. 88(89).52.
68 Matt. 23.38; Luke 13.35.
69 Cf. *Commentarioli in ps.* 88.53.

HOMILY 67

ON PSALM 89(90)

THE EIGHTY-NINTH PSALM has just been read and its title is: 'A prayer of Moses, the man of God.' This psalm serves as an introduction to the fourth book of the psalter, which is divided into five books.[1] The first to the fortieth psalm constitute the first book; the fortieth to the seventieth, the second; the seventy-first to the eighty-eighth, the third; the eighty-eighth to the hundred-fifth, the fourth; the hundred-fifth to the end, the fifth book. The fourth book opens with a prayer of Moses, the man of God. The Hebrews think that, not this psalm only, but also the next ten that follow consecutively and have no title of their own, were composed by Moses.[2] They believe that those without a title are his because they seem to be connected sequentially to the eighty-ninth.

'A prayer of Moses, the man of God.' If all men were men of God, there would have been no need for the qualification in: 'A prayer of Moses, the man of God.' Would you like evidence that not all men are men of God? 'Man, for all his splendor, does not understand; he resembles the beasts that perish.'[3] It is a noble tribute, indeed, to be called men of God, or servants of God.[4] When anyone is so designated, it is a sign, not of his lowliness, but of his dignity, for it is not the condition of servitude that is emphasized, but the distinc-

1 Cf. *Commentarioli in ps.* 40.14.
2 Cf. *Commentary on Malachia,* PL 25.1542 (941-942), Preface; Letter 140.2, PL 22.1167(1050).
3 Cf. Ps. 48.13.
4 Cf. Homily 40 on Ps. 115, p. 298.

tion of serving well. 'A prayer of Moses, the man of God.' By Moses, the Law is written; by Moses, the creation of the world is described; from Moses, we learn how man is made to the image of God. What, then, is the import of: 'A prayer of Moses, the man of God'? Well, Moses writes on how man was made and how he fell from his estate; hence, now he prays that he who fell down into death may be lifted up into life; and that he who had fallen through sin, prompted by the devil, may rise again through Christ to glory. Moses, therefore, prays thus to God:

'O Lord, you have been our refuge.' Refuge always implies that there has been a persecution,[5] for unless someone were persecuting us, there would be no need to take refuge in another. 'O Lord, you have been our refuge.' Because the intense and burning heat of tribulation is exhausting us, we seek refuge under the shadow of Your wings. 'O Lord, you have been our refuge.' We fly to Your protection because a monstrous beast is upon us, because we have many adversaries and enemies, do You, at least, be our refuge. 'Through all generations.' In this verse, just listen to the hydra hissing![6] Those who claim that souls were made before the world and before they were sent into bodies[7] quote Scripture after this fashion: O Lord, You have been our refuge through all generations, before mountains were made, or the earth took form; before this world was created, You have been our refuge. Their punctuation is wrong;[8] their understanding is at fault. It should read: Lord, You have been our refuge through all generations. Here comes the division; then the next part follows: 'Before the mountains were begotten and the earth and the world were brought forth, from everlasting to everlasting you are God.' This, then, is the proper reading; not

5 Cf. Letter 140.5, PL 22.1169(1052).

6 Cf. *Against Jovinian* 1.4, PL 23.224(241); Homily 75 on the beginning of Mark's Gospel 1, p. 130; Letter 130.16, PL 22.1120 (992).

7 Cf. Homily 66 on Ps. 88, pp. 65-66, 68.

8 Cf. Homily 19 on Ps. 89, pp. 147-148; cf. Letter 140.6, PL 22.1169-1170(1053).

that the soul of man has existed before the world, but that the Lord God be known to have existed always and from everlasting. The next versicle says fittingly: 'From everlasting to everlasting you are God'; from eternity unto eternity You are the Eternal, without beginning, without end.

'Do not turn man back to dust.'[9] Moses is praying for man and what is he saying? Do not allow man to perish whom You have made to Your own image. 'Do not turn man back to dust'; do not consider the worthlessness of the body, but the worth of the soul. Let it be enough for us to have heard once: 'Dust you are and unto dust you shall return,'[10] and be humbled because of the consciousness of our sin. 'Do not turn man back to dust.' Do not turn, but convert, for: 'You have said,'[11] through all the prophets: 'Return, O children of men.' Let it be the end of sin; repent, that salvation may be yours. 'Do not turn man back to dust.' Send Your Son that He may lift up the body of our lowliness and, through a new manner of life, raise it up to heaven released from the bondage of earth.

'A thousand years in your sight are as yesterday, now that it is past.' Compared to the eternity of God, man's whole life-span is brief; however long it may seem to us, in comparison to eternity, it is reckoned as nothing, for it comes to an end.

'As a watch of the night.' The night consists of four watches divided into periods of three hours, as, for example, the Gospel says: 'In the fourth watch of the night Jesus came to them,'[12] which is interpreted to be about the time of cock-crow. This, then, is the meaning of the versicle: a thousand years in Your sight are to be compared, not merely to the shortness of a day, but to the short span of three hours. 'Their years are of no account.'[13] In the beginning of the

9 Cf. Ps. 89(90).3.
10 Gen. 3.19.
11 Cf. Ps. 89(90).3.
12 Matt. 14.25; cf. Letter 140.8, PL 22.1172(1056).
13 Cf. Ps. 89(90).5.

world, man lived nearly a thousand years, and a thousand years in the sight of God are about as long as a watch in the night. But I have explained enough; yes, the ages of man are as nothing compared to divine eternity.

Would you like to know to what degree human life is nothing? Listen to what follows. 'The next morning they are like the changing grass.' Just as quickly as the morning dew disappears, so passes the life of man. Our morning is youth: 'which at dawn springs up anew.' In young manhood and in the perfect age, we blossom forth; but in old age, we wane and the flower of our strength wilts and fades. Who of us, for instance, knows when our time of life will pass away? Almost before we realize it, behind our very back, old age seizes upon us: 'By evening wilts and fades.' Evening is our old age, dried and withered and trembling with various diseases, after the flower of youth has been broken off. 'All mankind is grass, and all their glory like the flower of the field. Though the grass withers and the flower wilts, the word of our Lord stands forever.'[14] We are still alive, and part of us has already perished in old age; even though our soul is the same, nevertheless, we who suffer the loss of the pristine vigor of youth are, in a real sense, other than we were.

'Truly we are consumed by your anger.' Because we have deserved Your anger through sin, the immortality that You had given us, we have lost in Adam, from whom, as it were naturally, by law of heredity, sin has been bequeathed to us. 'By your wrath we are put to rout.' Accurately said, 'put to rout,' for he who is put to rout does not perish. He is shaken violently in terror so that he feels the power of Him whom he had scorned by sinning, and with humble submission takes refuge in penance. 'By your wrath we are put to rout.' Because of our offenses, we are greatly disturbed, but because we believe in Your Christ and acknowledge Him, we are comforted.

14 Cf. Isa. 40.6, 8; cf. Letter 140.9, PL 22.1173(1057).

'You have kept our iniquities before you'; not one of our sins escapes You; all the evils that we have committed are exposed before You. 'Our life in the light of your scrutiny.'[15] Every moment of our life, everything we do, lies open before Your eyes; darkness itself does not hide from You.

'All our days have passed away.'[16] The days so pass away and death draws near, that our whole lifetime, and life itself, slips away almost imperceptibly, so frail a thing it is. In fact, what I am saying now[17] and you are hearing, is terminating a part of our life; and however much we believe that anyone has profited for his soul, nevertheless, because an interval of time has been used up, it is a loss of a portion of one's life. So it happens that where we think we have gain, there rather is an occasion for loss.

'Our years will be considered as a spider.'[18] The prophet could not have more aptly described human life and all our solicitude and endeavors for which we run hither and thither, store up resources, seek wealth, build houses, and procreate children;[19] and to what is all this compared! 'Our years will be considered as a spider,' for just as we observe a spider on the wall spin threads, weave a web that is destroyed by a sudden gust of wind, even so the achievements of a lifetime are destroyed by a sudden attack of trouble or death. 'Seventy is the sum of our years.' See how gradually human life has been contracted! At first in Paradise, we had received the gift of eternal life which we lost through disobedience; afterwards, the life of the ancients was reduced to a thousand years; now, in our days, a lifetime scarcely reaches seventy.

'Seventy is the sum of our years, or eighty, if we are strong, and most of them are fruitless toil.'[20] Most of our years are fruitless toil; that is what we said before, for where we expect

15 Cf. Ps. 89(90).8; cf. Letter 140.11, PL 22.1174(1058).
16 Cf. Ps. 89(90).9.
17 Cf. Homily 19 on Ps. 89, p. 150; cf. Letter 140.12, PL 22.1174(1059).
18 Cf. Ps. 89(90).9; cf. *Commentarioli in ps.* 89.9.
19 Cf. Homily 19 on Ps. 89, p. 150.
20 Cf. Letter 10.1, PL 22.343(23).

gain in our life, there we find trouble and loss. Where there is an increase of years, there is old age; where there is old age, there is disease; where there is disease, there is pain and anguish; where there is anguish, there is a longing for death.

'Meekness overtakes us, and we shall be chastened.'[21] What is this meekness in which we are chastened? 'Remember, O Lord, for David all his meekness.'[22] What is this meekness? 'Learn from me for I am meek and humble of heart.'[23] 'Meekness overtakes us.' The prophet did not say, the 'meek one comes,' but 'meekness comes,' because he refers to our Lord Jesus Christ who, as in another place in Scripture is called not wise but Wisdom,[24] is here called not meek, but Meekness.

'Make known your right hand, that restrained we may gain wisdom of heart.'[25] May Your right hand with which You fashioned the world bring light to the world. 'To whom has the arm of the Lord been revealed?'[26] May Your right hand with which You formed man take on a human body and save man. 'That restrained we may gain wisdom of heart.' We may interpret these words to mean: May those who formerly wandered about at will be curbed by Your wisdom. It is better to be well fettered than to be disastrously free; better to stand still than to run into ruin. The colt in the Gospel, for example, when it was free and unrestrained, dashed about among the precipices, but afterwards, when our Lord sat upon it, it was bridled and brought under control; so, likewise, we beg You to make Your right hand known to the world, that the restless and inconstant be reined in by Your wisdom.

'Return, O Lord! How long?' Return, O Lord, and look upon Your image; do not turn to us Your back, but show us

---

21 Cf. Ps. 89(90).10.
22 Cf. Ps. 131.1; cf. Letter 76.1, PL 22.689(456); 82.1, PL 22.736(513).
23 Matt. 11.29.
24 Cf. 1 Cor. 1.24; cf. Letter 53.4, PL 22.543(274).
25 Cf. Ps. 89(90).12; cf. *Commentarioli in ps.* 89.11; Letter 140.16, PL 22.1177(1062).
26 Isa. 53.1.

Your face. 'Return, how long!' He who says, 'how long,' proves that he is full of longing and cannot endure the delay of his desire.

'We are filled at daybreak with your kindness.'[27] Mysteries are revealed in the psalm, replete with allegorical figures. Moses, a type of the human race, is pleading that the Son of God deign to come down to earth. Because he had prayed: 'Make your right hand known,' and now perceives that his prayer has been granted, he takes up his prayer again and says: We were filled at daybreak with Your kindness when, on the third day, Your Son rose from the dead. Because in the evening, He descended for our sake into the shadows of death to draw us forth at daybreak; at that hour, we experienced the fullness of Your kindness. It is in this sense that Psalm 21 is entitled: 'For the protection at dawn.'[28] Your kindness has always been manifest to Your faithful servants, but never has it been so clear and lavish, as when the Redeemer of all rose from the dead for the salvation of each and every one. 'That we may shout for joy and gladness.' After the joy of the Resurrection of our Lord, by which we believe that we have been redeemed and shall rise again on the day of judgment, we rejoice for the rest of our days and exult with the fullness of trust; and in hymns and spiritual songs, we give praise to God through Jesus Christ our Lord, to whom be glory forever and ever. Amen.

27 Cf. Ps. 89(90).14.
28 Cf. Ps. 21.1; cf. *Commentarioli in ps.* 21.1.

HOMILY 68

ON PSALM 90(91)

PSALM OF PRAISE FOR DAVID.'[1] In the first place, it is necessary to know that from the eighty-eighth to the hundredth psalm, eleven psalms[2] are without title in the Hebrew text, and that these, for the reasons that we mentioned recently when discussing the preceding psalm, belong to the same author as the one entitled: 'A prayer of Moses, the man of God.'[3]

'You who dwell in the shelter of the Most High.' It is ours to begin a work,[4] it is God's part to further it, for He does not give a crown to the slothful, but to those who toil.[5] 'Who abide in the shadow of the God of heaven.'[6] Where we read, 'God of heaven,' the Hebrew has SADDAI;[7] hence, we may gather that the words of Ezechiel: 'I heard the voice of the Lord Saddai speaking,'[8] mean that he heard the voice of the Lord, the God of heaven, speaking, since the translation of SADDAI is 'of the God of heaven.'

'My refuge, my God.'[9] Rightly said, refuge; for there are many persecutors, and You alone are refuge; there are many

1 Cf. Ps. 90(91).1.
2 Cf. *Against Rufinus* 1.13, PL 23.426(469); Letter 140.2, PL 22.1167(1050); *Commentary on Malachia*, Preface, PL 25.1542(941-942).
3 Ps. 89.1.
4 Cf. Homily 63 on Ps. 83, p. 47; 2 on Ps. 5, p. 17; 34 on Ps. 107, p. 252; 61 on Ps. 15, p. 29; cf. *Against the Pelagians* 3.1, PL 23.596 (781); 1.5, PL 23.523(700); Letter 130.12, PL 22.1130(1005).
5 Cf. Homily 63 on Ps. 83, p. 48.
6 Cf. Ps. 90(91).1.
7 Cf. *Commentarioli in ps.* 90.1.
8 Cf. Ezech. 10.5.
9 Cf. Ps. 90(91).2.

wounds, but You only are physician. 'In him will I trust. For he will rescue me from the snare of the fowler.'[10] In this generation, there are many fowlers eager to ensnare our souls, as the prophet says: 'We were rescued like a bird from the fowlers' snare.'[11] We have noted many times that, in Sacred Scripture, hunters play an unfavorable role. Nemrod, for example, that giant who was always rebelling against God, was a hunter,[12] as was Esau, also. 'For he will rescue me from the snare of the fowler.' We read in Proverbs: 'The eyes of the harlot, the snare of the sinner.'[13] 'Anyone who even looks with lust at a woman has already committed adultery in his heart.'[14] There are as many snares as there are sins; as many hunters as there are snares. The teachings of heretics are the traps of death. The psalmist, in fact, goes on to say: 'and from the sharp word.'[15] You see that he is speaking of heretics. Instead of our word for sharp, the Hebrew has 'concealed,' for heretics always promise deep, dark secrets in order to ravage and tear in pieces what is true and clear.

'With his pinions he will cover you.' Who will cover you? The God of heaven, of course, just as the hen covers her young[16] and the eagle its nestlings. In this same strain, the song in Deuteronomy[17] says that He bore the people of Israel upon His shoulders and like the eagle guarded them. This same versicle may be interpreted also of the Savior because on the cross He gave us the shelter of His wings. 'Under his wings you shall take refuge.' 'All the day long I stretched out my hand to a people unbelieving and contradicting.'[18] The hands of the Lord lifted up to heaven were not begging for help, but were sheltering us, His miserable creatures.

10 Cf. Ps. 90(91).2, 3.
11 Ps. 123.7.
12 Cf. Homily 20 on Ps. 90, pp. 156-157.
13 Cf. Prov. 6.25; cf. LXX.
14 Matt. 5.28.
15 Cf. Ps. 90(91).3.
16 Cf. Matt. 23.37.
17 Deut. 32.11.
18 Rom. 10.21.

'His faithfulness shall compass you with a shield,'[19] that is, His faithfulness will protect you on all sides. What comes next? 'You shall not fear the terror of the night.' The just man does not fear the night, but the day. 'Come, children, hear me; I will teach you the fear of the Lord.'[20] They who are the children of the prophets have no fear of the night nor the darkness, but of the light and the day. 'To shoot in the dark at the upright of heart.'[21] The devil does not shoot his arrows in the daytime lest he be seen, for everything that is done in the light is made manifest by the light.[22]

Someone may object, however: If the devil does not shoot in the daylight, what, then, in the following versicle does the psalmist mean: 'Nor the arrow that flies by day'? What is this arrow that flies by day? It is the teaching of the heretics[23] that flies hither and thither throughout the day—throughout all God's law—in their anxious search to gather testimony against us that they may rob us of all truth by their interpretation. 'Not the pestilence that roams in the darkness.' He did not say stands, but roams, for heretics are never constant in their convictions, but are forever changing their opinions,[24] shifting back and forth.

'Nor the devastating plague at noon.' We read in Genesis that Joseph held a feast for his brothers at noon, and in the Canticle of Canticles it is written: 'Where do you pasture your flock, where do you give them rest? At midday.'[25] No less than the saints, who have a midday light where they pasture their flocks and give them rest, the devil, transformed into an angel of light,[26] has his servants disguised as false ministers of justice. When, for example, you hear a heretic

19 Cf. Ps. 90(91).4.
20 Ps. 33.12.
21 Ps. 10.2.
22 Cf. Eph. 5.13.
23 Cf. *Against the Pelagians* 2.20, PL 23.583(766).
24 Cf. Homily 2 on Ps. 5, p. 21.
25 Cf. Cant. 1.7; cf. Letter 108.12, PL 22.887(701); 122.1, PL 22.1039(890).
26 Cf. 2 Cor. 11.14; cf. Letter 15.4, PL 22.357(41).

declaiming, 'This, Moses said,' 'this is written in the Prophets,' 'this, in the Gospels,' would it not seem to you, if you were unaware of their treachery, that it is the Savior's messenger speaking? Some inexperienced and credulous men think that there is a real midday demon that has more power to attack men at that time; we, however, shall interpret the noonday devils as the heresiarchs who, while simulating angels of light, preach dogmas of darkness. Would you have us make a neat application? Arius and the other heretics that come from Alexandria are called noonday devils.[27]

'Though two thousand fall at your side, ten thousand at your right side.'[28] 'At your side,' and 'at your right side.' The psalmist did not say at your left side because the just man has no left side, even as it is written in the Gospel: 'If someone strike thee on the right cheek, turn to him the other also.'[29] The Lord did not say, turn to him the left, since, indeed, the sheep will stand on the right side and the goats on the left.[30] 'Though two thousand fall at your side and ten thousand at your right side.' At the side of the just man, we may infer bodily weaknesses; on the right side, however, integrity of soul. By the sufferings of the body, by fasts and chastity, a thousand fall; but on the right where, through the freedom of the soul, doctrine is pure and holy, the greatest number of the enemy fall. 'Near you they shall not come.'[31] Imagine here that an armed mob of enemies is heading for the just man and of them the psalmist is saying: 'Near you they shall not come.' That means they shall perish before they reach you.

'Rather with your eyes shall you behold and see the requital of the wicked.' You will look upon the corpses of the dead and wonder at the divine majesty of the Lord Savior.

27 Cf. *Against Rufinus* 2.17, PL 23.460(509).
28 Cf. Ps. 90(91).7.
29 Matt. 5.39.
30 Cf. Matt. 25.33.
31 Cf. Ps. 90(91).7.

You will see the condign punishment of sinners. The sinners' fall is their death. What this all means is that you, who have made the Lord your refuge, look in safety upon the requital of heretics, for you have protected yourself against their teachings.

The words above have been said to the just man in the name of the Lord; now, however, there is a change in persons and the just man in contemplation answers the Lord: 'You, O Lord, are my hope.'[32] He who says this is a just man. 'You have made the Most High your stronghold.' Once more persons change, and it is this frequent change in persons that adds to the obscurity of the psalms.[33] Now, while the just man is praying to the Lord and saying: 'You, O Lord, are my hope,' he hears from the Lord the answer: 'You have made the Most High your refuge.' The following verse, therefore, continues appropriately.

'No evil shall befall you, nor shall affliction come near your tent.' It did not say, shall not make a noise,[34] but shall not 'come near your tent,' for it is not possible to keep the persecutions of the devil from resounding about the just man. If the Lord Himself was scourged and harassed by tribulations and temptations, who of the just will not be stung with the devil's lash? Let us consider the meaning of: 'Nor shall affliction come near your tent.' It means that the devil has certainly produced an uproar on the outside and has tried to arouse sensuous passions, but the tent of the soul, or the mind which is the tabernacle of faith, he does not subvert.

'To his angels he has given command about you, that they guard you in all your ways. Upon their hands they shall bear you up, lest you dash your foot against a stone.' If ever heretics interpret anything from Holy Writ against us, we must not be disturbed,[35] for the devil has quoted these verses

32 Cf. Ps. 90(91).9.
33 Cf. Homily 13 on Ps. 80, p. 97; 22 on Ps. 93, p. 179.
34 Cf. *Commentary on Nahum* 3.2-4, PL 25.1255(564).
35 Cf. *Against the Luciferians* 28, PL 23.190(201-202).

against the Lord Savior, saying: 'If thou art the Son of God, throw thyself down; for it is written, "He will give his angels charge concerning thee." '[36] The devil, you see, interprets Holy Writ just like the devil, for he applied to the person of the Lord this psalm that does not refer to the Lord at all, but to any just man. However, I concede to you, devil, that of the Lord above it is written: 'Upon their hands they shall bear thee up.' Why did you not also quote the verse that follows: 'You shall tread upon the asp and the viper'? O the stupidity of the enemy-werewolf! He quoted what seemed to appeal to the weakness of the Savior and the vulnerability of man; but what he perceived was directed against himself, he suppressed with his ancient cunning. You are wrong, devil, and you are catching yourself in the trap of your deceit. In this passage, your lie is of benefit to the Church; although your intention was maliciously to tempt, nevertheless, you have revealed that the children of God, all the just, are borne upon the hands of angels—for protection—at the Lord's injunction.

The rest of the psalm follows along in this same manner of exposition. That to the just and the beloved of God is given, moreover, the power to tread upon that ancient, contemptible snake and to crush his whole army under their heel, we shall find stated very clearly in the Gospel, for the Lord says to the apostles: 'Behold, I have given you power to tread upon serpents and scorpions.'[37] We shall be able to appreciate what power has been given to us as well, when we realize that we have been girded against serpents and scorpions by our apostolic way of life. Let us pray the Lord, therefore, that He who gave power to the just may give to us, who are still very little children, the shelter of His justice, so that we may follow the example of the apostles and be helped by their merits, in Christ Jesus our Lord. To whom be glory forever and ever. Amen.

---

36 Cf. Matt. 4.6.
37 Luke 10.19.

HOMILY 69

ON PSALM 91(92)

T IS GOOD TO CONFESS[1] to the Lord, to sing praise to your name, Most High.' Why did not the psalmist say first: 'It is good to sing praise,' and after that 'to confess'? Because the other is the order of true praise: it is good for man, first, to repent and confess his sins to the Lord, and when he has acknowledged his sins, then, sing praise to Him, for by penance he has merited the power to burst forth into the praise of God, unrestrained by the consciousness of sin.

'To proclaim your kindness at dawn and your faithfulness throughout the night.' Why is kindness to be sung at dawn and faithfulness at night? Listen attentively, because these are matters not easily understood. First, he said: 'It is good to confess to the Lord'; praise follows the acknowledgment of sin. The man who by repentance for sin has rendered himself worthy to give praise begins also to proclaim Him whom he praises. What does it mean, however, that kindness is proclaimed at dawn and faithfulness is praised at night in song? Wherever there is the mercy of the Lord, there is light, there is dawn, there is the hour when the sun rises and the blind shades of night vanish. 'Your faithfulness throughout the night.' Where there is faithfulness, there is justice; where there is justice, there is judgment; when the sentence has been passed, there is no more room for mercy; where mercy has been eliminated, there threatens the disaster of sin; there it is

1 Cf. Ps. 91(92).2.

night and not day; as the prophet says: 'What will this day of the Lord mean for you? Darkness and not light!'[2] On that day, the scrutiny of each life will be made known as he deserves; hence, in another versicle, the prophet says, this day is to be dreaded . . . 'for great is the day of the Lord and exceedingly terrible; who can bear it?'[3]

'With ten-stringed instrument and lyre, with melody upon the harp. For you make me glad, O Lord, by your deeds; at the works of your hands I rejoice.' No one can utter this except a man of learning, a man who knows that everything whatsoever has been created by the providence of God and who is not scandalized by any created thing, but who recognizes that there is reason for everything, and glorifies the Creator saying: 'For you make me glad, O Lord, by your deeds, at the works of your hands I rejoice.' Take heed, Mani; listen, Marcion, Valentine, and the rest of the heretics who dare to insult the Creator. See, where you take scandal, the prophet exalts and rejoices at the works of the Creator! He knows that anything that appears evil is not so by nature, but has become so by the free choice of the will.

'How great are your works, O Lord! How very deep are your thoughts!' This is the sentiment of the apostle who exclaims: 'Oh, the depth of the riches of the wisdom and of the knowledge of God!'[4] Because Your thoughts are unfathomable, no human pondering, no human thought is able to grasp Your work. Another psalm says: 'All your works are trustworthy.'[5] Mark well: 'Your works are trustworthy.' If our knowledge of the creature depends more on faith than on reason, how much more is this true of our knowledge of the Creator and the Maker of all things? Since Scripture says: 'All your works are trustworthy,' then I, too, who am speaking am trustworthy, inasmuch as I am a part of His works.

---

2 Cf. Amos 5.18.
3 Cf. Joel 2.11; cf. Ps. 129.3; cf. *Commentary on Joel* 2.11, PL 25.966(190).
4 Rom. 11.33; cf. *Against John of Jerusalem* 10, PL 23.379(417).
5 Cf. Ps. 32.4.

I, too, am a subject of faith and not of reason; for I cannot know the principle whereby I walk and talk, make decisions; why my will commands; why my body is obedient to the will; how an immortal soul is united to a mortal body; why my soul wanders hither and thither and cannot be limited by the compass of the world, yet is confined in a body.

Why am I saying all this? Because I heard that, among the brethren, there was a dispute, nay, rather a discussion, on faith. A discussion I say, not a dispute, for where there is strife,[6] there is sin; but where there is discussion, there is conscientious desire for knowledge. Indeed, it was not a case of everyone trying to prove what he did not know; for the brethren deferred to my knowledge and experience. It was not their intention to teach what they did not know,[7] but to learn what they did not know; hence, their discussion is no different from an argument stirred up over the mercy of the Lord. In reference to the Lord Savior, Isaia says: 'Who can describe his generation?'[8] Since it says, 'who,' every creature is excluded, for the prophet did not say: Who of men can describe His generation, but, in general, 'who,' which means not the angel, not the archangel, not the cherubin, not the seraphin. If His generation has been hidden in God from heavenly creatures, what wonder if it seems unknown to us who have been made from the slime of the earth?

It has come to my attention, brethren, that certain brothers had raised the question among themselves and were arguing about how the Father, the Son, and the Holy Spirit are both three and one. You realize from the problem how dangerous such a discussion is. An earthen vessel of potter's clay that cannot even arrive at the principle of its own nature, argues about the Creator and curiously seeks to know about the mystery of the Trinity which the angels in heaven do not understand. In fact, what do the angels say? 'Who is this king

6 Cf. *Against the Pelagians* 1.33, PL 23.551(731).
7 Cf. *Against Rufinus* 2.10, PL 23.451(498).
8 Isa. 53.8, LXX.

of glory? The Lord of hosts; he is the king of glory.'[9] Similarly, in Isaia: 'Who is this that comes from Edom, in radiant garments?'[10] Notice what the angels do: they proclaim His beauty, but are silent about His essence.

Now let us put this query into ordinary language. Do you want to know the nature of God? Do you want to know what God is? Know this, that you do not know.[11] Do not, either, be sad because you do not know, for even the angels have not known, nor any other creature. Someone may object: Why do I believe, then, what I do not grasp? Why am I a Christian, since I do not know how I have become a Christian? I shall answer straightforwardly before we propose any considerations from Holy Writ. My Christian, why does it seem to you that you know nothing? If you know this very fact, that you do not know a thing, does it not seem to you, on the contrary, that you are one who has greater knowledge? A heathen sees a stone and he thinks it is his God; philosophers look up at the sky and think it is their God; others gaze at the sun and think it is God. Truly now, see how much knowledge you have beyond them, you who say: A stone cannot be God; the sun that moves in haste at another's command cannot be God! See, in the very recognition of your lack of knowledge is hidden a greater knowledge; the heathens, on the contrary, do not know what they say they know because their knowledge is false. At the same time, consider what you are called: a believer, not a reasoner.[12] Furthermore, after the reception of baptism, we say: A faithful servant of God has been made, or, I have become a faithful servant of God. I believe what I do not understand; therefore, I have knowledge because I am conscious of my lack of knowledge. Still, someone may say: That is no explanation, but an evasion;[13]

9 Ps. 23.10.
10 Cf. Isa. 63.1; cf. *Commentary on Isaia* 63, PL 24.609(745); *on Abdia* 1.1, PL 25.1101-1102 (366).
11 Cf. *Commentary on Ezechiel* 42.1-13, PL 25.408(510).
12 Cf. Homily 26 on Ps. 98, pp. 210-211.
13 Cf. *Against Rufinus* 2.10, PL 23.451(498).

besides, we already knew that we know that we do not know something; teach us that we may know what is hidden from our understanding.

Is it not better openly to declare ignorance than rashly assume knowledge from pride? On the day of judgment, I shall not be condemned because I shall say: I did not know the essence of my Creator; on the other hand, if I shall have made any rash statement, remember, temerity has its penalty, ignorance deserves pardon. Let us cite proof from Holy Writ and follow, not reason, but the authority of the Lord Savior. When He is about to ascend into heaven, what does He say to His apostles to whom, as Master and Lord, He is giving instructions? No one can speak thus about his own nature except Him who is Himself God; let it be enough for us to know of the Trinity only what the Lord had deigned to reveal. What does He say to the apostles? 'Go, baptize all nations in the name of the Father, and of the Son, and of the Holy Spirit.'[14]

I hear three names, and yet 'name' is singular, for He did not say in the names, but in the name.[15] He mentioned three names; why, then, does He use the singular and say: 'In the name of the Father, and of the Son, and of the Holy Spirit'? The name of the Father, and of the Son, and of the Holy Spirit is one name, but it is the name belonging to the Trinity.[16] If He says, in the name of God the Father, in the name of God the Son, in the name of God the Holy Spirit, then Father, Son, and Holy Spirit is the one name of the Godhead. Do you still ask me how three are called by one name? I do not know, and I frankly acknowledge my ignorance because Christ did not wish to reveal anything about it. This only I know: I am a Christian because I acknowledge one God in Trinity. If, on the contrary, I should maintain that the Father, and the Son, and the Holy Spirit is only one

14 Cf. Matt. 28.19.
15 Cf. *Commentary on Ephesians* 4.5, 6, PL 26.528(610).
16 Cf. *Commentary on Matthew* 28.19, PL 26.227(244).

person, I would be called a Sabellian, and I would begin to be a Jew, not a Christian, for the Jew says there is one God, but because he does not know the Father, the Son, and the Holy Spirit, he does not believe in the mystery of the Trinity. If, therefore, we speak of one God in a sense to exclude the Father, the Son, and the Holy Spirit from the mystery of the Trinity, we become Jews.

I admit frankly, not on my own authority, but on the statement of the Savior, that a stumbling block does spring up in the soul of the listener, namely, 'How can there be one in three?' How is it that the Father, the Son. and the Holy Spirit are undivided in the Godhead? Whenever I use the term persons, I beg you not to think that I mean human persons. I do not speak of persons in the Father, the Son, and the Holy Spirit as being human persons, but as persons according to appropriation. I say the person of the Father because there is a Father; of the Son because there is a Son; of the Holy Spirit because there is a Holy Spirit. The Father is not Son, nor the Son Father, nor the Holy Spirit Father or Son; they are divided by their proper attributions, but are united in their nature. See, this is the obstacle Philip the Apostle was up against when he said to the Lord: 'Lord show us the Father and it is enough for us.'[17] The Lord answers him: 'Philip, have I been so long a time with you, and you do not know the Father? He who sees me sees also the Father.'[18] It would be wrong to say that the Father is the same as the Son, but if you hear the word Son, think also of the Father, for the Son cannot be called Son if He did not have a Father. The name Father, on the other hand, would be meaningless if there did not exist a Son.

There are many things to be said, but for the faithful it is enough to have heard only a little on the mystery of the Trinity.[19] I beg of you, let there be greater rivalry among us

17 John 14.8.
18 Cf. John 14.9.
19 Cf. Homily 70 on Ps. 92, p. 99.

in the monastery in seeking to know how we may triumph over the devil, how we may fast, deplore our sins, prevent our thoughts from drawing us into the captivity of lust, be patient over every injury; how not to revile when a brother has wronged us, but how we may strive to conquer him with the humility that we have learned from Christ: 'who when he suffered did not threaten.'[20] If ever the thought comes and persists, 'What is God, and what is the nature of the Trinity,' let us be content to believe in the fact that the Trinity is. We must not be presumptuous in seeking to know the nature and reason, but we must pray to the Lord in fear without ceasing. Let us display all our skill and knowledge in singing praises of the Trinity day and night. To whom be glory and empire forever and ever. Amen.

20 1 Peter 2.23.

HOMILY 70

ON PSALM 92 (93)

THE TITLE OF THE PSALM before us is: ' A song of praise for David on the Sabbath day when the earth was inhabited.'[1] The Sabbath day is the day of our rest, and the day of the indwelling of our clay. 'The Word was made flesh and dwelt among us,'[2] so our earth has been inhabited. Let us see, therefore, what is the result of this indwelling, by what praises it is proclaimed.

'The Lord is king, in splendor robed; robed is the Lord and girt about with strength; and he has made the world firm, not to be moved.' These three versicles are spoken of the Lord Savior by the prophet, but the rest of the psalm is addressed directly to the Lord Himself. 'The Lord is king, in splendor robed.' The Lord, who first had been a servant, is king; He is robed in splendor. What does Isaia say? 'We have seen him and there was in him no stately bearing, a man of suffering accustomed to infirmity.'[3] The Lord reigns as king; He is robed in splendor. The meaning, then, is that He whose appearance before had been frightful in the meanness of the flesh, now is resplendent in the majesty of the Godhead, for whatever unsightliness there is in Him is to be ascribed to our estate, but whatever there is of beauty shall be applied congruently to His majesty.

'Girt about.' The expression, 'girt about,' must signify some mystery. When we are ungirdled, our tunic flows down

1 Cf. Ps. 92(93).1.
2 John 1.14.
3 Cf. Isa. 53.2, 3.

about our feet; unless a garment is held in by a girdle, it hangs loosely. Because, therefore, we could not bear the full strength of the Lord,[4] He girt His majesty with flesh. This same thought appears in another place in Holy Writ: 'You may see my back; but my face is not to be seen.'[5] Again, the Book of Kings[6] says of Elias that he stood in the entrance of a cave on Mt. Sinai, and from there beheld the Lord as He passed. Note that it says he saw the back of the Lord Savior when he stood in the hollow of a rock. If rock is a symbol for Lord and Savior . . . 'The rock was Christ,'[7] says the apostle. Since, truly, we are set in the hollow of the Rock, through the flesh, we perceive God. Why have I said all this? Because in this same interpretation, we are including also the verse: the Lord is robed in beauty, and girdled. As through the opening of the Rock the Lord and Savior is discerned, so also through the girdle is His majesty perceived.

'He has made the world firm, not to be moved.' If we take this to mean that this world has been made so firm by the Lord that it is never disturbed by any commotion, what does it mean elsewhere in Scripture where it says: 'Heaven and earth will pass away'?[8] If heaven and earth will pass away, what is the meaning here of: 'He has made the world firm, not to be moved'? 'Oikouménē' in this passage, translated as 'the inhabitated earth,' seems to me to be the Church, of which it says in the Gospel: 'I and my Father will come and make our abode with him.'[9] Rightly is that called a habitation which has the Father, Son, and Holy Spirit as inhabitant. What we have come to know, therefore, about 'the inhabited earth,' that is, about the world having been made firm for all eternity, let us also apply to our soul, for if we have the

4 Cf. *Commentarioli in ps.* 64.7.
5 Cf. Exod. 33.23.
6 Cf. 3 Kings 19.11, 12.
7 1 Cor. 10.4.
8 Matt. 24.35.
9 Cf. John 14.23; cf. *Against Jovinian* 2.19, PL 23.327(356).

Father, Son, and Holy Spirit[10] as indweller, our earth shall be immovable for all eternity.

The psalmist has spoken of the kingship of the Lord and of the glory of His garment; he has mentioned His strength, and the world that will not be moved; and now he turns to the Lord Himself, reigning and resounding. What does the prophet say? 'Your throne stands firm, from then, from everlasting you are.'[11] The statement: 'Robed is the Lord and girt about with strength,' proceeds from the meanness of the flesh, nevertheless, Your kingdom has always been. Your throne stands firm, always established, never beginning. 'From then.' From when? From what time? It cannot be specified because it has no beginning. Whenever you say, 'from then,' time never runs out, but is undetermined; when you say, 'then,' it is proper that you be asked, when? So you see that the prophetic utterance was set down without limitation, and you perceive that it contains a syllogism. From then, from everlasting, You are. Excellently said, 'You are'; it did not say, from everlasting 'You began,' but from everlasting 'You are.' You are who always are, who said to Moses: 'This is what you shall tell the Israelites: I AM sent me to you.'[12]

'The floods lift up, O Lord, the floods lift up their voice. More powerful than the roar of many waters, more powerful than the breakers of the sea.'[13] There are as many meanings here as there are words; as many secrets, as versicles. 'The floods lift up their voice.' We find this concept paralleled in another psalm: 'There is a stream whose runlets gladden the city of God';[14] also in: 'Let the rivers clap their hands.'[15] I think the floods that water the world are the apostolic and prophetic offices. 'The floods lift up their voice,' broadcasting the praise and glory of the Lord, proclaiming His judg-

10 Homily 23 on Ps. 95, p. 189.
11 Cf. Ps. 92(93).2.
12 Exod. 3.14.
13 Cf. Ps. 92(93).3, 4.
14 Ps. 45.5.
15 Ps. 97.8.

ments throughout the world. 'Through all the earth their voice resounds, and to the ends of the world, their message.'[16] 'More powerful than the roar of many waters.' The voices of many waters announce to us three mysteries. Let us see what they are.

'More powerful than the roar of many waters, more powerful than the breakers of the sea—powerful on high is the Lord. Your decrees are worthy of trust indeed.' We may interpret sea mystically to mean this generation . . . for it is bitter and full of tempests, and the seafaring meditate upon the many wonderful works of the Lord. That is why the psalmist says: 'More powerful than the breakers of the sea.' Many a man, indeed, we have witnessed raised on high upon the surging billows and suddenly dashed to the bottom; then, again, we witness others, who have been crushed by the floods, just as suddenly elevated to greater heights. We find nothing constant in this world, nothing stable. Where you think there is a calm, there awaits shipwreck. Where there is the appearance of peace, there lurks the violence of storm and hurricanes, and unless we cry out: 'Master, save us,'[17] that very moment we are lost. 'Powerful on high is the Lord.' The man who is able to withstand the stormy billows of this world with his dwelling firmly fixed upon the rock is the one who is able to experience how 'powerful on high is the Lord.' 'The Most High dwells on high who is Holy among the holy';[18] just as it says elsewhere: 'For I, the Lord, am your God; and you shall make and keep yourselves holy, because I am holy.'[19] But to the man laid low by the consciousness of sins and unable to raise his eyes to heaven with Jesus, the Lord is not wonderful on high, but terrible to those plunged below.

'Your decrees are worthy of trust indeed.' There is a similar

16 Ps. 18.5.
17 Cf. Matt. 8.25.
18 Isa. 57.15, LXX.
19 Lev. 11.44.

verse in Psalm 17: 'The decree of the Lord is trustworthy, giving wisdom to the simple.'[20] Who are these simple? 'I praise thee, Father, that thou didst hide these things from the wise and prudent, and didst reveal them to little ones.'[21]

'Holiness befits your house, O Lord.' Just realize what it says. If anyone thinks that he is dwelling in the house of the Lord and is not pure and holy, he is estranged from it, because he does not possess the proper adornments. 'Holiness befits your house, O Lord.' If, according to the apostle, we are the temple and the house of God, then, the holiness of our conduct ought to be an honor and ornament of the Church; if, on the contrary, sins and vices are discovered in us, then, we are the dishonor and pollution of the house of the Lord, not its beauty. 'Holiness befits your house, O Lord.' The house of the Lord is the Church. Now, the Church, by mystical interpretation, has already been prefigured in the flood by the ark in which, at the Lord's command, the clean animals were multiplied. Although, on account of the clean and unclean animals, many different species lived therein, nevertheless, the clean befitted the house of the Lord, and by the unequal number[22] of the sexes prefigured the oblation of virginity. From among the clean animals, Noe offered a worthy holocaust to the Lord after his delivery from the perils of the flood. Many are the things that should be said,[23] but time prevents, and so let these few remarks on the praise of the Lord suffice. To whom be glory forever and ever. Amen.

---

20 Ps. 18.8.
21 Matt. 11.25.
22 Cf. *Commentary on Aggai* 1.1, PL 25.1389(738); Letter 123.12, PL 22.1054(909).
23 Cf. Homily 69 on Ps. 91, p. 93.

HOMILY 71

ON PSALM 93(94)

'The god of vengeance, the Lord, God of vengeance, has acted boldly.'[1] Whether you call Him the Father, the Son, or the Holy Spirit, according to the nature of the Trinity which we have expounded in the Gospel, He is both God and Lord. The God of vengeance has acted boldly. He who was despised in His humility shall take vengeance afterwards in His majesty.

'Rise up, judge of the earth.' You judge the earth because judgment is not proper to heaven. Hear, heretic, that the Lord judges the earth. If there is evil in heaven, why is there not also judgment in heaven? If the souls in heaven have sinned,[2] why is earth only to be judged?[3] 'Render their deserts to the proud.' All sins must be avoided, to be sure, because all sins are contrary to God, but they vary in degree. The proud, for example, are God's enemies. 'God resists the proud, but gives grace to the humble.'[4] The devil is the prince of the proud. 'Lest he be puffed up with pride,' says Holy Writ, 'and incur the condemnation passed on the devil,'[5] for everyone who glorifies himself in his heart is partner to the devil, who used to say: 'By my own power I have done it, and by my wisdom, for I am shrewd. I have moved the boundaries of peoples.'[6] The rest of the passage, in which

1 Cf. Ps. 93(94).1.
2 Cf. Homily 88 on the Nativity of the Lord, p. 223.
3 Cf. Homily 14 on Ps. 81, p. 108.
4 James 4.6; cf. Letter 76.1, PL 22.689(455).
5 1 Tim. 3.6.
6 Isa. 10.13; cf. *Commentary on Ezechiel* 16.48-49, PL 25.154(181-182).

the prophet describes the pride of the devil, is too long to quote. All other failings deserve the mercy of the Lord because, in humility, they are submitted to the tribunal of God; pride alone, because it honors itself beyond its power, resists God. The adulterer or the fornicator[7] does not dare to raise his eyes to heaven; in dejection of soul, he looks for God's mercy; yet this man whom conscience bows down and humbles to the ground, it also elevates to heaven. When pride and inordinate desire for glory raise up a man, they, at the same time, abase him, for by his sin they make him an enemy of God.

'How long, O Lord, shall the wicked, how long shall the wicked glory?' The sinner who supplicates God merits pardon, but the man who vaunts himself in wickedness is proud, and pride makes God an enemy. The Latin, *usquequo,* must be taken in the sense of 'apò xunôn' so that we understand *'Usque quo,'* 'how long,' shall the wicked continue to glory? How long shall they continue to mouth their insolence? How long shall all evildoers continue to boast of their deeds? Human impatience marvels at the patience of God, and says: I, a sinner, do not endure sinners; You who are just, how can You bear with them all? How long, Lord, shall the wicked go on vaunting their wickedness? He did not say, how long shall sinners sin. His is the monstrous sin, who sins and boasts of his sin besides. 'Mouthing insolent speeches.' They veil their wickedness in fine speech; but pride betrays evildoing in the very glorification of evil.

'Your people, O Lord, they trample down, your inheritance they afflict.' Who? The proud. 'Widow and stranger they slay.' History, obviously; but, if according to the anagogical interpretation, every day the proud devil with his satellites persecutes and harasses the humble in the Church. 'They say, "The Lord sees not; the God of Jacob perceives not."' The patience of the Lord they took for lack of knowledge.

7 Cf. Homily 95 on Obedience, p. 256.

'Understand, you senseless ones among the people; and, you fools, when will you be wise? Shall he who shaped the ear not hear? or he who formed the eye not see?'[8] The prophet rebukes and vanquishes sinners with an argument from nature. O you, who think that human affairs do not concern God, who maintain with Epicurus that God is aloof from the matters of mankind, listen to his reasoning. Because you are but children, I shall give you children's examples. Shall He who gave man hearing not Himself hear? Note exactly what it says. The prophet did not match like to like, for he did not say: He who shaped the ear, does He not Himself have an ear; or He who formed the eye, does He not Himself have an eye? Because God does not have the members of a body, the prophet speaks in this way so that whenever we read of such members, as we do frequently in Holy Writ, we may recognize a reference to the faculty and not to the member itself. In Solomon we read: 'Death and life are in the hand of the tongue.'[9] Does the tongue have a hand? We have cited this expression that we may more easily reach a higher degree of comprehension; certainly, with the same reasoning by which you have granted a hand to the tongue, you will grant to God all members of the body without exception.

'Shall he who instructs nations not chastise?' This means that He who gave the law gave it to instruct those who obey or to punish the contemptuous. 'He who teaches men knowledge.' The prophet did not add: Does He not Himself have knowledge, but what did he say?

'The Lord knows the thoughts of men, and that they are vain.' Men are carried away in admiration of philosophers and poets when they say: 'O the thoughts of mankind, how much vanity in human affairs!'[10] Yet, the psalm of David expressed the same judgment many ages before! The Lord knows the thoughts of men, and that they are vain. So long

8 Cf. *Commentarioli in ps.* 93.9.
9 Cf. Prov. 18.21.
10 Persius, *Satire* 1.1; cf. Letter 58.7, PL 22.584(324).

as we are men, our thoughts are vain. 'I said: You are gods, all of you sons of the Most High.'[11]

'Happy the man whom you instruct, O Lord, whom by your law you teach.' You realize that the law must be taught in order that its obscurities may be carefully cleared away; furthermore, the apostle says: 'the Law is spiritual';[12] and David: 'Open my eyes, that I may consider the wonders of your law.'[13] The psalmist repeats: 'Happy the man whom you instruct, O Lord, whom by your law you teach.' Why do you teach him? Tell us why.

'To give him rest from evil days.'[14] That is why You teach him, to spare him in the future; that is why You correct him in the present, that You may not condemn him in the future. The sentence of the judge is a torment, indeed, to the sufferer,[15] not because the judgment is harsh, but because a just and saving sentence does seem severe to the one suffering it while he feels the sting of punishment. 'Till the pit be dug for the wicked.' Who digs the pit for wrongdoers? Let us see what the prophet says in another psalm: 'He has opened a hole, he has dug it deep, but he falls into the pit which he has made.'[16] Certainly, then, it is not God who makes the pit, but the sinner, with the result that he falls into it. 'If a blind man guide a blind man,' declares the Lord, 'both fall into a pit.'[17]

'Who will rise up for me against the wicked? Who will stand by me against the evildoers?' When it says, 'who,' either it implies an extraordinary person, or no one at all, for the prophet speaks thus in the name of frail mankind: 'Who will rise up for me against the wicked?' Moses came and he could not improve matters; the prophets came and they did not release me from the snares of sinners. Who, then, will

11 Ps. 81.6; cf. *Commentary on Matthew* 16.13-27, PL 26.119-121(123).
12 Rom. 7.14; cf. Letter 53.4, PL 22.543(274).
13 Ps. 118.18; cf. Letter 58.9, PL 22.585(325).
14 Cf. Ps. 93(94).13.
15 Cf. *Commentary on Amos* 3.3-9, PL 25.1016(255).
16 Ps. 7.16.
17 Matt. 15.14.

rise up for me? Neatly put, 'will rise up,' as if He were sleeping or resting. 'Awake! Why are you asleep, O Lord?'[18] 'Master, save us! we are perishing!'[19] Who will rise up for me against the multitude of devils? Who will come to my assistance? 'Who will stand by me against the evildoers?' Excellently said: 'Who will stand by me,' for unless the Lord who was prostrate in His Passion stands by us, unless He rises up who was sleeping in death, we cannot overcome our enemies. That is why Stephen, while contending against the Jews who assailed him, saw Jesus standing at the right of the Father. He saw Him standing because He was fighting in behalf of His martyr. 'Were not the Lord my help.' If Christ had not risen from the nether world, my soul would have descended into hell.

'When I say, "My foot is slipping," your kindness, O Lord, sustains me.' Acknowledgment of helplessness promptly wins the help of God, for He is as much appeased by humility as He is offended by pride. When I say, 'My foot is slipping,' when I confess my sins, when I do not trust in my own power, when I do not boast that I am strong, at once Your kindness is as a hand to sustain me.

'When cares abound within me, your comfort gladdens my soul.' This is as the prophet said above; he continues in the same strain and from the same motive. When cares abound within me, Your comfort gladdens my soul. You will give me of Your kindness in proportion to the sorrow that You have perceived in my heart from its cry of repentance, for the magnitude of sorrow becomes the occasion for comfort.

'How could the tribunal of wickedness be leagued with you?' You who judge justice, can you have wrongdoing for a colleague? 'Which creates burdens in the guise of law?'[20] The commandments of God carry the burden of repentance, a salutary burden because it contains medicine for sinners, for it

18 Ps. 43.24.
19 Cf. Matt. 8.25; Luke 8.24.
20 Cf. Letter 133.7, PL 22.1155(1035).

is only by sweat and labor that we shall fulfill the precept of God. Certainly, no one expects to be crowned in pleasures. 'The widow who gives herself up to pleasures is dead while she is still alive.'[21] From what the apostle has said of one person, let us make application to all. The apostle was not concerned with the care of widows alone; he was a teacher of the whole Church. Merely because he did not mention by name the virgin, the monk, nor the churchman, is such a one, therefore, free to give himself unrestrained to pleasures? If, indeed, the widow is human, I presume the others are human, too, men who by their common frailty may incur through pleasures what the widow greatly fears. Listen, then, to the psalmist: 'Which creates burdens in the guise of law.' We have, for example, the precept to fast, to be sober, to offer the other cheek when we receive a blow, to give our mantle to the one who steals our tunic. These laws are not observed without cost. 'According to the words of your lips I have kept hard ways.'[22] You see, then, that no one receives a crown in pleasures. 'How narrow the gate and close the way that leads to life!'[23] No matter what the virtues, they are not acquired without difficulty. By great toil and effort, we reach the top of a mountain; how much more labor is necessary to reach heaven? The Gospel says: 'The kingdom of heaven has been enduring violent assault.'[24] It has been 'enduring violent assault,' because what nature[25] failed to subjugate in us, grace subdues; that whence angels have fallen, men may ascend; that where bodily integrity has been preserved, souls may hasten to their bodies.

Someone may ask: How will our same bodies go to heaven? If Christ reigns, we shall reign with Christ; what He already possesses is promised us after the resurrection. If the first-

21 Cf. 1 Tim. 5.6.
22 Cf. Ps. 16.4; cf. Letter 133.7, PL 22.1155(1035).
23 Matt. 7.14.
24 Matt. 11.12.
25 Cf. *Commentary on Matthew* 11.12, PL 26.74(70).

fruits[26] reign, the rest also shall reign. Why should not the flesh that reigns in Christ, reign in those who believe in Christ?[27] 'When Christ, your life, shall appear, then we, too, shall appear with him in glory.'[28] If flesh is worshiped by angels in heaven, why should it not reign in men who have merited the honor of the kingdom? Another psalm says: 'Worship at his footstool; holy is he!'[29] There are some who believe that 'at his footstool' refers to earth; but to me, it seems that, in comparison to the divine majesty, the Incarnation of the Savior is justly called a footstool on account of its submissiveness and humility. Because it is Christ's, it is worshiped, for nothing is lacking to divinity. Whatever is [proper] 'oikonomía' to Christ is not added to Him, but is for our benefit. He ascends in glory that for us who shall reign with Him may be manifested the grace of future hope. To whom be glory and empire forever and ever. Amen.

26 Cf. 1 Cor. 15.20
27 Cf. Homily 54 on Ps. 143, p. 381.
28 Cf. Col. 3.4.
29 Ps. 98.5.

HOMILY 72

ON PSALM 95(96)

BEFORE WE TAKE UP THE GOSPEL for discussion, a few words are in order, it seems to me, on the title of the psalm; then, after that, let us comment on one or more of the versicles. We want to have the same understanding of each entrance to the mansion that we had of the main entrance itself.[1]

The title of the psalm is: 'A song for David, when the house was being built after the captivity.'[2] Whose house was being built after the captivity? Who of us, do you suppose, has been captured and destroyed in the tempest of the captivity, so that after captivity, he is being rehabilitated? If God has shut up all men under sin, and all sins are found in unbelief,[3] wherever there is sin, there is captivity; wherever captivity, there is destruction and need for restoration. We must, therefore, give our mansions very careful attention lest, by chance, they collapse in some part and need to be rebuilt after captivity. We must strain every effort and use all knowledge at our command to prevent their complete collapse, that what is written in Exodus may be fulfilled in us: 'Because the midwives feared God, they built up houses for themselves.'[4] Note: Because they feared God, they built up houses. Without the fear of God, a house cannot be built. If, then, with the fear of God, houses were built by those who had not

1 Cf. Homily 1 on Ps. 1, p. 3.
2 Cf. Ps. 95(96).1.
3 Cf. Rom. 11.32; Gal. 3.22; cf. *Against the Pelagians* 2.30, PL 23.596(780).
4 Cf. Exod. 1.21.

committed sin, but rather did their building at God's pleasure, we who have been captured, what must we do? Listen, sinner; we must fear God, indeed, to avoid sin; but after shipwreck, there is the second plank of repentance.[5] 'When the house was being built after the captivity.' 'When the house was being built'; not 'was built,' for repentance is without limit. To the just man who has died, repentance naturally is rendered superfluous. Wherever there is sin, always there is remorse of conscience; hence, the psalmist says, was 'being built.' While time lasts, the door is always open to repentance, for however long you shall live, as long as you live, you will fall into sin.

'Sing to the Lord a new song.' The old man is pulled down and a new one built up; therefore, a new song is sung. 'Sing joyfully to the Lord, all the earth!'[6] Earth that has been wholeheartedly converted to the Lord, continually sings His praises of thanksgiving with the sweetness of a young voice.

We must not forget our promise, but must turn our attention to the Gospel lesson, for it is difficult. In a word, let it be enough to have said that the psalm is uttered in the name of the penitent; to this concept, the rest of the psalm will lend itself.

---

5 Cf. Homily 23 on Ps. 95, p. 184; cf. Letter 122.4, PL 22.1046(899); 130.9, PL 22.1115(986).
6 Cf. Ps. 95 (96).1; cf. *Commentarioli in ps.* 95.11.

HOMILY 73

ON PSALM 96(97)

The title-superscription of this psalm is: 'When his land was restored to him.'[1] Since it says, 'was restored,' it is evident that the land had been his before, was afterwards lost, then recovered again. What land is this that was restored to David? David's land is holy Mary, the mother of the Savior: 'who was born to him according to the flesh of the offspring of David.'[2] The promise made to David was fulfilled in the virginity of Mary and in her child-bearing, when a virgin was born of a virgin. The announcement of the Gospel: 'The Word was made flesh, and dwelt among us,'[3] thus came to pass, so that what had been promised to David was restored to us through holy Mary.

'The Lord is king; let the earth rejoice.' Let the earth rejoice; may the earth, that previously was held by many kings, have but one king. 'Let the many isles be glad.' A certain prophet says: 'Speak to the inhabitants of this isle,'[4] meaning, to the inhabitants of Jerusalem. You notice that Jerusalem is called an isle. Before David's land was restored, therefore, only one island of Judea rejoiced; but now, when the land has returned to him, we find: 'Let the many isles be glad.' We might say that the many isles are separate provinces or cities of the faithful, or interpret them as the individual churches, for even as islands are lashed and beaten on all

1 Cf. Ps. 96(97).1.
2 Rom. 1.3.
3 John 1.14.
4 Cf. Isa. 20.6; cf. Homily 24 on Ps. 96, p. 192; 26 on Ps. 98, p. 205.

sides[5] by the surging billows of the sea, so are the churches buffeted by various storms of temptations without being torn from their foundation.

'Clouds and darkness are round about him.' There is no doubt but that the clouds and darkness round about Him was the body that the Lord Savior deigned to assume, although in the Gospel of John, He is said to have appeared: [He] 'has appeared to us.'[6] True, He appeared to the apostles, but He was veiled to the Jews. He is revealed to the former on the mountain; from the latter in the valley of lowliness, He is hidden; He edifies the former with the beatitudes; to the latter, He speaks in parables, that seeing, they might not see because of their treachery. 'Clouds and darkness are round about him.' He appeared just as He willed to appear and not in accordance with His divine nature. 'He made darkness the cloak about him.'[7] If God is light, how is light able to dwell in darkness? In that passage, darkness represents our imperfect knowledge and our infirmity, for we cannot gaze upon His majesty. If human eyes cannot, in fact, look upon the rays of the sun of this world, a creature, our fellow slave, how much more are there shades and darkness round about the Sun of Justice that He may not be observed nor looked upon by us? We read about holy Moses: 'He approached the cloud'[8] so that he might see God whom he was not able to behold outside of the cloud; and Isaia says: 'The Lord is riding on a swift cloud on his way to Egypt,'[9] that is, in holy Mary. 'On a swift cloud,' because she was not heavy[10] with human seed. 'Justice and judgment are the correction of his throne.'[11] 'Correction' shows that previously the throne was

5 Cf. Homily 24 on Ps. 96, p. 192; *Commentary on Isaia* 41.1-7, PL 24.412(496); 42.1-5, PL 24.422(508); 51.5, PL 24.484(587).
6 1 John 1.2; cf. Homily 9 on Ps. 75, p. 67.
7 Ps. 17.12.
8 Cf. Exod. 20.21.
9 Cf. Isa. 19.1.
10 Cf. Homily 11 on Ps. 77, p. 88; 24 on Ps. 96, p. 193.
11 Cf. Ps. 96(97).2.

unbalanced: 'justice and judgment, the correction of his throne.' Before the Lord came in the flesh, there was inequality, for God was known only in Judea. He came, and all the earth recognized the one and same Creator that Judea had known, and the correction of His throne was accomplished.

'Fire goes before him.' The Lord is pure: 'the Holy One dwells in holiness';[12] we cannot devote ourselves to Him until fire has consumed our vices. 'The fire will assay the quality of everyone's work.'[13] 'Consumes his foes round about.' God does not consume His foes as enemies, but as friends, for He burns away the vices of His foes that He may make of them His friends.

'His lightnings illumine the world.' Jeremia says: 'The Lord who established the world by his wisdom, and brings up clouds from the end of the earth; he makes the lightning flash in the rain.'[14] 'His lightnings illumine the world.' The philosophers,[15] who are always discoursing on the nature of things, say that unless the winds cause a collision among the clouds, fire cannot escape from them; but when they have been aroused to a kind of rivalry in thundering, lightning flashes forth. We can observe a similar phenomenon in producing fire from stones. We have called attention to this to note more easily a similar marvel in the mystery of the Savior. We have our clouds, prophets and apostles, as another psalm says: 'Your truth, to the clouds.'[16] If to the clouds of this sky He transmits His truth, what does the prophet mean in still another psalm when he says: 'Truth shall spring out of the earth'?[17] Now, 'Your truth, to the clouds' is certainly a figure of the prophets and the apostles, for, unless these clouds collide, they cannot give forth their brillance, but if they meet

12 Cf. Isa. 57.15; cf. Homily 70 on Ps. 92, p.
13 1 Cor. 3.13; cf. *Against Jovinian* 2.22, PL 23.331(360).
14 Cf. Jer. 51.15, 16.
15 Cf. Homily 24 on Ps. 96, p. 195.
16 Cf. Ps. 35.6.
17 Ps. 84.12.

to thunder together in one teaching, their lightning shall flash forth throughout the world.

Would you like to know in what way the faithful are called clouds in Holy Writ? Isaia says: 'I will command the clouds not to send rain upon them.'[18] Moses was a cloud; therefore, he said: 'May my instruction soak in like rain.'[19] The letters of the apostles are spiritual rain for us. As a matter of fact, what does Paul say in his Letter to the Hebrews? 'For the earth that drinks in the rain that often falls upon it';[20] and again: 'I have planted, Apollos watered.'[21] 'The earth sees and trembles.' The earth, that before was unyielding and unreceptive to the word of the Lord, felt the flash of His words throughout and trembled. The Lord looked upon the earth: 'who looks upon the earth, and it trembles.'[22] What is the import of, 'it trembles'? 'Upon whom shall I find rest, except upon the lowly and peaceful man who trembles at my word?'[23]

'The mountains melt like wax before the Lord.' Mountains, he calls the high and mighty rulers. They who before rose as high as the sky in their pride are brought low at the coming of the Savior; they who hardened exceedingly by vain boasting, afterwards, softened in the heat of divine wisdom.

'The heavens proclaim his justice, and all peoples see his glory.' These two versicles convey two instructions: the heavens proclaim the justice of the Lord, and all peoples see His glory. Unless heaven were a person, it could not proclaim the Lord's justice. Besides, if it is said to the sinner: 'Dust you are and unto dust you shall return,'[24] why may it not be said to the just man: Heaven you are and unto heaven you shall return? We do not bear the likeness of the

18 Cf. Isa. 5.6.
19 Deut. 32.2.
20 Heb. 6.7.
21 1 Cor. 3.6.
22 Ps. 103.32.
23 Cf. Isa. 66.2.
24 Gen. 3.19; cf. Homily 66 on Ps. 88, p. 67; 46 on Ps. 133, pp. 350-351.

earthly, but the likeness of the heavenly,[25] for 'our citizenship is in heaven.'[26] Consequently, if man is as a pilgrim on earth, in the flesh certainly, yet not according to the flesh, he may sincerely proclaim the justice of the Lord. Now, if anyone should suffer a scruple through lack of knowledge and complain, 'Why is it that in this life we see the just in want and crushed under the burden of toil, and sinners abounding in riches and all comforts?' unless the man of the Church is learned in divine Scripture, how, in such cases, is he able to prove the justice of God? If, however, he has labored in meditation on the Law day and night, he will readily reply that the brief time of abasement in the present world must be balanced against eternal rewards hereafter. It is far better, indeed, to endure voluntary poverty for the Lord's sake during the short span of this life, in order to enjoy the riches of the future life, than to abound with luxuries here and be tortured hereafter with unbearable punishments. 'All peoples see his glory.' They who at first took scandal in the cross of the Lord because, of themselves, they were unable to recognize Him, presently, after the heavens proclaimed the justice of God, glorified Him.

'All who worship graven things are put to shame.' If the prophet is a blessed man, he knows that the blessed never revile. When, therefore, he says, 'are put to shame,' he is not praying against those who are put to shame, but for them. He prays that they will be put to shame in their error and be converted to the true God who is sole Creator.

'The daughters of Juda rejoice because of your judgments, O Lord.'[27] Does this mean that the daughters of Juda rejoice and not the sons? Let us be sure, first, of the meaning of the name Juda, and when we know that, we may consider the interpretation of daughters. Juda betokens profession of faith. Every soul that acknowledges God is a daughter of Juda;

25 Cf. 1 Cor. 15.49.
26 Phil. 3.20.
27 Cf. Ps. 96(97).8; cf. Letter 39.2, PL 22.467(179); 22.31, PL 22.417(116).

hence, we may say that the daughters of Juda are the souls of the faithful that rejoice in the judgments of God, for unless one has faith, he does not rejoice in God's judgments. My house has tumbled down; I have lost all my wealth in a shipwreck; my son has died; a servant has fled with my possessions; I who was a rich man am now wasting away in want: unless I am a daughter of Juda, I do not rejoice in the judgments of God.

The soul of blessed Job was a daughter of Juda. In the loss of his property, he consoled himself thus: 'The Lord gave and the Lord has taken away; blessed be the name of the Lord! Naked I came forth from my mother's womb, and naked shall I go back again'[28]—into dust. From a man of wealth, he became a pauper; he lost his property with his children; he was crushed under the weight of want and bereavement; finally, he reached the peak of misery and was struck by jaundice and an incurable ulcer—incurable to man, that is, but curable by God. What human medicine could not cure, patience and faith healed. He sat on a dung heap, but in his soul he was wandering about in Paradise. With his entire body rotting away, his tongue alone was spared, that with it he might blaspheme God.[29] Do not miss the cunning of the ancient enemy. In cruel plundering, he robbed a just man of his substance, took his sons in a sudden disaster, and struck him with palsy and a grievous ulcer. The devil left him nothing but his tongue and his wife, for her to tempt him, and for his tongue to blaspheme. The devil had not forgotten that old craftiness by which he deceived Adam through a woman; therefore, he attacks Job through his wife, reckoning that he can always deceive man through woman, not considering that, because one man has been mortally wounded through a woman, now the whole world is saved through a woman. You remember Eve, but consider Mary; the

28 Cf. Job 1.21; cf. Letter 118.2, PL 22.961(793); 22.31, PL 22.417(117); 39.2, PL 22.467(179).

29 Cf. Homily 6 on Ps. 66, p. 48.

former cast us out from Paradise, the latter leads us back to heaven. Let us return now to the order of the psalm.

'You who love the Lord, hate evil.'[30] If the Lord is good . . . What is it that we read? 'The good shepherd lays down his life for his sheep';[31] and again in another parable: 'Friend, art thou envious because I am generous?'[32] 'You who love the Lord, hate evil.' There cannot be two contradictory loves in one man.[33] Just as there is no harmony between Christ and Belial, between justice and iniquity,[34] so it is impossible for one soul to love both good and evil. You who love the Lord, hate evil, the devil; in every deed, there is love of one and hatred of the other. 'He who has my commandments and keeps them, he it is who loves me.'[35] On the other hand, what is said in regard to the devil? 'By the envy of the devil, death entered the world, and they follow him who are on his side,'[36] or, in simple language: You who love the things that are good, hate the things that are bad. You cannot love good, unless you hate evil.

'The Lord guards the souls of his faithful ones.'[37] Excellent sequence! He who loves good and hates evil, what does he deserve from the Lord but His guardianship? 'From the hand of the wicked he delivers them.' Here, the question arises: If the Lord guards the souls of His faithful and delivers them from the hand of the wicked, how does it happen that martyrs are destroyed in persecution? How did the impious Nero condemn to death in one day[38] Peter and Paul, if the Lord guards the souls of His faithful? Listen carefully now. The Lord guards the souls of His faithful ones; the

30 Cf. Ps. 96(97).10.
31 John 10.11.
32 Cf. Matt. 20.15.
33 Cf. *Commentarioli in ps.* 96.10.
34 Cf. 2 Cor. 6.14, 15; cf. *Against the Luciferians* 5, PL 23.168(176); *Against Jovinian* 2.2, PL 23.296(322).
35 John 14.21.
36 Cf. Wisd. 2.24.
37 Cf. Ps. 96(97).10.
38 Cf. *Lives of Illustrious Men* 5, PL 23.647(837).

souls, it said, not the bodies. 'Do not be afraid of those who kill the body but cannot kill the soul. But rather be afraid of him who is able to destroy both soul and body in hell.'[39] How does the Lord guard the souls of His faithful? In martyrdom. 'Precious in the eyes of the Lord is the death of his faithful ones.'[40] In martyrdom, I say, blood is shed that the soul may be delivered from temptations; that it may forsake a short life and enter eternity; that it may leave all persecution behind and hasten to our Lord Jesus Christ for its crown. To whom be honor and glory forever and ever. Amen.

39 Matt. 10.28.
40 Ps. 115.15.

FRAGMENT OF HOMILY 74

ON PSALM 93(94)

Easter Homily of St. Jerome

'THE GOD OF VENGEANCE, LORD, God of vengeance, has acted freely.'[1] Truly, He alone has acted freely who today has revealed to us what He has done. Freely, indeed, has He acted, He of whom much had been prophesied of old: 'I am a man without strength, free among the dead.'[2] Would you like to know, moreover, what He has done? Just listen. Without any necessity, freely, of His own choice, He permitted Himself to hang from a tree; He did not refuse to have His body pierced with nails; He gave up His spirit and endured death; He laid His body in a tomb, and with His soul He descended into hell; He made captive the prince of death and confounded all his legions; He shattered the iron bars of the gates of hell and released all the just who were being held captive by original sin; He recalled the prisoners to their first freedom; He bathed in brilliant light all those blinded by the darkness of sin. You have now heard why our Defender, the Lord of vengeance, is represented as having acted freely. Briefly, after He had been lifted up, that is suspended on the cross by the Jews, no sooner did He yield up the spirit than, united to the soul of His divinity, He descended at once to the depths of the nether world; and when to the uttermost bound of the infernal regions like a plunderer. . .

1 Cf. Ps. 93(94).1.
2 Cf. Ps. 87.5, 6.

HOMILIES ON THE GOSPEL OF ST. MARK ON VARIOUS TOPICS

(75-84)

HOMILY 75(I)

ON THE BEGINNING OF THE GOSPEL OF ST. MARK (1.1-12)[1]

THE FOUR-FACED (tetrámorphon) creature that we met in the Apocalypse of John[2] and in the beginning of Ezechiel's[3] prophecy, that had the face of a man, the face of a calf, the face of a lion, the face of an eagle, has also special significance for the text we are considering. In Matthew, this human being has the face of a man; in Luke, an ox; in John, an eagle; in Mark, the lion crying in the desert.[4] 'The beginning of the Gospel of Jesus Christ, the Son of God. As it is written in Isaia the prophet, "The voice of one crying in the desert, 'Make ready the way of the Lord, make straight his paths.' " ' The one crying out in the desert is, indeed, the lion whose roar fills all the other animals with terror and huddles them together in a paralysis of fear. At the same time, ponder well that John the Baptist is called the voice, but our Lord Jesus the word; the servant comes before the master.

'The beginning of the Gospel of Jesus Christ, the Son of God,' and, therefore, not the son of Joseph. The beginning of the Gospel is the end of the Law; the Law is ended and the Gospel begins. 'As it is written in Isaia the prophet, "Behold, I send my messenger before thee, who shall prepare thy way." ' 'As it is written in Isaia.' Now, as far as I recall[5] by going back in my mind and sifting carefully the work of the

1 Sunday Sermon; cf. the beginning of Homily 76 on Mark 1.13-31, p. 132.
2 Apoc. 4.6-8.
3 Ezech. 1.5-8; cf. *Commentary on Ezechiel* 1.5, 6, PL 25.20(8); and Prologue to *Commentary on Matthew*, PL 26.19(5-6).
4 Cf. Letter 60.3, PL 22.591(333).
5 Cf. *Commentary on Ezechiel* 32.17-32, PL 25.314(390).

seventy translators as well as the Hebrew scrolls, I have never been able to locate in Isaia, the prophet, the words: 'Behold I send my messenger before thee,' but I do find them written near the close of the prophecy of Malachia.[6] If, therefore, this statement is written at the end of Malachia's prophecy, on what grounds does Mark, the evangelist, take for granted here: 'As it is written in Isaia the prophet'?[7] The utterances of the evangelists are the work of the Holy Spirit. This Mark who writes is not to be esteemed lightly; in fact, Peter the Apostle says in his letter: 'The Church chosen together with you, greets you; and so does my son Mark.'[8] O Apostle Peter, Mark, your son–son, not by the flesh, but by the Spirit–informed as he is in spiritual matters, is uninformed here, and credits to one prophet of Holy Writ what is written by another. 'As it is written in Isaia the prophet, "Behold I send my messenger before thee." '

This is the very passage that the ungodly Porphyry, who has vomited forth his venom in so many volumes written against us, attacks in his fourteenth scroll.[9] 'The evangelists,' he asserts, 'were such ignorant men, not only in secular matters, but even in divine Scripture, that they cited the testimony of one prophet and attributed it to another.' That is what he hurls at us; now, what shall we answer him? I think this is the answer inspired by your prayers. 'As it is written in Isaia.' What is written in Isaia the prophet? 'The voice of one crying in the desert, "Make ready the way of the Lord, make straight his paths." ' This is written in Isaia; but there is a clearer explanation of this text in another prophet, and the evangelist is really saying: This is John the Baptist, of whom Malachia has also said: 'Behold, I send my messenger before thee, who shall prepare thy way.' The phrase, 'it is

6 Cf. Mal. 3.1.
7 Cf. Letter 57.9, PL 22.575(313); *Commentary on Malachia* 3.1, PL 25.1564(969).
8 Cf. 1 Peter 5.13.
9 Cf. *Commentary on Matthew* 3.3, PL 26.29(17).

written,' refers only to the following verse: 'The voice of one crying in the desert, "Make ready the way of the Lord, make straight his paths."' To prove, moreover, that John the Baptist was the messenger who was sent, Mark did not choose to attest on his own word, but to adduce proof from the word of a prophet.

'John has been in the desert, baptizing and preaching.'[10] John has been; our God was. That which has been, has ceased to be; that which has been, before it had been, was not; but He who was, was before and always was, and He was, without ever having had a beginning. Of John the Baptist, it is said, 'he has been,' 'egéneto'; but of the Lord Savior, 'He was.' When it says, 'He was,' He always was without beginning. It is He Himself who said: 'He who is has sent me,'[11] for BEING never had a beginning. 'John has been in the desert baptizing and preaching.' The voice that is about to proclaim the Lord has been in the desert; its first and foremost mission has been to announce the coming of the Savior. 'John has been in the desert.' Happy that way of life: to despise men, to search for angels; to desert cities and, in the wilderness, to find Christ. John has been in the wilderness baptizing and preaching, baptizing with his hand, teaching with his word. The baptism of John preceded the baptism of the Savior. Even as John the Baptist was the precursor of the Lord Savior, so was the baptism of John the Baptist the precursor of the baptism of the Savior.[12] The former was given in repentance; the latter, in grace. On that occasion, repentance is granted; on that occasion, pardon; on this, victory is conferred.

'All the country of Judea went out to him.' Judea comes to John in crowds; Jerusalem hastens to him; the entire world flocks to Jesus the Lord Savior. 'God is renowned in Juda; in Israel great is his name.'[13] To John, then, run Judea and

10 Cf. John 1.4.
11 Cf. Exod. 3.14; cf. Letter 15.4, PL 22.357(40).
12 Cf. *Against the Luciferians* 7, PL 23.470(179).
13 Ps. 75.2.

Jerusalem; but to the Savior, the whole world. All the inhabitants kept on coming: 'and they were baptized by him in the river Jordan, confessing their sins.' They were baptized by John. John the Baptist offers them the protection of the Law; hence, the Jews are baptized only in respect to the Law. They were coming to Jerusalem and were baptized by him in the Jordan, in the river flowing downstream. The Law, indeed, is downstream; although it baptizes, it is still downward. That is what the name of Jordan means—the river flowing downwards;[14] but our Lord and the mystery of the Trinity is upwards. Someone may object: If the baptism of the Law is from below, then, is the Lord from below who was baptized in the Jordan? But I say, rightly was He baptized in the Jordan, for He observed the precepts of the Law; He was circumcised by the Law and He was baptized by the Law.

'John was clothed in camel's hair, with a leathern girdle about his loins, and he ate locusts and wild honey.' Just as the apostles set the example for the priesthood, so John the Baptist set the example for monks.[15] As far as tradition goes in the writings of the Hebrews and in the memory of this very day, John's name appears among the names of the priests and of the chief priests. It is evident, then, that he was a holy man and a priest. Furthermore, we read in the Gospel according to Luke that John had been born of a priestly class. 'There was a priest,' Luke says, 'named Zachary, and in the order of his course. . .'[16] Nor, moreover, was his privilege fittingly allotted except to the foremost of the priests, that is, to the chief priests. Now, why have I said all this? That we may know that this was a chief priest who knew that Christ was to come, and he was not looking for Christ in the temple, but had withdrawn from the crowds to the desert. It is only proper that the eyes expecting to behold Christ should

14 Cf. Letter 78.41, PL 22.722 (495).
15 Cf. Letter 22.36, PL 22.421(121).
16 Cf. Luke 1.5, 8.

look upon nothing except Christ.[17] John was clothed in camel's hair, not in wool. Do not imagine he had soft garments. Our Lord Himself is witness in the Gospel of his 'askēseōs' [asceticism]. 'Behold,' He says, 'those who wear soft garments are in the houses of kings.'[18]

Now with the guidance of your prayers, let us turn to the spiritual understanding of this passage. 'John was clothed in camel's hair, with a leathern girdle about his loins.' It is the same John who says: 'He must increase, but I must decrease. He who has the bride is the bridegroom; but the friend of the bridegroom rejoices exceedingly if he sees the bridegroom.'[19] And again: 'One mightier than I is coming after me, the strap of whose sandals I am not worthy to stoop down and loose.'[20] The meaning of the words: 'He must increase, I must decrease,' is that the Gospel must increase, but I, the Law, must decrease. John, that is, the Law in John, was clothed, therefore, in the hair of a camel; he could not wear a tunic of the lamb of whom it is said: 'Behold the lamb of God who takes away the sins of the world';[21] and again: 'He is led like a lamb to the slaughter.'[22] In the Law, we cannot wear a tunic from that lamb.

In the Law, John had a leather girdle because the Jews thought that to sin in act was the only sin. On the other hand, in the Apocalypse[23] of John, our Lord Jesus, who is seen amidst the seven-lamp stands, also wore a girdle, a golden girdle, not about his loins, but about the breasts. The Law is girdled about the loins; but Christ, that is, the Gospel and the fortitude of monks, is binding, not only in wanton passion, but also in mind and heart. In the Gospel, it behooves

17 Cf. *Against the Luciferians* 7, PL 23.170(179); cf. Letter 125.7, PL 22.1076(936).
18 Matt. 11.8.
19 Cf. John 3.30, 29.
20 Mark 1.7.
21 John 1.29.
22 Cf. Isa. 53.7.
23 Apoc. 1.13.

one not even to think evil; in the Law, the fornicator is accused for judgment. 'Amen, Amen, I say to you, that anyone who even looks with lust at a woman has already committed adultery with her in his heart.'[24] 'It is written,' He says, 'in the Law, "Thou shalt not commit adultery." '[25] This is the leather girdle clinging about the loins: 'I say to you, anyone who even looks with lust at a woman has already committed adultery with her in his heart.' This is the golden girdle that is girt about the mind and heart.

Clothed in camel's hair, 'he ate locusts and wild honey.' The locust is a tiny creature midway between bird and reptile.[26] It does not lift itself up far enough from the ground to be a bird, for if it rises ever so little, it is not flying but jumping. When it takes off just a wee bit from the ground, it falls back again, for its wings fail. So with the Law; it seemed to depart from the error of idolatry, but it could not fly to heaven. We, certainly, never read of the kingdom of heaven in the Law.[27] Would you like evidence that the kingdom of heaven is proclaimed only in the Gospel? 'Repent,' it says, 'for the kingdom of heaven is at hand.'[28] The Old Law lifted men up a little from the ground, but it could not carry them to heaven. 'Wherever the body is, there will the eagles be gathered together.'[29]

'Locusts.' He was also eating honey, not the cultivated kind, but wild honey, among wild animals, among brute beasts; not in the house nor in the Church, but outside it. In other words, in the Law, he was consuming wild honey, though we never read that honey was offered in sacrifices.[30] Someone may wonder at this and ask: Why, since oil, wheat,

---

24 Cf. Matt. 5.28.
25 Cf. Matt. 5.27.
26 Cf. *Commentary on Jona* 4.6, PL 25.1149(427).
27 Cf. *Against the Pelagians* 1.31, PL 23.548(728); *Commentary on Matthew* 3.3, PL 26.29-30(17).
28 Matt. 3.2.
29 Matt. 24.28.
30 Cf. Lev. 2.11; cf. Letter 128.2, PL 22.1096-1097(962); 31.1, PL 22.445(151).

a ram, lamb, the blood of cattle, and all the other things are offered in sacrifice to God, why is honey alone not offered?[31] What does the Law say? Salt is the seasoning of every sacrificial offering.[32] 'Let your speech be seasoned with salt.'[33] Under no circumstances is there an offering of honey. 'Whatever happens,' it says, 'will be impure.'[34] Honey is a sign of pleasure and sweetness, and believe me, sensual pleasure always bring death; sensuality is never pleasing to God. Anything sweet may not be offered to God in sacrifices. Naturally, honey is sweet and caresses the senses with sweetness, just as sense gratification does, and lust, and wantonness. Everybody knows, of course, that honey is gathered here and there from flowers; but if you should examine carefully those same flowers, you would discover that they contain dead bodies, putrid matter and the like. . . . So honey is not only from flowers, but from anything that is full of gratification; it seems to be sweet and pleasing, but if you consider its nature it is deadly. Why have I said all this? Because the Law was only the beginning of the Covenant; the Gospel is the fulfillment.

'One mightier than I is coming after me, the strap of whose sandals I am not worthy to stoop down and loose.' This seems to be an expression of humility as though he were saying, I am not worthy to be His servant, but, in these very simple words, there is evidence of another mystery. We read in Exodus, Deuteronomy,[35] and the Book of Ruth,[36] that if a man did not want to accept a kinswoman who proposed that he marry her, his next of kin came forward and, in the presence of judges and elders, said: 'You are qualified to marry; you ought to accept her.' If the man was still unwilling, then,

---

31 Cf. Letter 128.2, PL 22.1096-1097(962); *Commentary on Joel* 1.5, PL 25.954(173-174); Letter 31.1, PL 22.445(151).
32 Cf. Lev. 2.13.
33 Cf. Col. 4.6.
34 In Exodus?
35 Deut. 25.7-10.
36 Cf. Ruth 4.7.

the rejected woman stripped off his sandal, shook it in his face, and spat at him. After that, she married her second kinsman. To inflict ignominy was the motive for her behavior (this, by the way, is the literal interpretation) so that if, perhaps, it was her poverty her kinsman had disdained, the dread of public disgrace might deter him from rejecting her. John, therefore, is showing plainly here the office of the priest. He himself says: 'He who has the bride is the bridegroom';[37] He has the bride, the Church; I, however, am the friend of the bridegroom; I cannot loose the strap of His sandal in the Law, for He has wedded the Church. 'I have baptized you with water.' I am the one who serves; He is Creator and Lord. I offer water. I, who as a creature, offer a creature; He, who is uncreated, gives the uncreated. I baptize you with water; I offer you what is seen; He, what is unseen. I, who am visible, give visible water; He, invisible, gives the invisible Spirit.

'It came to pass in those days, that Jesus came from Nazareth in Galilee.' Notice the careful articulation and meaning of the words. It did not say, Christ came, or the Son of God came, but Jesus came. Someone may say: Why did it not say Christ? I am speaking in the manner of the flesh; on the other hand, God is always holy and is not in need of sanctification. Now, we are speaking of the man, Christ; He had not yet been baptized and anointed by the Holy Spirit. I speak in terms of the flesh, of Him who came in the form of the servant; let no one be scandalized, for I am speaking of Him who came to be baptized as though He were a sinner. Not that I may divide Christ; not that there is one Christ, another Jesus, another Son of God; but that the One and the Same is distinguished by us according to the divisions of time. 'Jesus from Nazareth in Galilee.' See the mystery? To John the Baptist, first, came Judea and Jerusalem. Our Lord changed the beginning of evangelical baptism and the

37 John 3.29.

sacraments of the Law into the sacraments of the Gospel; He did not come from Judea nor Jerusalem, but from Galilee of the Gentiles. Jesus came from Nazareth in Galilee. NAZARA means flower.[38] The Flower came from a flower. He 'was baptized by John in the Jordan.' The compassionate kindness of the Mighty One! He who had not committed sin is baptized as if He were a sinner. In the baptism of the Lord, all sins are forgiven, but of the Savior's baptism, one might say that it is prevenient; true remission of sins is in the blood of Christ, in the mystery of the Trinity.

'Immediately on coming up from the water he saw the heavens opened.' Every word of this is written for us. Until we receive baptism, our eyes are closed; we do not discern the divine. 'The Spirit, as a dove, descending and remaining upon him. And there came a voice from the heavens, "Thou art my beloved Son, in thee I am well pleased." ' Jesus Christ is baptized by John; the Holy Spirit descends upon Him in the likeness of a dove; the Father from heaven bears witness. Take note, Arius; mark this, heretics; the mystery of the Trinity is also in the baptism of Jesus. Jesus is baptized; the Holy Spirit descends under the appearance of a dove, the Father speaks from heaven. 'He saw the heavens opened.' Since it says, He saw, it gives us to understand that the others had not seen, for all of them do not see the heavens opened. In fact, what is it that Ezechiel says in the beginning of his prophecy? 'Now it came to pass while I was among the exiles by the river Chobar, the heavens opened, and I saw divine visions.'[39] I saw, but others did not see. Let no one imagine that the heavens opened in the simple, physical sense. No, we ourselves, who are sitting here now, see the heavens opened or closed according to our different degrees of worthiness. Full faith opens the heavens; doubt closes them.

---

38 Cf. Letter 46.12, PL 22.497(209); *Commentary on Matthew* 21.10, PL 26.155(163).

39 Cf. Ezech. 1.1; cf. *Commentary on Ezechiel* 1.2, PL 25.18(5); *on Matthew* 3.16,17, PL 26.31(19).

'The spirit, as a dove, descending.' It is the practice of the Manichaeans, Marcionites, and the other heretics to quarrel with us over this text and say: If Christ is in a body and the same flesh that He assumed has not been laid aside, nor has He laid it aside, the Holy Spirit that descended is, therefore, in the dove. Do you hear the hissing of the ancient serpent?[40] Do you recognize that snake that drove man from the Garden of Paradise and is eager to hurl us from the paradise of faith? The evangelist did not say, He assumed the body of a dove; but the Spirit 'as' a dove. Whenever it says 'as' (*tamquam*), it is pointing out, not a truth, but a likeness. In regard to the Lord, however, it is not written that He was born as a man, but He was born man; here, moreover, it actually says, 'as a dove,' which expresses a comparison, not a reality.

'Immediately the Spirit drove him forth into the desert,' the Spirit that descended in the appearance of a dove. 'He saw,' the Gospel says, 'the heavens opened and the Spirit, as a dove, descending and remaining upon him.' Notice that it says remaining, abiding continuously, never departing. John says, in fact, in his Gospel: 'But he who sent me said to me, "He upon whom thou wilt see the Spirit descending, and abiding upon him." '[41] The Holy Spirit descended upon Christ and remained; He descends upon men, assuredly, but does not remain. Furthermore, in the scroll of Ezechiel, who is properly a type of the Savior[42]—no other prophet, I mean of the major prophets, is called, 'Son of man'; the title is given strictly to Ezechiel—in Ezechiel, then, after almost every twenty or thirty verses, it says regularly: 'The word of the Lord came to the prophet Ezechiel.'[43] Someone may ask: Why is that so frequently repeated in the prophecy? Because the Holy Spirit certainly descended upon the prophet, but again withdrew from him. Whenever it says: 'the word came,' it

40 Cf. *Against Jovinian* 1.4, PL 23.224(241); Letter 130.16, PL 22.1120(992); Homily 67 on Ps. 89, p. 76.
41 Cf. John 1.33.
42 Cf. *Commentary on Ezechiel* 47.6-12, PL 25.471(591).
43 Cf. Ezech. 1.3; 2.3; 3.1.

indicates that the Holy Spirit departed from him and came back again to him.[44]

When we give way to anger, yield to detraction, surrender to a sadness that leads to death, entertain thoughts of the flesh, do we think that the Holy Spirit is abiding in us? Do we suppose that we may hate a brother with the Holy Spirit dwelling in us? That we may call to mind and dwell upon anything evil? On the other hand, when our thoughts are good thoughts, let us realize that the Holy Spirit is dwelling in us. If, however, we contemplate evil, it is a sign that the Holy Spirit has left us. That is why in respect to the Savior, Scripture says: 'He upon whom thou wilt see the Spirit descending, and abiding upon him, he it is.'[45]

'Immediately the Spirit drove him forth into the desert.' How many monks there are living at home with their parents; if the Holy Spirit descends and abides upon them, it is the Spirit that drives them out into the desert. The Holy Spirit drives them from their home, and leads them into the wilderness. The Holy Spirit does not will to dwell where there are confusion, crowds, quarrels, and dissensions. No, the proper abode of the Holy Spirit is solitude. When our Lord and Savior wanted to pray, Holy Writ says: 'Alone, he went out to the mountain, and continued all night in prayer.'[46] During the day, He was with His disciples; at night, He dedicated His prayer to the Father in our behalf. Why do I say all this? Because not a few of the brothers often complain: If I stay in the monastery, I cannot pray alone; did not our Lord send His disciples away? He, certainly, was with His disciples, but when He wanted to pray intently, He withdrew alone. If we want to pray more than the common prayer, we have our cell, the fields, the desert. We may have both solitude and the good example of the brothers.

44 Cf. *Commentary on Ezechiel* 35, PL 25.333(415); *on Philemon*, Prologue, PL 26.637(741-742).
45 John 1.33.
46 Cf. Luke 6.12; cf. Letter 58.4, PL 22.582(322).

HOMILY 76(II)

ON MARK 1.13-31

THE PASSAGE FROM THE GOSPEL that we considered previously, closed with the words: 'He was with the wild beasts, and the angels ministered to him.' Since there was not enough time last Sunday to go as far as this text, we ought to begin with it today, for all of Holy Writ is animated and held together by one Spirit. It is not unlike a necklace held together by the union of its links, so that whichever link you pick up, another suspends from it. 'He was with wild beasts, and angels ministered to him.' Jesus was with beasts, and on that account angels ministered to Him. 'Give not to the beasts,' Scripture says, 'the soul of thy confessor.'[1] These are the beasts that the Lord trampled down with the foot of the Gospel—the lion and the dragon.[2] 'Angels ministered to him.' Not that it should seem grand and wonderful if angels ministered to God, for there is nothing remarkable about servants paying homage to their master; but this is all expressed in the language of the Incarnation. He was lodging with beasts. God cannot lodge with beasts, but the body that He assumed could, that flesh subject to human temptations; that body, that flesh that thirsted, hungered, is tempted, conquers, and in which we are triumphant.

'After John had been delivered up, Jesus came into Galilee.' The historical sense is clear enough to those who are listening without any explanation on our part. Let us ask Him: 'who has the key of David, he who opens and no one shuts, and

1 Cf. Ps. 73.19.
2 Cf. Ps. 90.13.

who shuts and no one opens,'[3] to open for us the inner chambers of the Gospel that we, too, may say with David: 'Open my eyes that I may consider the wonders of your law.'[4] To the multitudes, the Lord spoke in parables; He spoke to them from the outside, not interiorly or in the spirit, but externally in the letter. So we beg the Lord to introduce us to His mysteries, to bring us into His chamber, to permit us to say with the spouse in the Canticle of Canticles: 'The king brought me to his chambers.'[5] The apostle says that a veil was placed over the eyes of Moses,[6] but I say, not only is there a veil over the Law, but also over the Gospel for the one who does not understand. The Jew hears, but does not comprehend; for him a veil has been placed over the Gospel; the Gentiles hear, heretics hear, but for them also there is the veil. Let us leave the letter, therefore, with the Jews, and follow the spirit with Jesus; not that we scorn the letter of the Gospel—for everything has come to pass that is written—but that, by mounting certain steps, we may climb to higher places.

'After John had been delivered up, Jesus came into Galilee.' When we were commenting upon the Gospel last Sunday, we distinguished John in the Law and Jesus in the Gospel,[7] for John says: 'One mightier than I is coming after me, the strap of whose sandals I am not worthy to stoop down and loose.'[8] And in another place, he says: 'He must increase, but I must decrease.'[9] He is drawing a comparison, therefore, between the Law and the Gospel. Farther, he says: 'I have baptized you with water,' that is, the Law; 'but he will baptize you with the Holy Spirit,'[10] that is, the Gospel. Jesus came, therefore, because John had been imprisoned; hence, it is the Old Law

3 Apoc. 3.7; cf. Letter 58.9, PL 22.585(326).
4 Ps. 118.18.
5 Cf. Cant. 1.4, LXX.
6 Cf. 2 Cor. 3.13-17.
7 Cf. Homily 75 (I) on Mark 1.1-12, p. 125.
8 Mark 1.7.
9 John 3.30.
10 Mark 1.8.

that is closed up. and gone is its freedom; from the Law, we have crossed over into the Gospel. Notice that: 'After John had been delivered up, Jesus came into Galilee'; by no means into Judea nor Jerusalem, but into Galilee of the Gentiles. 'Jesus came into Galilee.' Galilee in our language means 'katakulistḗ' [rolling down]. There was nothing sublime nor lofty there before the coming of the Savior; everything base was tolerated: luxury, filth, impurities, the wallowing place for the muck of swine.

'Preaching the gospel of the kingdom of God.' As far as I am able to recall[11] reading the Law, perusing the prophets, reciting the psalter, I have never heard of the kingdom of heaven except in the Gospel. Only after He came, by whom it was said: 'the kingdom of God is within you,'[12] the kingdom of God was opened. 'Preaching the gospel of the kingdom of God.' 'From the days of John the Baptist the kingdom of heaven has been enduring violent assault, and the violent have been seizing it by force.'[13] Before the advent of the Savior and the glory of the Gospel, until Christ with the robber opened the door of Paradise, all the souls of the faithful were consigned to the nether world. As a matter of fact, even Jacob says: 'I will go down mourning to the nether world.'[14] If Abraham[15] descended to the land of the dead, who did not?[16] In the Law, Abraham is in hell; in the Gospel, the robber is in heaven.[17] We are not depreciating Abraham in whose bosom we all long to find rest, but we prefer Christ to Abraham, the Gospel to the Law. We have read that, after the Resurrection of Christ, many of the saints appeared in the holy city.[18] Our Lord and Savior preached on earth and also

---

11 Cf. Homily 75 (I) on Mark 1.1-12, pp. 121-122.
12 Luke 17.21.
13 Matt. 11.12.
14 Cf. Gen. 37.35.
15 Cf. Luke 16.22, 23; cf. Letter 129.2, PL 22.1101(968).
16 Cf. Letter 60.3, PL 22.590-591(333).
17 Cf. Letter 60.3, PL 22.591(333); 78.34, PL 22.718(490).
18 Cf. Matt. 27.52, 53.

among the dead, for that is why He died and why he descended into hell: to release the souls that had been confined there.

'Preaching the gospel of the kingdom of God, and saying, "The time [of the Law] is fulfilled," ' the Gospel has begun ' "and the kingdom of God is at hand." ' He did not say, the kingdom of God has already arrived, but the kingdom is at hand. Until I suffer and shed My blood, the kingdom of God is closed; it is near at hand, therefore, because not yet have I suffered the Passion. 'Repent and believe in the gospel': by no means in the Law, but in the Gospel; nay, rather through the Law into the Gospel, as it is written: 'From faith unto faith.'[19] The faith of the Law has confirmed the faith of the Gospel.

'Passing along the sea of Galilee, he saw Simon and his brother Andrew, casting their nets into the sea (for they were fishermen).' Simon, not yet Peter—for not yet had he followed the Rock that he should be called Peter—Simon and his brother, Andrew, were at sea and were casting their nets. Scripture does not say that they cast their nets and caught fish. He saw Simon, it says, and his brother, Andrew, casting their nets into the sea, for they were fishermen. The Gospel reports, to be sure, that they were casting nets; still it does not say that they caught anything; hence, it is clear that before the Passion, they cast nets, but it is not recorded that they caught anything. After the Passion, however, they let down their net and drew up a catch, so great that it broke the nets.[20] 'Casting their nets into the sea, for they were fishermen.'

'Jesus said to them, "Come, follow me, and I will make you fishers of men." ' Happy exchange of fishing! Jesus fishes for them that they may become fishers of other fishermen. First, they become fish that they may be caught by Christ; afterwards, they will fish for others. Jesus says: 'Come, follow me

19 Rom. 1.17.
20 Cf. Luke 5.6; John 21.11.

and I will make you fishers of men.' 'And at once they left the nets, and followed him.' 'At once.' True faith does not hesitate; it responds at once, believes at once, it follows at once, becomes a fisherman at once. 'At once they left the nets.' I think that in the nets, they left behind the vices of the world. It was impossible, indeed, for them to keep their nets and follow Jesus.

'Going on a little farther, he saw James the son of Zebedee, and his brother John; they also were in their boat mending the nets.' The fact that it says 'mending' shows that the nets were torn. They were casting their nets into the sea, but, because they were torn, they could not catch any fish. They were mending their nets in the sea; sitting in a little boat in the sea, with their father, Zebedee, they were mending the nets of the Old Law. That, by the way, is the spiritual interpretation. 'They also were in their boat mending the nets,' 'they also who were in the boat.' They were in the boat, not on the shore where it was steady and firm, but in a boat washed back and forth by the waves.

'Immediately he called them. And they left their father Zebedee in the boat with the hired men, and followed him.' Someone may remark: Faith is rash. What sign had they seen, what majesty had they beheld, that they should follow Him immediately upon being called? Certainly, there is evidence here that Jesus' eyes and countenance radiated a certain divinity that readily attracted those whom He met.[21] Even without Jesus ever saying, 'Follow Me,' they would have followed Him, for if they had followed Him without cause, it would not have been faith as much as temerity. If I were seated and anyone passing by should say to me, 'Come, follow me,' and I should follow him, is that faith? Why do I make such a point of all this? Because the very speech of the Lord was efficacious. Whatever He spoke accomplished His purpose, for if: 'he spoke and they were made, he commanded

21 Cf. Mark 11.15-19; Matt. 9.9.

and they were created,'[22] assuredly, He is the same and the very One who called; therefore, they followed.

'Immediately he called them. And they left their father Zebedee.' 'Hear, O daughter, and see; turn your ear, forget your people and your father's house. So shall the king desire your beauty.'[23] 'They left their father Zebedee in the boat.' Take heed, O monk, and imitate the apostles; listen to the voice of the Savior and pay no attention to your temporal father. Recognize your true Father of the soul and of the spirit, and leave your natural father. The apostles leave their father; they leave the boat; in a moment, they leave all their wealth. They leave the world and innumerable possessions. They surrendered all that they had. God does not consider the extent of property, but the disposition of the soul that renounces it; they who have given up little would have given up much just as promptly.

They left their father Zebedee in a boat with the hired men, and followed Him. This goes back to what we said a little earlier in allegory about the apostles, that they were mending the nets of the Law. By now the nets had been torn and could not hold a catch, by now they had been eaten away by the brine of the sea and could no longer have been repaired if the blood of Jesus had not come and renewed them. They leave, then, their father Zebedee; they forsake the Law that in truth had begotten them; they abandon the Law in the boat, in the midst of the billows of the sea. Note, also, that they leave their father—that is the Law—with the hired men. Everything the Jews do, they do for the sake of the present life; hence, they are hired men. 'The man who carries out the Law will find life through it.'[24] Scripture did not say, he will find life through it, in the sense that through the Law he will live in heaven, but he will find life through it to the extent that what he merits, he reaps in the present world. It is

22 Cf. Ps. 148.5.
23 Ps. 44.11, 12.
24 Cf. Lev. 18.5; Rom. 10.5.

written for a fact in Ezechiel: 'I gave them statutes that were not good and regulations not the best, which they shall observe and thereby find life.'[25] The Jews find life in them, for they look for nothing else than to have children, to possess health and wealth. They seek the things of earth; they give no thought to those of heaven; they are hired men. Would you be convinced that the Jews are hired men? That son who had squandered all his fortune, and who, by interpretation, prefigures the Gentiles, exclaims: 'How many hired men there are in my father's house!'[26] 'They left their father Zebedee in the boat with the hired men, and followed him.' They left their father—the Law—with the hired men in the boat. To this very day, the Jews are navigators, navigating in the Law and in the sea, but they cannot reach the harbor. They have not believed in the harbor; hence, for them there is no arriving in haven.

'They entered Capharnaum.' O happy and grand and glorious exchange! They quit the sea; they abandon the ship; they renounce the bonds of the nets and enter Capharnaum. The first change is to give up the sea, to surrender the boat, to desert their father, to reject their earlier errors. In the nets, I say, and in the attraction of the nets, all vices are left behind. Just realize the exchange! They renounce them and, because they have renounced them, what do they find? They enter, Holy Writ says, Capharnaum, the field of consolation. Now CAPHAR means field; NAVM, consolation. If, however, we mean Naum—in Hebrew there are multiple meanings, and the sense differs according to the difference in pronunciation—it can be taken as either consolation or beautiful. Capharnaum, therefore, may be translated as field of consolation or most beautiful land.[27] In Scripture, where we read: 'Behold, how good it is, and how pleasant,'[28] where we

25 Cf. Ezech. 20.25.
26 Cf. Luke 15.17; cf. Letter 21.14, PL 22.386(77).
27 Cf. *Hebrew Names*, PL 23.888(94); *Commentary on Matthew* 11.23, 24, PL 26.77(73).
28 Ps. 132.1.

say, 'terpnón [pleasing], and Aquila translates, 'eúprepés [fitting], the Hebrew has NAVM, which means beautiful.

'They entered Capharnaum. And immediately on the Sabbath he went into the synagogue and began to teach them,' in order that they might forsake the leisure of the Sabbath and take up the work of the Gospel. 'He was teaching them as one having authority, and not as the Scribes.' He was not saying, for instance, 'This the Lord says,' and He who sent me says that; He was speaking Himself in person who previously had spoken by the prophets.[29] It is one thing to say, 'it is written,' and another to say, 'the Lord says this,' and still another to say, 'amen I say to you.' In another passage: 'It is written in the Law: thou shalt not kill, thou shalt not dismiss thy wife.' 'It is written.' By whom is it written? By Moses at God's command. If it is written with the finger of God, how dare you say: 'Amen I say to you,' unless you are He who first gave the Law? No one ventures to change the law except the king himself. But did the Father give the Law, or the Son? Answer, heretic. Whichever you say, I gladly support; for me, it is one as well as the other. If the Father gave the Law and changes it, the Son who changes it with Him who gave it, is equal to Him. Whether, moreover, He is the one who gave or the one who changes, it takes equal authority to have given and to have changed—a thing which no one is able to do except the king.

'They were astonished at his teaching.' Now I ask what new doctrine had He taught, what had He said that was new? He was saying the same things that He had spoken by the prophets, but that is exactly why they were astonished; He was teaching as one who had authority, and not as the Scribes. He was not speaking as a teacher, but as the Lord; He was not speaking in reference to a greater authority, but He was teaching that which was His very own. In fine, He was speaking in this manner because He who had spoken by

29 Cf. Heb. 1.1, 2.

the prophets was talking now in person. 'It is I who have foretold it: Here I am!'[30]

The unclean spirit that before had been in the synagogue and had led them into idolatry, of whom it is written: 'the spirit of harlotry has led them astray';[31] the spirit that had gone out of a man and was roaming in the dry places in search of a resting place and could find none, and that took with him seven other demons and returned into his former[32] dwelling place; all these spirits were in the synagogue and could not bear the presence of the Savior. Indeed: 'What harmony is there between Christ and Belial?'[33] Christ and Belial could not abide in the same assembly. 'Now in their synagogue there was a man with an unclean spirit, and he cried out, saying, "What have we to do with thee?" ' Who is asking: 'What have we to do with you?' He is only one, but he cries out the recognition of many. He is aware that, in his own defeat, his devils have been vanquished with him.

'He cried out,' like one undergoing torture, gripped in pain, unable to endure scourging. 'He cried out, saying, "What have we to do with thee, Jesus of Nazareth? Hast thou come to destroy us? I know who thou art, the Holy One of God." ' He was in extreme torture and, by his cry, betrayed the excess of his torments, but there is no end to his guile. He is driven to utter the truth; the torments compel him, but malice forbids: 'What have we to do with thee, Jesus of Nazareth?' Why do you not admit that it is the Son of God? Is it a Nazarene who torments you and not the Son of God? Do you feel the punishments, but refuse to confess the name? 'Jesus of Nazareth, have you come to destroy us?' What you are saying is true: 'You have come to destroy us. I know who You are.' Let us examine the title you give Him: the Holy One

30 Isa. 52.6.
31 Osee 4.12.
32 Cf. Matt. 12.43-46.
33 2 Cor. 6.15; cf. *Commentary on Ephesians* 4.27, PL 26.544(630); *Hebrew Names*, 2 Cor., PL 23.898(110).

of God. Was not Moses the holy one of God? Was not Isaia? Was not Jeremia? 'Before I formed you in the womb, I sanctified you.'[34] That is said to Jeremia, and he yet was not the holy one of God? If not they, then, who were holy men? But why do you not say to them, 'I know who you are, the Holy One of God'? O perversity of heart! He is held in the midst of scourgings and torments and knows what is true but will not admit it. 'I know who you are, the Holy One of God.' Do not say: 'Holy One of God'; but, 'Holy God.' You pretend to know, but you do not know, for either you know and are guilefully silent, or actually you are ignorant. Indeed, He is not the Holy One of God, but Holy God. Why do I stress all this? That we may not give assent to the testimony of demons.

The devil never tells the truth, since he is a liar, the father of lies. 'Your father is a liar, and from the beginning he is a liar just as the father of lies.'[35] The father, Holy Writ says, is a liar and does not speak truth, the father of lies, the father of the Jews. The devil is certainly a liar from the beginning. Who is the devil's father? 'For his father is a liar and from the beginning spoke lies, just as the father of lies.' This means that the devil is a liar and utters lies, and, therefore, is the father of lies. Not that the devil has another father, but the devil is the father of untruth.[36] Scripture says, therefore: He is a liar and, from the beginning of the world, does not tell the truth; what he speaks is a lie and he is its father; he is the father of lying itself. We have digressed on this point, because we must not give credence to the testimony of demons. The Lord and Savior teaches: 'This kind can only be cast out by much prayer and fasting.'[37] But look here, I see many dissipated in drunkenness who belch up wine and, in the midst of feasting, get rid of demons and the demons cry out: we also believe that Christ has lied, for He said: This kind can

34 Cf. Jer. 1.5.
35 Cf. John 8.44; cf. Letter 22.1, PL 22.395(88).
36 Cf. *Commentary on Isaia* 14.22, 23, PL 24.226(259).
37 Matt. 17.20.

only be cast out by much prayer and fasting. My purpose in saying all this is to warn you against too readily believing in the testimonies of demons.

What does the Savior say next? 'Jesus rebuked him, saying, "Hold thy peace, and go out of the man."' Truth has no need for the witness of falsehood; I have not come to give proof to your testimony, but to cast you out of My creature. 'Unseemly is praise on a sinner's lips.'[38] I do not need the witness of one whose torture I have commanded. Silence! Let your silence be My praise. I do not want your voice to praise Me, but your torments; your punishment is My praise. Not because of your praise do I rejoice, but because you are departing. Hold your peace and go out of the man. It is as if He were saying: Go out from My dwelling place; what are you doing in My guest chamber? I wish to enter it; be silent and go out from the man, from the rational animal. Go out from the man; leave the guest chamber that has been prepared for Me. The Lord desires His own dwelling place; depart from the man, from a rational animal. 'Go out of the man.' In another place in Holy Writ, He commanded a legion to come out of a man and go into swine.[39] Realize how precious is the soul of man! This contradicts those who think that we and brute animals have one and the same soul and receive one and the same spirit.[40] He is driven out of one man and is sent into two thousand swine; the precious is saved, and the mean is destroyed. Go out of the man, go into the swine; go into brute creatures; go into whatever else you wish; go into the bottomless pits. Relinquish man, My own proper possession. Go out of man; it is not My will that you take possession of him; it is a wrong to Me for you to dwell in him since he is My dwelling place. I have assumed a human body, I dwell in man; the body that you are holding in possession shares in My body; depart from the man.

38 Sir. (Ecclus.) 15.9.
39 Cf. Matt. 8.32.
40 Cf. *Commentary on Matthew* 8.31-33, PL 26.56(48).

'The unclean spirit, convulsing him.' By this sign, he reveals his anguish; he threw the man into a convulsion. He could not wound the soul; the body he afflicted, yes, because in no other way could it be perceived that the demon was coming out of him; by such bodily contortions, he reveals that he is departing. 'The unclean spirit, convulsing him.' Because the clean spirit was holding its own steadfastly, the unclean spirit fled. 'Crying out with a loud voice, went out of him.' He protested his departure with a loud cry and the convulsion of the body. 'They were all amazed, so that they inquired among themselves.' Let us read the Acts of the Apostles and the miracles that the ancient prophets performed. Moses works wondrous signs, and what do Pharao's magicians say? 'This is the finger of God.'[41] Moses performs, and they acknowledge the power of another. The apostles, too, worked miracles: 'In the name of Jesus, arise and walk';[42] 'In the Spirit of Jesus, go out';[43] always in the name of Jesus. But here, what does He say? 'Go out of the man.' Not in the name of another, but by His own power, He compels them to depart. 'They were all amazed, so that they inquired among themselves, saying, "What is this? What new doctrine is this?"' It was nothing new that a demon had departed; it was usual for the Hebrew exorcists to expel evil spirits.[44] What new doctrine is this, then? What is new? 'With authority he commands even the unclean spirits.' He does not command in the name of another, but He gives the command Himself; not in the name of another does He speak, but in His own.

'Rumor concerning him went forth immediately into all the region round about Galilee.' Not into Judea nor Jerusalem did the Jewish rabbis, in envy of Jesus' fame, suffer the rumor to enter. Besides, Pilate and the others had known that the

41 Exod. 8.15.
42 Cf. Acts 3.6.
43 Cf. Acts 16.18.
44 Cf. *Commentary on Matthew* 12.27, PL 26.82(79).

Pharisees had delivered Jesus up out of envy.[45] Fame finds entrance only into ears that are not closed up by envy. Why do I say all this? Because rumor concerning Him went forth into all regions of Galilee. It reached all Galilee. It reached all Galilee, but did not enter into one little village of Judea. Again, why do I say this? Because once the soul has been possessed by envy, it is very difficult for it to receive virtue; it is almost impossible to restore the soul that envy has mastered. It was, in fact, envy that caused the first fratricide. There were two men in the world, Abel and Cain; the Lord accepted the gift of Abel, but not Cain's. He who should have made virtue his model did not, but immediately killed him whose gift had been acceptable to the Lord.

'As soon as they came out of the synagogue, they, with James and John, came into the house of Simon and Andrew.' The Lord had drawn up His team of four and was carried above the Cherubim—and entered in the house of Peter, whose soul was worthy to receive so great a guest. They 'came into the house of Simon and Andrew.' 'Now Simon's mother-in-law was keeping her bed sick with a fever.' O, may He come to our house and enter in and by His command cure the fever of our sins! Each one of us is sick with a fever. Whenever I give way to anger, I have a fever; there are as many fevers as there are faults and vices. Let us beg the apostles to intercede for us with Jesus, that He may come to us and touch our hand, for if He but does so, at once our fever is gone. Excellent physician and truly the chief physician! Moses is a physician; Isaia, a physician; all the saints are physicians, but He is the archphysician. He knew how carefully to touch veins and thoroughly search out the hidden secrets of diseases. He does not touch the ear or any other part of the body; He touches only the hand. The cause of sickness and fever is the lack of good works. So, first of all, deeds are made right; afterwards, the fever is lifted. The fever cannot be dissipated

45 Cf. Matt. 27.18.

unless works are amended. When our hands are guilty of evil deeds, we are sick in bed; we cannot rise or walk; we are sick all over.

'Drawing near' to her who was sick . . . she could not rise, for she was lying sick upon a couch, unable to go to meet Him, but this compassionate physician went Himself to her couch; He who had carried the sick lamb upon His shoulders went Himself to the sick bed. 'Drawing near.' Of His own will He approaches, so that of His own will He may heal. 'Drawing near.' It is as if He says: Certainly, you ought to have come to meet Me. You ought to have come to the door and received Me so that your cure might be the result, not only of My kindness, but also of your desire. Because, however, you are lying prostrate from the violence of the fever and cannot get up, I come to you Myself. 'Drawing near, he raised her up.' Because she could not rise of herself, the Lord raises her up. 'He took her by the hand and raised her up.' He took her hand. Peter, too, when he was in danger in the sea and was drowning, is raised up by the touch of His hand. He raised her up by touching her hand. He takes her hand in His. O happy friendship! O beautiful kiss! He raised her up by taking her hand! He healed her hand with His hand. He took her by the hand as if He were a physician; He touched her veins; He recognized the intensity of the fever; He is both doctor and cure. At Jesus' touch, the fever is put to flight.

May He also touch our hand, that our works may be cleansed. May He enter our house. Let us now, at last, rise up from the couch; let us not lie prostrate. Jesus stands before our couch, and do we lie down? Let us rise up and stand. It is disgraceful for us to be indolent in the presence of Jesus. Someone may ask: Where is Jesus? He is here in our midst. 'In the midst of you there has stood one whom you do not know.'[46] 'The kingdom of God is within you.'[47] Let us have

46 John 1.26.
47 Luke 17.21.

faith, and we shall see Jesus in our midst. If we cannot touch His hand, let us fall at His feet. If we are unable to reach His head, let us, at least, wash His feet with our tears. Our penitence is perfume to the Savior. Just see how great is the compassionate kindness of the Savior! Our sins are malodorous, putrid; still, if we do penance for our wrongdoings, if we weep over them, our foul offenses become the fragrant perfume of the Lord. Let us, therefore, beg the Lord to take us by the hand.

'The fever left her at once.' As soon as He took her by the hand, the fever fled. Mark what follows. 'The fever left her at once.' Be hopeful, sinner, if only you rise up from the couch! Even holy David who had fallen, who lay on the couch with Bethsabee, the wife of Urias the Hethite, and was feverishly sick of adultery, the Lord cured as soon as he said: 'Have mercy on me, O God, in your goodness,'[48] 'for I acknowledge my offense, and my sin is before me always';[49] 'free me from blood guilt, O God, my saving God. . . .'[50] David had shed the blood of Urias because he had commanded his death. 'Free me,' he said, 'from blood guilt, O God, my saving God, and a steadfast spirit renew within me.'[51] Notice that he said, 'renew.' When I committed adultery, when I perpetrated homicide, the Holy Spirit in me had grown old. 'Wash me, and I shall be whiter than snow.'[52] Because you have washed me with my tears, my tears and my repentance were for me as baptism. See, then, what is wrought of repentance? He repented and wept; therefore, he was cleansed. What follows directly? 'I will teach transgressors your ways, and sinners shall return to you.'[53] He is made the teacher of repentance.

Why now have I said all this? Because it is written here in

48 Ps. 50.3; cf. Letter 122.3, PL 22.1043(805).
49 Ps. 50.5.
50 Ps. 50.16.
51 Ps. 50.16, 12.
52 Ps. 50.9.
53 Ps. 50.15.

our text: 'The fever left her at once, and she began to wait on them.' It is not enough that her fever leave her, but she is elevated to the service of Christ. 'She began to wait on them.' She served Him with her feet and with her hand; hither and thither she ran; she worshiped Him by whom she had been cured. Let us also wait on Jesus. Gladly does He accept our service even though we have soiled hands; because He has healed us, He deigns to look upon what He has healed. To Him be glory forever and ever. Amen.

HOMILY 77(III)

ON MARK 5.30-43

'WHO TOUCHED ME?'[1] He inquires and looks around to see the woman who had touched Him. Did not the Lord really know who had touched Him? Why, then, does He look around for her? He knew, of course, that she would declare publicly what had happened. 'The woman, fearing and trembling, knowing what had happened within her. . . .' If He had not asked: 'Who touched me,' no one would have known that a miracle had taken place. They could even have insisted that He did not work any miracles, but was only vaunting Himself and seeking His own glory. He asks the question, therefore, that the woman may acknowledge the favor and give glory to God.

'She came and fell down before him, and told him all the truth.' Note the separate stages; mark the progress. As long as she was hemorrhaging, she could not come into His presence; she was healed and then came before Him. She fell at His feet; not yet did she dare to look up into His face. As long as she has been cured, it is enough for her to cling to His feet. She 'told him all the truth.' Christ is truth. Because she had been healed by Truth, she gave praise to Truth. 'He said to her, "Daughter thy faith has saved thee." ' She whose faith is so great deserves to be called daughter. The crowd that presses upon Him cannot be called daughter, but she who falls at His feet and acknowledges Him merits to receive that title. Your faith has saved you. Just see His humility! He it is

1 Mark 5.31.

who heals, and yet He ascribes the healing to her. Your faith has brought your salvation. 'Thy faith has saved thee. Go in peace.' Before you could believe in Solomon, the peacemaker, you had no peace; but now go in peace. 'I have overcome the world.'[2] Peace is yours; do not be troubled, for the people of the Gentiles have been healed.

'There came some from the house of the ruler of the synagogue, saying, "Thy daughter is dead. Why dost thou trouble the Master further?"' The Church has come to life, and the synagogue is dead. Though the girl is dead, nevertheless, the Lord says to the ruler of the synagogue: 'Do not be afraid, only have faith.' Let us this very day say to the synagogue, to the Jews: Yes, the daughter of the ruler of the synagogue is dead; but have faith and she will be restored to life. 'He allowed no one to follow him except Peter and James, and John the brother of James.' Someone may wonder and ask: Why are these apostles always chosen[3] and the others sent away? Even when He was transfigured on the mountain, these three were with Him. Yes, three are chosen: Peter, James, and John. In the first place, there is the mystery of the Trinity in this number, a number sacred in itself; secondly, according to the Hebrew truth, Jacob set three green boughs in the watering troughs;[4] finally, it is written: 'A three-ply cord is not easily broken.'[5] Logically, then, Peter is chosen upon whom the Church is to be built, and James, the first of the apostles who is to be crowned with martyrdom, and John, who initiates the state of virginity.

'They came to the house of the ruler of the synagogue and he saw a tumult, people weeping and wailing greatly.' Right down to this day, there is uproar in the synagogue. Although the Jews assure us that they chant the psalms of David, never-

2 John 16.33.
3 Cf. *Commentary on Matthew* 17.1, PL 26.121(129).
4 Cf. Gen. 30.37; cf. *Hebrew Questions on Genesis* 30.37, PL 23.1034(353-354).
5 Eccles. 4.12; cf. Letter 82.11, PL 22.742-743(521).

theless, it is the song of their lamentation. 'Going in he said to them, "Why do you make this din, and weep? The girl is asleep, not dead." ' The girl who is dead to you is alive to Me; to you, she is dead; to Me, she is asleep. Because she is sleeping, she can be awakened. 'They laughed him to scorn.' They certainly did not believe that the ruler's daughter could be brought back to life by Jesus: 'But he, putting them all out, took the father and mother of the girl.' Let us address our remarks to the holy men who work signs and wonders, to whom the Lord has granted certain miraculous powers. Christ, who is going to restore life to the ruler's daughter, dismisses all the others to prevent their thinking He is doing it for vainglory. In truth, He put the others out, and He took with Him the father and mother of the girl. Perhaps He would have sent them off likewise, except that, because of their love, the parents were to behold their daughter being restored to life.

'He entered in where the girl was lying. And taking the girl by the hand. . . .' First, He touched her hand; He healed her works and thus brought her back to life. Then, in truth, were the words fulfilled: 'Until the full number of Gentiles shall enter, and thus all Israel shall be saved.'[6] Then, He says: 'Talitha cumi,' which is interpreted, 'Girl, I say to thee arise.' If He said, 'Talitha cum,' the translation would be: 'Girl arise'; but because He said, 'Talitha cumi,' the Aramaic and Hebrew phrase means: 'Girl, rise up for Me.'[7] 'Cumi,' means, in other words, 'I say to thee arise.' See what mystery there is in the Aramaic and Hebrew language?[8] It is as if He said: Girl, you whose duty it was to become a mother, have been made a maiden on account of your infidelity. We may also express the thought: Because you shall be reborn, you shall be called girl. Girl, I say to you arise; not by your own merit,

6 Cf. Rom. 11.25, 26.
7 Cf. Letter 57.7, PL 22.572(310).
8 Cf. *Hebrew Names*, PL 23.888(94).

but with My grace; for Me, therefore, arise; you are healed, but your return to life [is] not the result of your virtuous acts.

'The girl rose up immediately and began to walk.' May Jesus touch us, also, and immediately we shall walk. Even though we are paralyzed; even though our deeds are evil and we cannot walk; even though we are lying on a couch sick in body and soul; if Jesus shall touch us, we shall recover at once. Peter's mother-in-law had been afflicted with fever; Jesus touched her hand, and she rose up and began to minister to Him. Notice the difference. The mother of Peter's wife is touched, and she rises up and ministers; for the girl, it is enough only that she walk.

'They were utterly amazed. And he charged them strictly that no one should know of it.' Do you see why He had dismissed the crowd when He was about to work the miracle? He charged them, and not only did He charge them, but He laid a strict injunction upon them, that no one should know. He admonished the three apostles, He warned the parents that no one was to know. The Lord gave the command to all; but the girl who arose from the dead could not keep the secret. 'He directed that something be given her to eat,' so that the resurrection might not be considered a phantasm. He, too, after His Resurrection ate some fish and honey comb.[9] He gave directions that they give her something to eat. I beseech You, O Lord, touch the hand of us who are lying ill, raise us up again from the couch of our sins, and make us walk. When we walk, bid that food be given us; lying sick abed, we cannot eat; unless we stand, we cannot receive the Body of Christ. To whom be glory with the Father and the Holy Spirit forever and ever. Amen.

9 Luke 24.42; cf. Letter 108.23, PL 22.901(717); *Against Jovinian* 2.17, PL 23.325(352); *Against John of Jerusalem* 34, PL 23.404 (444).

HOMILY 78(IV)

ON MARK 8.1-9

IN THOSE DAYS WHEN AGAIN there was a great crowd, and they had nothing to eat, he called his disciples together and said to them, "I have compassion on the crowd, for behold, they have now been with me three days, and have nothing to eat." ' In an earlier part[1] of the Gospel, we read that the Lord fed five thousand men with five loaves, and from the broken pieces left over, they picked up twelve full hampers. On that occasion, we discussed what seemed to be the meaning of the miracle. This simple record of fact that we have just read is different; yet in some respects, the same as the previous occurrence; in fact, they are alike in part and in part unlike. In the former account, we read that they were fed in the desert; here, however, upon a mountain. First, I want to draw your attention to their difference. We have to know the very flesh and blood of Holy Writ, so that, when we understand exactly what is written, we can grasp its import. There, five thousand were fed; here, four thousand; there, five loaves of bread; here, seven; there, according to St. John's Gospel, the five loaves were of barley;[2] here, the seven, of corn. You see the difference, the same account, yet not the same. Consequently, we must not be careless in reading Scripture.

Is what we have noted the only dissimilarity? Is there no other? Let us see. There, we read that the people fed by Jesus have been with Him only one day, and they are fed, not

1 Mark 6.35-44.
2 Cf. John 6.9.

at noon, but toward evening at sunset. Of the four thousand who are fed with seven loaves of corn, what does Jesus Himself say, not the apostles as in the earlier situation? There, it is the apostles who say: Behold, the whole day, they are in attendance upon You; here, the Savior Himself says: Behold they have now been with Me three days. Note the difference between one day and three days. There, the apostles ask the Lord to feed them; here, the Lord reminds the apostles to feed them. What does He say here? 'If I send them away to their homes fasting, they will faint on the way.' They who had been attendant upon Him for three days are worthy of the solicitude of the Lord.

Now, let us consider some other points. Five thousand men eat five loaves, and twelve baskets are filled with what is left over. Four thousand men—the number certainly is less; there, five thousand; here, four thousand—eat seven loaves. A smaller number plainly eats more: 'for many are called, but few are chosen.'[3] Note: four thousand men eat seven loaves. From five loaves, twelve baskets are filled; from seven loaves, seven hampers. From the lesser number of men, less remains; from the greater number, more is left over. Four thousand men—fewer certainly in number, but greater in faith. The man who is greater in faith eats more, and because he does, there is less left over. I wish that we, too, might eat more of the corn bread of Holy Writ, so that there would be less left over for us to learn. There are many things to be said, but, because they have already been discussed in connection with the first event, it was our intention on this occasion merely to point out the differences between the two, for the other time, we also took into account the meaning. Now, let us follow in the footsteps of the venerable priest and, since he has explained for us so adequately the beginning of the psalm, we shall run quickly over the rest of it.[4]

3 Matt. 20.16.
4 Cf. Homily 59 on Ps. 149, p. 424.

HOMILY 79(V)

ON MARK 8.22-26

SINCE THE VENERABLE PRIEST has made known to us the divine message of the psalm, we shall share the Gospel, and incorporate into our portion what we were going to say about the psalm.

'They came to Bethsaida and they brought him a blind man and entreated him to touch him.' The apostles came to Bethsaida, to those to whom the Lord had said: 'How is it that you do not yet understand?'[1] This was, in fact, the question that concluded the narration of the preceding event. They came, then, to Bethsaida, into the village of Andrew and Peter, James and John. Bethsaida means 'house of hunters,'[2] and, in truth, from this house, hunters and fishermen are sent into the whole world.

Reflect upon the text. The historical facts are clear, the literal sense is obvious; we must search into its spiritual message. That He came to Bethsaida, that there was a blind man there, that He departed, what is there great about all that? Nothing, but what He did is great; striking, however, only if it should take place today, for we have ceased to wonder about what happened at that time. 'They came to Bethsaida'; the apostles came into their own village where they had been born. 'They brought to him a blind man.' Watch this very carefully; note exactly what is said. In the home village of the apostles, there is a blind man; where the apostles were

1 Mark 8.21.
2 Cf. *Commentary on Ezechiel* 28.20-26, PL 25.275(339).

born, there is blindness. Do you grasp what I am saying? This blind man that was in the very home of the apostles is the Jewish people. 'They brought to him a blind man.' This is the blind man who was sitting by the wayside in Jericho;[3] not in the road, but on the wayside; not in the true law, but in the law of the letter. They entreat the Lord to touch the blind man. When the man in Jericho heard Jesus passing by, he began to cry out and say: 'Son of David, have mercy on me,' and those who were passing by angrily tried to silence him. But Jesus does not rebuke him, for He has not come except to the lost sheep of the house of Israel.[4] Jesus commanded that he should be brought to Him. He, hearing that Jesus was calling for him: 'sprang to his feet, and throwing off his cloak ran to him.'[5] He could not go to Him in his garments. Why did he throw off his cloak and run without it to Jesus? He could not go in his old clothes; naked he ran to the Lord. He was blind; his garments were soiled and tattered; so he ran like a blind man, and he was healed. Now, just as there was in Jericho this blind man on the wayside who was healed, a blind man is healed here, also, in Bethsaida.

'Entreated him to touch him.' The disciples entreated the Lord Savior to touch him; because of his blindness, he did not know the way; he could not walk up to Christ to touch Him. The apostles entreat Jesus and say: Touch him, and he will be healed. 'Taking the blind man by the hand, he led him forth outside the village.' 'Taking his hand.' Because his hand was full of blood, Jesus took his hand and cleansed it. He took his hand as He would a blind man's—He, the way and the guide[6]—and led him outside the village. Do you think that we are doing violence to the Scriptures? Perhaps someone is thinking secretly: That man is always going after allegory; he forces the Sacred Scriptures. Why—let him answer

3 Cf. Mark 10.46, 47.
4 Cf. Matt. 15.24.
5 Cf. Mark 10.50; cf. Letter 147.9, PL 22.1202(1092).
6 Cf. Homily 33 on Ps. 106, p. 242.

me who is harboring that thought—why, I ask, should He go to Bethsaida and why should a blind man be brought before Him? He does not cure him in the village, but outside, for he cannot be healed of his blindness in the Law, but in the Gospel. If this very day, Jesus should enter Bethsaida, the synagogue of the Jews, if Jesus—I mean the Divine Word—should go into the synagogue of the Jews, into their council, as long as that blind man is in the synagogue, in the letter of the law, he cannot be healed unless he is led outside.

'He led him forth outside the village; and applying spittle to his eyes, he laid his hands upon him.' Christ's spittle is medicine. 'Applying spittle to his eyes, he laid his hands upon him, and asked him if he saw anything.' Knowledge is always progressive. One cannot taste of perfect wisdom in an hour, however experienced he may be. One cannot arrive at perfect knowledge without expending a great deal of time in long pursuit of it. First, the dirt is removed; then, the blindness is lifted, and light comes. The Lord's spittle is the perfect doctrine that proceeds from His mouth to instruct perfectly. The Lord's spittle, if I may so speak, is knowledge as from His very essence, for just as the word that comes forth from His mouth is medicine, so even does His spittle seem to come forth from the very substance of God. This, then, is the meaning of our passage: with a penetrating contact, He wipes away the errors from his eyes. 'Applying spittle to his eyes, he laid his hands upon him.' Spittle cures his eyes, hands are imposed upon the head; spittle drives out blindness, hands impart a blessing.

'He asked him if he saw anything.' Jesus knew what he could see and what he could not, yet He asked him if he saw anything. When He asked him that, He knew that he was not yet seeing perfectly. 'The man looked up, and said.' Splendidly has Scripture said 'anablépsas,' looking up. He who, as long as he was blind, looked downward, looked upwards and was healed. 'The man looked up, and said, "I see men as though they were trees, but walking about."' He is neither totally blind nor does he have the full use of his eyes. 'I see men like trees walking about'; I still see shadow, not yet truth. The saying: 'I see men as though they were trees, but walking,' means: I see something in the Law, but I do not yet behold the clear light of the Gospel. To this very day, the Jews see men as if they were trees walking about; they see Moses, and still they do not see him; they read Isaia and do not understand. They see men, for Isaia is a man; Jeremia and all the prophets are men in comparison to brute beasts. 'A man, when he is in honor, does not realize it: he resembles the brute beasts and is made like unto them';[7] hence, they see the prophets, not as men, but as trees, that is, as irrational, unintelligent creatures.

'Then again he laid his hands upon the man's eyes.' You who think that I am doing violence to Holy Writ; you who say, 'You are forcing the Scripture, for this text contains only what the letter says,' is there nothing deeper within? He lays His hands upon his eyes and asks him whether he sees anything.

'Then again he laid his hands upon the man's eyes, and he began to see.' Note: He laid His hand upon his eyes and the man began to see. If it were merely a matter of human power, surely, even if he had sight, he could not see if hands were covering up his eyes, but the hand of the Lord is clearer than all eyes. He laid His hands upon his eyes, and he began to see: 'and was restored so that he saw all things plainly,' all things—I repeat—that we see; so that he discerned the mystery of the Trinity and perceived all the secret mysteries that are in the Gospel. 'So that he saw plainly.' Unless there were some who could see, but not clearly, Scripture would never say: 'so that he saw plainly.' Now, what he saw clearly, we all, likewise, see, for we believe in Christ who is the true Light. There is, however, a vast degree of difference among those who see. According to the faith of each one who be-

7 Cf. Ps. 48.13.

lieves, Jesus is either great or small. If I am a sinner and I repent of my sins, I touch His feet; if a saint, I bathe His head.

'He sent him to his house, saying, "Go to thy house, and do not enter the village, tell nobody." '[8] Listen carefully. This blind man was in Bethsaida; he is led outside and cured, not in Bethsaida, but outside. Because he is healed, it is said to him: Return to your house, but do not go into the village. He is taken out of Bethsaida; there he was, there they find him. How, then, is his house not in Bethsaida? Note the text exactly. If we consider the literal interpretation only, it does not make any sense. If this blind man is found in Bethsaida and is taken out and cured, and he is commanded: Return to your own house, certainly, he is bid: Return to Bethsaida. If, however, he returns there, what is the meaning of the command: Do not go into the village? You see, therefore, that the interpretation is allegorical. He is led out from the house of the Jews, from the village, from the Law, from the traditions of the Jews. He who could not be cured in the Law is cured in the grace of the Gospel. It is said to him, 'Return to your own house'—not into the house that you think, the one from which he came out, but into the house which was also the house of Abraham, since Abraham is the father of those who believe. 'Abraham saw my day and was glad.'[9] To your own house return, that is, to the Church. 'That thou mayest know, until I come, how to conduct thyself in the Church which is the house of God.'[10] Now, you see that the Church is the house of God; therefore, the Lord says to him: Go to your own house, the house of faith, the Church; do not return to the village of the Jews.

8 Cf. Mark 8.26.
9 Cf. John 8.56.
10 Cf. 1 Tim. 3.15.

HOMILY 80(VI)

ON MARK 9.1-7

'AMEN I SAY TO YOU, there are some of those standing here who will not taste death.'[1] 'Amen I say to you.' Christ is making a solemn promise. We must trust in Christ's promises. The Old Testament, 'As I live says the Lord,' is equivalent to the New Testament, 'Amen amen I say to you.' 'Amen, amen,' means truly, truly. Truth speaks truth to vanquish falsehood. 'Amen I say to you, there are some of those standing here.' I say to you, disciples; to the Jews, however, I am not speaking, for their ears are closed and My words cannot penetrate them. 'There are some of those standing here who will not taste death, till they have seen the kingdom of God.' It is very well said of those who are standing that they will not taste death, for the man who stands, by the very fact that he is standing, does not taste death. Moses, for example, says in Deuteronomy: 'Forty days and forty nights I stood on the mountain with the Lord.'[2] Alone he stood for forty days, and thereby merited to receive the Law. It is given to those standing; to those lying down, it is not given. We shall inquire into the significance of the words in order to fathom the mystery contained in the text. If the entrance courts are so beautiful, what will the house itself be like!

'Who will not taste death.' There are many kinds of death: some taste death; others see death; still others eat it;

1 Mark 8.39.
2 Cf. Deut. 10.10.

some are glutted with it; others again are renewed by it. The apostles, on the contrary, because they were standing and were apostles, for that very reason did not even taste death. We are speaking according to tropology and in harmony with the words: 'What man shall live, and not see death.'[3] The connotation of 'what man' indicates that it is impossible or difficult not to see death. 'Who will not taste death.' There are some, certainly, who will not taste death, but it is not easy to find those who shall not see death. Death we must understand here as the death of sin. 'Only the one who sins shall die.'[4] It is difficult, then, for anyone to live and not see death. There is a difference between seeing death and tasting death. He who sees, sees assuredly, but does not taste; he who tastes, however, must necessarily see.

Let us reflect upon what it means to taste death, what it means to see death. I saw a beautiful woman, my whole being longed for her; the fear of God drives away the desire. I have seen death, but I have not tasted it. If, however, I look at her and covet her, I have already committed adultery in my heart; see, I have tasted death. That is tasting death; not eating, not refreshing oneself, but rather partaking of death with the soul. The apostles, as apostles, did not even taste death. If, however, I have yielded a second and a third time, and commit fornication a number of times, no longer have I merely tasted death, but I am glutted with it. Comprehend, therefore, what the prophet said. He did not say: What man shall live, and not taste death; but, What man shall live, and not see death? It is hard to find the man who is not gripped by concupiscence, not shaken by temptations. So far, we have been following a more lofty form of exegesis; now, let us speak on the historical plane. The Lord said to His disciples that there are many of those standing here who will not taste death until they see the kingdom of God coming in power.

3 Ps. 88.49; cf. *Against the Pelagians* 3.11, PL 23.607(794).
4 Ezech. 18.4.

What He is actually saying is that they shall not die before they have seen Him ruling as King. This is according to history. The Gospel moves right along.

'Now after six days Jesus took Peter, James and John, and led them up a high mountain off by themselves, and was transfigured before them.' This, they say, is Christ ruling; the apostles saw what kind of king Christ was going to be. When they saw Him transfigured upon the mountain, they saw Him in the glory that would be His. This, therefore, is the meaning behind the words: They shall not taste death, until they have seen the kingdom of God—which came to pass six days later. The Gospel according to Matthew[5] has: 'Now it came to pass on the eighth day.' There seems to be a difference in the chronology, for Matthew says eight days, Mark, six. What we have to understand is that Matthew counted the first day and the last, but Mark reckoned only the time between.[6] The historical facts are that He ascended a mountain; He was transfigured; Moses and Elias were seen speaking with Him; Peter said to Him that he was delighted with this glorious vision: 'Lord, if thou wilt let us set up three tents here, one for thee, one for Moses, and one for Elias.'[7] Immediately, the evangelist adds: 'For he did not know what to say, for they were struck with fear.' Next, he says that a cloud appeared, that this same bright cloud overshadowed them, and there came a voice from heaven, saying: ' "This is my beloved Son; hear him." And suddenly looking around, they no longer saw anyone with them, but Jesus only.' That is history.

The lovers of history, who accept only the judgment of the Jews, who follow the letter that kills and not the spirit that gives life. . . .[8] We are not denying the historical event, but prefer a spiritual explanation. Nor are we merely expressing our own opinion; we follow the judgment of the apostles, and

5 Cf. Luke 9.28; cf. Matt. 17.1.
6 Cf. *Commentary on Matthew* 17.1, PL 26.125(129).
7 Cf. Mark 9.4, 5; cf. Matt. 17.4.
8 Cf. 2 Cor. 3.6.

especially of the 'chosen vessel'[9] who apprehended unto life the same words that the Jews interpreted unto death. I am referring, of course, to the apostle who says that Sara and Agar are types of the two covenants, Mount Sinai and Mount Sion. It is by a spiritual interpretation that they typify the two covenants. 'For these are the two covenants.'[10] Now, was there not an Agar, a Sara? Is there not a Mount Sinai, a Mount Sion? He has not rejected history, but has revealed its mystical meaning; furthermore, he did not say that these are explained as the two covenants, but: 'These are the two covenants.'

'Now after six days Jesus took Peter, James and John.' 'After six days.' Pray the Lord that these words may be expounded in the same Spirit in which they were uttered. It came to pass six days later. Why not nine days later? Why not ten, twenty, four, five? Why not some number before or after; why six? 'It came to pass after six days.' They who are standing with Jesus—of whom He says: 'there are some of those standing here'—will not see the kingdom of God except after six days. Not until this world shall pass away—that is the force of the six days—shall the new kingdom appear. When the six days have passed, he who is Peter, that is, he who, like Peter, has received his name from the Rock, Christ, will merit to see the kingdom, for by the same token that we are called Christians from Christ, Peter is named from the Rock, 'pétrinos.' If anyone of us shall be 'pétrinos' and have such faith that the Church of Christ may be built upon him; if anyone shall be as James and John, brothers, not so much in blood as in spirit; if anyone shall be Jacob, 'pternistḗr,' the supplanter, and John, meaning 'favor of the Lord,'[11] (for we shall merit the favor of Christ when we have supplanted our adversaries); if anyone shall have a more sublime doc-

9 Acts 9.15.
10 Gal. 4.24; cf. Letter 123.13, PL 22.1055(910).
11 Cf. *Hebrew Names*, PL 23.825(12).

trine and superior understanding and deserve to be called the Son of Thunder; it is necessary that he be led by Jesus into the mountain.

Consider, too, that as long as Jesus is down below, He is not transfigured; He ascends and is transformed. 'He led them up a high mountain off by themselves, and was transfigured before them. And his garments became shining, exceedingly white as snow.' To this very day, Jesus is down below for some and up above for others. They who are below, the crowd who cannot climb the mountain, have Jesus down below—only the disciples climb the mountain, the crowd remains below—if anyone, I say, is one of the crowd, he cannot see Jesus in shining garments, only in soiled. If anyone follows the letter and is completely of the earth and looks at the ground in the manner of brute beasts, he is unable to see Jesus in a shining vestment, but for him who follows the word of God and ascends the mountain, climbs to the top, for him, Jesus is instantly transfigured and His garments shine exceedingly.

Now, if we read and take all this literally, what is the value of 'shining,' of 'white,' of 'on high'? If we ponder it spiritually, Holy Writ, that is, the clothing of the word, is transformed immediately and becomes as white as snow: 'as no fuller on earth can whiten.' Take any prophetical witness, any evangelical parable, if you consider merely the letter, there is nothing shining in it, nothing white. If, however, you follow the apostle with deep spiritual perception, immediately the clothing of the word is changed and becomes white; Jesus is completely transformed on the mountain, and His garments become exceedingly white as snow: 'as no fuller on earth can whiten.' The earthly man cannot whiten his garments; but he who abandons the world and ascends the mountain with Jesus, and meditating mounts to heavenly contemplations, that man is able to make his garments white as no fuller on earth can do.

Someone may say to me, although he may not say it actually, but be thinking it within himself: You have given us the meaning of mountain; you have discussed the word of God; you have called the garments Holy Writ; tell me who these fullers are who cannot make garments as white as those of Jesus? It is the work of fullers to whiten what is soiled, and they cannot do that except with great effort. They have to tread upon the dirty garments, wash them, expose them to the sun, for not without much toil do garments that are soiled become white.[12] Plato deliberately set out, and Aristotle, too, and Zeno, the founder of Stoicism,[13] and Epicurus, the advocate of pleasure, to whiten their sordid doctrine with dazzling white words. They could not, however, make garments as white as those of Jesus on the mountain; because they were of the earth, their treatises are all of earth. No fuller, therefore, no arbiter of secular literature, could fashion garments such as Jesus possesses on the mountain.

'There appeared to them Elias with Moses, and they were talking with Jesus.' Until they had seen Jesus transfigured, until they had seen His white garments, they could not see Moses and Elias. 'They were talking with Jesus.' As long as we limit our perception as do the Jews, and follow only the letter that kills, Moses and Elias are not talking with Jesus; they do not know the Gospel. If, however, they shall have followed Jesus and have deserved to see the Lord transfigured with His white garments and to penetrate the Sacred Scripture with spiritual insight, at once, Moses and Elias come—that is, the Law and the prophets—and talk with the Word. 'There appeared to them Elias with Moses, and they were talking with Jesus.' The Gospel according to Luke adds: 'They spoke to him of his death, which he was about to fulfill in Jerusalem.'[14] That is what Moses and Elias are discussing, and they speak with Jesus, that is, with the Word, and announce

12 Cf. Homily 18 on Ps. 86, p. 139.
13 Cf. Letter 132.1, PL 22.1148(1026).
14 Cf. Luke 9.31; cf. *Against Jovinian* 2.15, PL 23.321(348).

to Him what He is going to suffer in Jerusalem, for the Law and the prophets proclaim the Passion of Christ. Do you see how the spiritual interpretation benefits our soul? Moses and Elias, notice, also appear in white garments. As long as they are not with Jesus, they do not have white garments. If you should read the Law, which is Moses, and the prophets, which is Elias, and do not appreciate them in Christ, nor comprehend how Moses and Elias speak with Jesus; but accept Moses and Elias without Him and do not perceive that they are announcing to Him the Passion, then, Moses and Elias do not ascend the mountain, nor do they have white garments, but those that are still soiled.

If you follow the letter[15] as do the Jews, what does it profit you to read that Juda has relations with Thamar, his daughter-in-law? What profit to you that Noe became intoxicated and exposed his nakedness? What profit that Onan, the son of Juda, committed so disgraceful an act that I blush to mention it; what, I ask, does it profit you? But if you have spiritual discernment, do you see how the soiled garments of Moses are made white? Peter, James, and John, who had seen Moses and Elias before without Jesus, now that they have seen them in white garments talking with Him, realize that they are themselves on the mountain. Truly, we are standing on the mountain with them when we understand the Scriptures spiritually. If I read Genesis, Exodus, Leviticus, Numbers, Deuteronomy, as long as I read carnally, I seem to be down below, but if I grasp their spiritual significance, I am climbing to the top of the mountain. You see, therefore, how Peter, James, and John recognize that they are on the mountain—in the discernment of the spirit—and despise, therefore, the lowly and the human, and long for the lofty and divine. They do not want to descend to earth, but to remain wholely with the spiritual.

'Peter addressed Jesus, saying, "Rabbi, it is good for us to be here." ' When I read Holy Writ and appreciate something

15 Cf. Letter 123.13, PL 22.1054(909); 52.2, PL 22.528(255).

more sublimely in its spiritual sense, neither do I want to descend, to come down to the lowly; I want only to build in my heart a tabernacle for Christ, the Law, and the prophets. But Jesus, who came to save that which had been lost, not to save saints, but those who are in sin, knows that if the human race is to be on the mountain, mankind will not be saved unless He descends to the earthly.

'Rabbi, it is good for us to be here. And let us set up three tents, one for thee, and one for Moses, and one for Elias.' Were there no trees on that mountain? Besides, even if there were trees and garments, do we suppose that Peter wished to build them a tent in order that they might dwell there, nothing else? No, he wanted to set up three tents, one for Jesus, one for Moses, and one for Elias, with the result that he was separating the Law and the prophets and the Gospel, a thing which cannot be done. He actually says: Let us set up three tents, one for You, one for Moses, and one for Elias. O Peter, even though you have ascended the mountain, even though you see Jesus transfigured, even though His garments are white; nevertheless, because Christ has not yet suffered for you, you are still unable to know the truth. Someone may say to the Lord: I shall set up a tent for You and similar tents for Your servants. Whenever the unequal are equally honored the greater suffers wrong by comparison.[16] 'Let us set up three tents.' Three apostles were on the mountain and they want to set up three tents. There was Peter; there were James and John; one wants to take one tent; another, another; the third, the third. He certainly did not realize what he was saying when he was conferring honor upon the servants equally with the Lord. There is, indeed, but one tent for the Gospel, the Law, and the prophets. Unless they dwell together, they cannot be in harmony.

'There came a cloud overshadowing them.' The cloud, ac-

16 Cf. *Against Jovinian* 1.3, PL 23.223(239); Homily 1 on Ps. 1, p. 3.

cording to Matthew, is a bright (phōtinē) cloud.[17] It seems to me that this cloud is the grace of the Holy Spirit. Naturally, a tent gives shelter and overshadows those who are within; the cloud, therefore, serves the purpose of the tents. O Peter, you who want to set up three tents,[18] have regard for the one tent of the Holy Spirit who shelters us equally. If you had built a tent, surely, it would have been made manlike; you would have made the kind that shuts out the light and shuts in the shade. That bright overshadowing cloud, however, the one tent, does not exclude, but is open to the Sun of Justice. So the Father says to you: Why do you set up three tents? Behold, you have one tent. See the mystery of the Trinity, according to my power of understanding, at any rate. Everything that I perceive, I want to understand in Christ, the Holy Spirit, and the Father. Unless I understand in the Trinity that will save me, no understanding can be sweet to me. 'There came a bright (phōtinē) cloud and there came a voice out of the cloud saying, "This is my beloved Son; hear him." '[19] This means: O Peter, you who say: 'Let me set up three tents, one for you, and one for Moses, and one for Elias,' I do not want you to set up three tents. Behold, I have given you a tent to protect you. Do not set up tents equally for the Lord and His servants.

'This is my beloved Son; hear him,' My Son, not Moses nor Elias. They are servants; this is the Son. This is My Son, of My nature, of My substance, abiding in Me, and He is all that I am. This is My beloved Son. They, too, indeed are dear to Me, but He is My beloved; hear Him, therefore. They proclaim and teach Him, but you, hear Him; He is the Lord and Master, they are companions in servitude. Moses and Elias speak of Christ; they are your fellow servants; He is the Lord; hear Him. Do not render the same honor to fellow

17 Cf. Matt. 17.5.
18 Cf. Letter 46.13, PL 22.491(209).
19 Cf. Mark 9.6.

servants as to the Lord and Master. Hear only the Son of God.

While the Father is speaking thus and saying: 'This is my beloved Son; hear him,' it has not been evident who was speaking. There was a cloud; a voice was heard; it said: 'This is my beloved Son; hear him.' Peter could have said, in error: It speaks of Moses or of Elias, but lest there be any doubt, the two vanish while the Father is speaking and Christ alone remains. 'This is my beloved Son; hear him.' Peter muses in his heart: Who is His Son? I see three; do you have any idea of whom He is speaking? While he is seeking to know whom to choose, he sees only One. Suddenly looking round expecting to see three, they find only One; nay more, losing three, they find One; I may even say by way of amplification, in One they find three. Moses, in fact, and Elias, too, are more apt to be found if they are brought together in one with Christ.

'Suddenly looking round, they no longer saw anyone with them.' When I read the Gospel and see there testimony from the Law and the prophets, I contemplate Christ alone. I have looked at Moses and Elias only that I might understand them as they speak of Christ. Finally, when I come to the splendor of Christ, and behold, as it were, the exceedingly brilliant light of the bright sun, I cannot see the light of the lamp.[20] Can a lamp give light if you light it in the daytime? If the sun is shining, the light of the lamp is not visible, so when Christ is present, the Law and the prophets, by comparison, are not even visible. I am not detracting from the Law and the prophets, rather I am praising them, for they proclaim Christ; I so read the Law and the prophets that I do not remain in them, but through them arrive at Christ.

20 Cf. Letter 48.14, PL 22.503(225).

HOMILY 81(VII)

ON MARK 11.1-10

How does it happen, according to Luke's Gospel,[1] that the tethered colt had so many owners? In what sense is it taken away from them and led to one master? Again, how was it outside at a door and, at the same time, in the cross-streets? Outside the door, it surely was; it had been prepared for the faith, but could not enter without the apostles. It was in a place, too, where streets meet; it was between paganism and Judaism and did not know which street to follow.

Why does Mark specify that upon it no man had yet sat? You may be sure that no one had yet broken in this colt. They all wanted to subdue and ride it, but no one could mount it because it had never been tamed. Here is something strange! It had been tethered, but could not be tamed. Jesus does something quite contrary; He looses it and in that way tames it. This is the same colt, by the way, that is led away from Bethany to Bethphage. Jesus, moreover, was in Bethany. Now, the evangelists do not agree on this point; some say that He was in Bethany; others that He was in Bethphage. Bethany is a locality, a small village where today Lazarus is [buried],[2] the village of Martha, Mary, and Lazarus. Here is something for your meditation. Jesus leads this unbroken colt thither where He had raised Lazarus back to life, into Bethany, the

1 Cf. Luke 19.33; cf. *Commentary on Matthew* 21.1-3, PL 26.152(160).
2 Cf. *Hebrew Names*, PL 23.931(182).

house of obedience.[3] The colt could not before be subdued; it is now led to obedience that Jesus may ride it.

We have commented on Bethany; let us turn to Bethphage, which means 'house of the jawbone.'[4] Notice the progress of faith. First, we believe and we come into Bethany, the house of obedience; then, we enter the house of the jawbones, the house of confession,[5] belonging to the priests. It was the custom, in fact, to give the 'siagóna' [jawbone] to the priests. Someone may ask: Why did the priest receive only the 'siagóna,' the jawbone? Nothing else does the priest receive [except] the 'siagóna,' the breast, and the shoulder;[6] mark well: the jowl, breast, and the shoulder. It is part of the priestly office to be able to teach the people; hence, the prophet says: 'Ask the priests the law of God.'[7] It is the priest's duty to answer questions on the Law; consequently, they receive the power of expression symbolized in the jawbone, the knowledge of the Scriptures symbolized in the breast. Words are of no use whatsoever if knowledge is lacking. When you have received the jawbone (siagóna) and the breast, then you receive also the muscles from the thigh, the symbol for deeds.[8] It is of no benefit to you to have facility with words, to have knowledge, if you do not translate them into works. Why have I said all this? Because this colt of an ass is led to the house of the jawbones, Bethphage. It is not led, first, to muscles or to the breast, but to the jawbone, to the word that is to train it.

The Savior mounted the colt. He sat upon it because He was weary. From Samaria of Galilee, He had come to Jericho, and from Jericho all the way to Bethany; He had just climbed

3 Cf. *Commentary on Matthew* 21.17, PL 26.158(166).
4 Cf. Letter 108.12, PL 22.887(701).
5 Cf. *Commentary on Matthew* 21.1, PL 26.152(159).
6 Cf. Lev. 7.31-34; 10.14-20; Num. 18.18, 19; Deut. 18.3.
7 Cf. Agg. 2.12; cf. Letter 53.3, PL 22.542(272); *Commentary on Aggai* 2.12, PL 25.1406(760).
8 Cf. Letter 64.1, 2, PL 22.608-609(354-355); *Commentary on Malachia* 2.3, 4, PL 25.1554-1555(956-957).

a mountain, yet he had not been wearied. He is too tired, however, to walk two miles and asks for the ass. From Jerusalem, He went into Galilee as far as Samaria on foot, and now He could not walk two miles. Everything that Jesus did points to our salvation. Truly, if the apostle says to us: 'Whether you eat or drink, or do anything else, do all in the name of the Lord,'[9] how much more are all the acts of the Savior sacraments for us, whether He walks, sits, eats, sleeps. So He mounts the ass. One of the evangelists says that He mounts a colt, but another, that He mounts, at the same time, both the ass and the colt.[10] I am going to ask a question that is quite absurd.[11] Was it possible for Him to have the same foot on both donkeys at the same time? I am saying all this to confound the Jews, for if He came upon a she-ass, He did not come upon a colt. The facts are general, to be sure, but have issued into distinct signs. He sits upon the untamed colt of an ass, one that could never be bridled, one that had never been ridden—upon the Gentiles; He sat upon an ass, upon those who were from the synagogue and believed in Him. Just grasp what it says: He sat upon an ass accustomed to the yoke, with its neck and shoulders worn down by the Law.

A crowd ran to meet Him. As long as He was on the mountain, the crowd could not come to Him; He began to descend and the crowd came. 'The crowds that went before him, and those that followed, kept crying out, saying, "Hosanna to the Son of David! Blessed is he who comes in the name of the Lord! Hosanna in the highest!" '[12] They who went before and they who followed, cry out aloud in one voice.[13] Who are they who go before? Patriarchs and prophets. Who follow? Apostles and Gentiles. In those who precede and in those who follow, however, it is Christ who speaks; Him they are praising; Him they acclaim with one harmonious voice. What is

9 Cf. 1 Cor. 10.31.
10 Cf. Matt. 21.7.
11 Cf. *Commentary on Matthew* 21.4, PL 26.152-153(160).
12 Matt. 21.9.
13 Cf. *Commentary on Matthew* 21.9, PL 26.154(161).

their cry? Hosanna to the Son of David! Blessed is He who comes in the name of the Lord! Hosanna in the highest! They say three things: Hosanna to the Son of David, that is, to beginners; Blessed is He who comes in the name of the Lord, to proficients; Hosanna in the highest, to those who are reigning.

Let no one imagine that we are dividing up Christ. That is the accusation of our calumniators, that we make two persons of Christ, one a man and one a God. We believe in the Trinity; we do not believe in a foursome, with two persons in Christ. If Christ, indeed, is two persons, then, by the same token, the Son, who is Christ, is twofold and so there are four persons. We believe in the Father, the Son, and the Holy Spirit. In regard to the Father and the Spirit, there is no question, for they did not assume a body, something mean or insignificant; but we are now speaking of Christ our God, the Son of God and the Son of man, of the one Son of God. He is the Son of God and the Son of man. Whatever is great refers to the Son of God; whatever slight refers to the Son of man; nevertheless, there is one Son of God. Why am I compelled to say this? O, I have heard certain ones uttering misrepresentations, who perhaps have an Arian bent to their mind. Because I refuse to refer to God the injustice of humanity, I am not dividing Christ. He is in the nether world and in heaven; at one and the same time, He descended into hell and entered paradise with the robber. He holds all the elements in His hand, and if they are in His hand, where is He not who holds all things?

We have done our best in this discussion, with the help of your prayers. May you know, moreover, that for 'Hosanna' we say in Greek, 'sôson dḗ.' In the Septuagint it becomes, 'ō kūrie sôson dḗ,' and in the Hebrew, אנא יהוה הושיעה נא, that is, Lord, grant salvation, I beseech thee.[14] To whom be glory forever and ever. Amen.

---

14 Cf. Letter 20, PL 22.377(66); *Commentary on Matthew* 21.9, PL 26.154(162); *Commentarioli in ps.* 117.25.

HOMILY 82(VIII)

ON MARK 11.11-14

'THE LORD JESUS WENT INTO JERUSALEM, into the temple. And when he had looked round upon all things, then, as it was already late, he went out to Bethany with the Twelve.'[1] The Lord went into Jerusalem and into the temple. He went in and, having entered, what does He do? He looks about at everything. In the temple of the Jews, He was looking for a place to rest His head and found none. 'He had looked round upon all things.' Why did it say, 'He had looked round upon all that was there'? He was looking for the priests; He wanted to be with them, but He could not find them; He always had regard for priests. So he surveyed all that was about Him, almost as though He were searching with a lantern; so says the prophet in Sophonia: 'I will explore Jerusalem with lamps.'[2] In this same way, the Lord, too, looked around at everything with the light of a lamp. He was searching in the temple, but He did not find what He wanted. When it was already evening, He was still exploring everything; He was looking round upon all things. Even though His search was unfruitful, nevertheless, as long as there was light, he remained in the temple; but when evening had come, when the shades of ignorance had darkened the temple of the Jews, when it was the evening hour, He went out to Bethany with the Twelve. The Savior searched; the apostles searched; in the temple, they found nothing, so they left it. Rejoice, O

1 Cf. Mark 11.11.
2 Soph. 1.12.

monk, be glad you who dwell in the desert, for He is not found in the temple, but outside it. He came into Bethany with the Twelve. The meaning of Bethany is house of obedience. He withdrew, therefore, from the temple of the Jews where there was pride, and came into the house of obedience. Where there is obedience, there is humility; He abandoned the pride of the Jews and went to the humility of the Gentiles.[3]

'The next day, after they had left'; on the next day, evidently when they had left Bethany. Now, he who departs on the next day was in Bethany on the day before. It was, therefore, the temple in which He did not remain; He came and stayed in Bethany. 'The next day, after they had left Bethany, he felt hungry.' He stayed in Bethany, but when He was leaving there, He hungered for the salvation of the Jews.[4] 'I was not sent except to the lost sheep of the house of Israel.'[5] To this day, Christ still hungers. Certainly, He has been filled with the Gentiles; in the Jews, He is still hungry. Even among us there are some who believe; others who do not. He is refreshed with the believers; in the non-believers, He hungers.

'Seeing in the distance a fig tree in leaf.' Unhappy Jew! 'God is renowned in Juda; in Israel great is his name.'[6] That was a while ago, among the patriarchs and prophets; but now, the God who said in Jeremia: 'I am a God near at hand, and not a God far off,'[7] that same Lord withdraws from the Jews and looks at them from a distance. In order to save them, however, He was drawing near. 'Seeing in the distance a fig tree in leaf'; in leaf, not with fruit; words, not their meaning; Holy Writ, not the understanding of it—they, indeed, possess the Scriptures, but we understand them. He sees, then, a fig tree in leaf. This fig tree always has leaves, but it never

3 Cf. *Commentary on Matthew* 21.17, PL 26.158(166).
4 Cf. *Commentary on Matthew* 21.18-21, PL 26.159(167).
5 Matt. 15.24.
6 Ps. 75.2.
7 Cf. Jer. 23.23.

has fruit, this fig tree that was in Paradise. Adam covered his nakedness with its leaves when he fell into sin, for it always had leaves. This fig tree is the synagogue of the Jews that can claim words only, but not the understanding of Scripture.

Let us see where else we read of it. In the Gospel according to Luke, we read: 'A certain man had a fig tree planted in his vineyard; and he came seeking fruit thereon, and found none. And he said to the vine-dresser, "Behold, for three years now I have come seeking fruit on this fig tree, and I find none. Let me alone, and I shall cut it down." '[8] Let Me alone. When He says to Moses: 'Let me alone and I shall destroy this people. . . .'[9] No one is holding You back, yet do You say, 'Let me alone'? When You say, 'Let me alone,' You are provoking the vine-dresser to hold You back. 'Let me alone, and I shall cut it down.' Behold, He says, I have come a third time and I find no fruit. I came, first, in the Law with Moses; I came the next time in the prophets; now I come Myself in person, and I find no fruit. This fig tree was not planted among thorns, nor was it planted outside, but within the vineyard of the house of Israel. I see something new to consider. The thorns of the Gentiles bear grapes, and the fig tree does not bear figs. Behold, He says, I have come a third time and I find no fruit; 'let me alone and I shall cut it down.' When the vine-dresser had been thus provoked, he understood that he could restrain his lord if he but asked. What does he ask? 'Sir, let it alone this year too, till I dig around it and manure it. Perhaps it may bear fruit. . . .' He does not say, 'If it should not then bear fruit'; but, 'you shall come and cut it down.'[10] The vine-dresser entreats him, and the lord grants what he had desired.

I have something new for you. When the Lord is entreated, He grants pardon, which He would have done anyhow, even

8 Cf. Luke 13.6-9.

9 Cf. Exod. 32.10; cf. Homily 26 on Ps. 98, pp. 211-212; Letter 128.4 PL 22.1099(965).

10 Cf. Luke 13.9.

if He had not been entreated. Let it alone, He says, this year. As soon, indeed, as the Savior suffered His Passion, Judea was saved; forty-two years were granted for repentance. Forty-two years are the one year, that is a short time; in other words, this opportunity was granted them for repentance. The vine-dresser dug around it; he manured it. Who are these vine-dressers? The apostles who dug and manured. The fig tree, however, did not bear fruit, but the vine-dresser himself says: 'Perhaps it may bear fruit.' It bore none. Note that he did not say, either let it alone or do not let it alone; either keep it in your vineyard or uproot it. He said no such thing. 'Perhaps it may bear fruit.' I do not know what it will do; I leave it to your judgment. He did not say that this fig tree will remain in the vineyard. If, in fact, it should bear fruit, it will not remain in Judea of Israel, but will be transplanted into the Church of the Gentiles.[11] 'If it should not bear fruit.' We behold with our eyes the fig tree that had been cut down, for the stony ruins that we see are the roots of the chopped down fig tree.

Why have we discussed all this? We wanted to show from this episode what fig tree this is from which the Lord desires fruit. 'He saw,' it says, 'a fig tree in leaf,' by the wayside, not in the way; in the Law, not in the Gospel. It did not bear fruit, because it was not in the way, but close to the way. Jesus goes up to it and looks for the fruit. Since it cannot go to Him, He goes to it. 'When he came up to it, he found nothing but leaves.' Even to this day, we find nothing else in the Jews except the words of the Law. They read Moses, Isaia, Jeremia, and the rest of the prophets; they read, 'This the Lord says,' and they do not understand what He says.

'It was not the season for figs.' A considerable problem—'it was not the season for figs.' Someone may say: If it was not the season for figs, the fig tree was not at fault in not producing fruit. If, moreover, it had not transgressed, it was

11 Cf. *Commentary on Habacuc* 3.17, PL 25.1333 (665).

unjustly withered, for it was not the season for figs. This fig tree had foliage, but no fruit. It had leaves; from a distance it gave the appearance of verdure, but it had no fruit. It was not the season for figs. The apostle elucidates this text to the Romans: 'I would not, brethren, have you ignorant of this mystery, that a partial blindness only has befallen Israel, until the full number of the Gentiles should enter. When the full number of the Gentiles has entered, then all Israel shall be saved.'[12] If the Lord had found fruit on this fig tree, the full number of the Gentiles would not have entered,[13] but, because the full number of the Gentiles shall have entered, in the end all Israel will be saved.

Someone may ask: Where does one read that all Israel will be saved? First, of course, there is the apostle: 'Until the full number of the Gentiles should enter; and thus all Israel should be saved.' In the second place, John says in his Apocalypse:[14] of the tribe of Juda, twelve thousand shall believe, of the tribe of Ruben, twelve thousand shall believe, and of the remaining tribes, he says the same; and the number of all who believe became a hundred and forty-four thousand. Then, too, Psalm 144, which is alphabetical, treats of this number saved.[15] If Israel had believed, our Lord would not have been crucified. If our Lord had not been crucified, the multitude of Gentiles would not have been saved. The Jews are going to believe, but not until the end of the world. It was not the time for them to believe in the cross; for if they had believed, the Lord would not have been crucified. It was not the time for them to believe. Their infidelity is our faith. By their downfall, we are raised up. It was not their time in order that it might be our time. We said that, at the end of the world, they will believe, and we have explained the words: 'It was not yet the season.'

12 Cf. Rom. 11.25-27.
13 Cf. *Commentary on Matthew* 21.18-20, PL 26.159(167).
14 Cf. Apoc. 7.5-10.
15 Cf. Ps. 144.15.

In regard to the sequel, however: 'The Lord spoke to it saying, "May no one ever eat fruit of thee henceforward forever,"' if the Jews are going to believe, how is it that no one will eat fruits of them? He did not say, in the future order; He did not say, for generations; but in the present generation.[16] This is what He means: In the present generation, you shall not believe, but when this world has come to its end, then, you shall believe. You shall believe, indeed, but not in His lowliness; when He is reigning, you shall believe, and you shall look on Him whom you had pierced.[17] In the present world, therefore, you shall not bear fruit, but in the future.

16 Cf. *Commentary on Habacuc* 3.17, PL 25.1333(665).
17 Cf. Apoc. 1.7; John 19.37; Zach. 12.10.

HOMILY 83(IX)

ON MARK 11.15-17

THEY CAME TO JERUSALEM. And he entered the temple, and began to cast out those who were selling and buying in the temple; and he overturned the tables of the money-changers and the seats of those who sold the doves.' In St. John's Gospel, we read this same historical account, and we find there a clearer record of the time when the event took place. 'Now the feast of Unleavened Bread—the Passover when the Jews ate unleavened bread—was at hand and Jesus went up,'[1] 'and making a whip of cords, he began to drive them out.'[2] It was, therefore, during the Passover, the days of unleavened bread, that He drove the money-changers out of the temple. During the days of the Pasch, moreover, it was prescribed by law for everyone to go to the temple, and if anyone did not go, he would be cut off from his people.[3] From the entire province of Palestine, then, from Cyprus and the other provinces, from all the regions round about, all the people assembled there. Meditate on and visualize the vast throng that would be gathered on that occasion.

Meanwhile, we shall first examine the episode as such. Some people there are who are amazed over Lazarus and his return to life, and astonished at the widow's son raised from the dead; others are in awe over other miracles. To bring life back to a dead body, truly, is cause for wonderment, but

1 Cf. John 2.13.
2 Cf. John 2.15.
3 Cf. Num. 9.13.

I marvel more at the present miracle.[4] Here was one man, believed to be the son of a carpenter, a beggar without a home, with no place to rest His head, without an army, not a commander nor a judge. What power did such a One have to make a whip of cords and drive out so vast a crowd; what power, that one man, I say, should drive out such a throng? What was the mob that He was expelling? Those who were selling and buying in the temple for their own profit. No one challenged Him, no one dared to, for no one dared resist the Son avenging the affront committed against His Father. It seems to me that in the eyes and in the very countenance of the Lord Savior there was something divine, and I shall give you my reason for thinking so. 'It came to pass,' Scripture says, 'that when Jesus was passing along the sea of Galilee, he saw two men mending their nets, the sons of Zebedee, and he said to them, "Leave your nets and come, follow me." And they immediately left their nets, the ship, and their father Zebedee and followed him at once.'[5] Unless there was something divinely compelling in the face of the Savior, they acted irrationally in following a man whom they had never seen before. Does one leave a father to follow a man in whom he sees nothing more than in his father? They leave their father of the flesh to follow the Father of the spirit; they do not leave a father, they find a Father. What is the point of this digression? To show that there was something divine in the Savior's countenance that men, seeing, could not resist. Let us cite other evidence. 'Now,' the Gospel says, 'as Jesus passed on from there, he saw a man named Matthew, and said to him, "Follow me," and he left everything and followed him.'[6] Matthew sees no miracle; the authority in the One calling him was the miracle.

'He began to cast out those who were selling and buying in the temple.' If this was true in the case of the Jews, how

4 Cf. *Commentary on Matthew* 21.15, PL 26.157-158(165-166).
5 Cf. Mark 1.16-20; cf. Homily 76 (II) on Mark 1.13-31, p. 136.
6 Cf. Matt. 9.9.

much more so is it for us? If this was in the Law, how much more is it in the Gospel? 'He began to cast out those who were selling and buying.' Christ, the poor man, casts out the rich Jews. The man who sells and the man who buys are similarly cast out. No one should say: I am offering what is my own; I am giving gifts to the priests just as God has prescribed. We read in another place: 'Freely you have received, freely give.'[7] The grace of God is not sold, but given. Not only is the man who sells at fault, but also the man who buys. Furthermore, Simon,[8] the magician, was condemned, not because he sold, but because he wanted to buy. Even today, in the temple, there are many who sell. Unhappy is the man who sells; happy the one who buys! The grace of Christ cannot be purchased with gold and silver. 'He overturned the tables of the money-changers.' There, where the showbread and the gifts of God were supposed to be, are the sacrifices of greed. 'The tables of the money-changers'; the greed-altars of the priests are not altars, but the tables of the money-changers.

'And the seats of those who sold the doves.' Doves, of course, are not caged in the seats, but in bird cages.[9] No one pens doves in seats, but in bird cages. What, then, is the meaning of: 'He overturned the seats of those who sold the doves'? Notice just what it says: they who were selling doves were sitting on chairs: 'The Scribes and the Pharisees have sat on the chair of Moses.'[10] These are the chairs the psalmist, also, means when he says: 'Nor sits in the chair of the insolent.'[11] Truly, is he a seat of insolence who sells doves, who sells the gift of the Holy Spirit. There are many in such seats this very day who sell doves. The man who sells doves is not standing, but sitting; he is not upright, but bent downward.

7 Matt. 10.8.
8 Cf. Acts 8.9-24.
9 Cf. *Commentary on Matthew* 21.12, 13, PL 26.157(165).
10 Matt. 23.2.
11 Cf. Ps. 1.1.

In selling the grace of God, he is bent over and lowly. Our Lord, who came to save that which had been lost, does not overthrow those who were selling, but overturns their seats; He overthrows their authority, but will save them.

'He would not allow anyone to carry a vessel through the temple.' At that time, He would not suffer vessels to be carried through an earthly temple, and, today, how many unclean vessels are there around in the temple of God? Then, no vessels could be carried, and it does not specify unclean vessels either, but vessels of any kind whatsoever. Nowadays, indeed, how much trafficking goes on within!

'Is it not written,' He says, ' "My house shall be called a house of prayer for all the nations"?' We read this in Isaia.[12] 'But you have made it a den of thieves.' O what unhappiness for us! O creatures to be lamented with every source of tears! The house of God has been made a den of thieves! This is the house of which Jeremia says: 'Has not my house become for me the den of a hyena?'[13] Here, we have: 'you have made it a den of thieves'; in Jeremia: 'the den of a hyena.' We have to know the nature of this animal; then, from that, we shall be able to learn why the prophet called God's house a hyena's den. The hyena is never seen in the daytime, but always at night; never is it seen in the light, but always in the darkness. Of its very nature, it has a craving to dig up the bodies of the dead and maul them to pieces.[14] In fact, if anyone is careless in burying the dead, the hyena digs up the body at night, carries it off, and feeds upon it. Wherever there are graves, wherever there are the bones of the dead, there you find the lair of the hyena. By its nature, too, it has a ravenous appetite for dogs; attacks and carries them off and devours them. Grasp what it says; pay strict attention. The hyena is a beast that devours blood, that is lured by bodies,

12 Cf. Isa. 56.7.

13 Cf. Jer. 12.9, LXX.

14 Cf. *Commentary on Isaia* 65.4, 5, PL 24.633(775); *on Jeremia* 12.9, PL 24.761(928).

that always wanders in the night, never in the day; its only pleasure is in the cadavers of the dead and in dogs. It wants to kill those who guard the house. They say, too, that by nature the hyena has a backbone all in one piece and, therefore, it cannot bend. If it wants to turn around, it must turn its whole body; it cannot twist itself about as other animals do. So you see, this is a creature that is always in the darkness, never turned, never converted. This is all said, however, in application to the priests of the Jews. You can easily lead the ordinary Jew to repentance, but not one of the priests nor the teachers, for they are always attracted by the corpses of the dead, of those whom they may seduce. It does not satisfy them that they are not themselves in the light, but they must strive to destroy those who are seeking shelter in the light. They have a single backbone; they cannot be converted: they do not repent; they are preoccupied with the corpses of the dead.

Where here we read: 'You have made it a den of thieves,' St. John's Gospel has instead: 'You have made it a house of business.'[15] 'A house of business.' Wherever there are thieves, there is a house of trafficking. Would that this had been said only of the people of the past! Would that it were applied only to the Jews and not to the Christians! We would, indeed, weep for them, but rejoice for ourselves. But now, in many places, the house of God, the house of the Father, has become a place of business. Notice how I speak with fear and trembling. The fact is so well known that it needs no explanation. I wish it were unknown and that we did not understand! In many places, the house of the Father is a house of business! I who am speaking and each one of you, priest, deacon, or bishop,[16] who yesterday was a poor man, who today is a rich man in the house of God; does it not seem to you that you have made the house of the Father a house

15 Cf. John 2.16.
16 Cf. *Commentary on Matthew* 21.12, 13, PL 26.157(164).

of commerce? Of these the apostle, too, has something to say: 'Supposing godliness to be gain.'[17] It is of all of us, therefore, that the apostle speaks. Christ is a pauper, let us blush with shame; Christ is lowly, let us be ashamed; Christ was crucified; He did not rule; He was crucified in order to rule. He conquered the world, not in pride, but in humility. He destroyed the devil, not by laughing, but by weeping; He did not scourge, but was scourged; He received a blow but did not give blows.[18] Let us, therefore, imitate our Lord.

But see, the days of fasting are over! Just think, the days of fasting, of penance, of purification, are past. Let us rejoice now and be glad! The man in the Gospel who carries a pitcher of water, comes out of the house and goes into the guest chamber.[19] You, too, who are going to receive baptism, begin your preparation now for tomorrow. They, who are going into battle, prepare themselves carefully beforehand. Each one sees whether he has a shield, a two-edged sword, or a spear; whether he needs arrows; whether his horse has been put into condition; he prepares his equipment and weapons ahead of time that he may be ready to fight. Your weapons are fasts; your battle is humility. If anyone has anything against another, let him forgive that he may be forgiven. No one, indeed, would think of approaching baptism to have his sins forgiven, without first forgiving his brother. If you have anything against your brother, forgive him. I did not say, if he has anything against you, let him forgive; but if you have anything, you forgive. Whether or not he forgives you is in his power, but you, because it is in your power, forgive that you may be forgiven. You are about to approach baptism. O happy you, who are to be reborn in Christ, who are going to receive the garment of Christ, who are to be buried with Him that you may rise again with Him!

During the remaining days, you are going to hear in its

17 1 Tim. 6.5.
18 Cf. Homily 2 on Ps. 5, p. 23.
19 Mark 14.13-16.

proper order all that pertains to the mystery. For the present, I have told you that you may know that from tomorrow on you must toil and labor very hard. May God Almighty Himself strengthen your hearts; may He render you worthy of His cleansing; may He descend upon you in baptism; may He sanctify the waters that you may be sanctified. Let no one approach with a hesitant heart; let no one say, 'Do you think my sins are forgiven me?' He who approaches in that spirit does not have his sins forgiven. It is better not to approach at all than approach with that attitude; especially you who are receiving baptism in order to serve God in a monastery.[20]

20 Cf. *Against John of Jerusalem* 42, PL 23.411(442).

HOMILY 84(X)

ON MARK 13.32, 33 and 14.3-6

THE GOSPEL READING DEMANDS considerable exposition. Before we get to the sacraments, we must remove a stumbling-block lest any obstacle lodge in the minds of those who are going to receive them. They who are going to be baptized must believe in the Father, the Son, and the Holy Spirit; yet right here Holy Writ says, in reference to the Son: 'Of that day or hour no one knows, neither the angels in heaven, nor the Son, but the Father only.' If we receive baptism equally in the Father, Son, and Holy Spirit, and must believe that it is in the one name of the Father, the Son, and the Holy Spirit, which is God, and if God is one, how in one Godhead are there different degrees of knowledge? Which is greater, to be God or to know everything? If to be God is, how can He be unknowing? Scripture says, in fact, of the Lord Savior: 'All things were made through him, and without him nothing was made.'[1] If all things were made through Him, then, the day of judgment that is to come was also made through Him. Is it possible that He does not know what He made? Can the workman be unknowing of his work? We read of Christ in St. Paul: 'In whom are hidden all treasures of wisdom and knowledge.'[2] Note: 'all treasures of wisdom and knowledge.' Not that some are and some are not in Him, but all treasures of wisdom and knowledge are in Him, but they are hidden. That which is in Him, therefore, is not lacking to Him,

1 Cf. John 1.3.
2 Col. 2.3.

even though it be hidden to us. If, moreover, the treasures of wisdom and knowledge are hidden in Christ, we must find out why they are hidden. If we men were to know the day of judgment, that, for example, it would not be for two thousand years, and if we knew it so long ahead of time, we would be more careless on that account. We would say, for instance, What is it to me if the day of judgment will not be here for two thousand years? Scripture says, therefore, for our benefit, that 'the Son does not know the day of judgment,' because we do not know when the day of judgment will be upon us; and further: 'Take heed, watch and pray, for you do not know when the time is.' Not, we do not know, but you do not know.

So far, we seem to be forcing Holy Writ and not really explaining it. After the Resurrection, the apostles ask the Lord Savior: 'Lord, when wilt thou restore the kingdom to Israel?'[3] O apostles, you heard before the Resurrection: I know not that day, nor the hour; do you, again, ask what I do not know? But the apostles do not believe the Savior, do not believe that He does not know. See now, there is a mystery. He who does not know before the Passion, does know after the Resurrection. What is His answer to the apostles when, after the Resurrection, they question Him about the time: When will you restore the kingdom to Israel? 'It is not for you to know the time,' He replies, 'which the Father has fixed by his own authority.'[4] Here, He is not saying: I do not know, but, It is not yours to know, it does not profit you to know the day of judgment.[5] Watch, therefore, for you know not when the master of the house will come. There is much more that could be said, but we have drawn your attention to this point in the Gospel to prevent anyone from being scandalized that there might be something unknown to Him in whom he was about to put his trust.

3 Cf. Acts 1.6.
4 Cf. Acts 1.7; cf. Letter 144.8, PL 22.1189(1076).
5 Cf. *Commentary on Matthew* 24.36, PL 26.188-189(199).

This same lesson from the Gospel says: 'When he was at Bethany, in the house of Simon the leper, and was reclining at the table, there came a woman with an alabaster jar of ointment, genuine nard of great value.'[6] This woman has a very special message for you who are about to be baptized. She broke her alabaster jar that Christ may make you 'christs,' His anointed. Hear what it says in the Canticle of Canticles: 'Your name spoken is a spreading perfume, therefore the maidens love you. We will follow you eagerly in the fragrance of your perfume!'[7] As long as the perfume was sealed up, as long as Christ was known only in Judea, in Israel alone His name was great,[8] the maidens were not following Jesus. When His perfume spread throughout the world, then, maiden souls of believers followed the Savior.

'When he was at Bethany, in the house of Simon the leper.'[9] Bethany means house of obedience. How, then, is the house of Simon the leper in Bethany, the house of obedience? What is the Lord doing in the house of one who is leprous? That is exactly why He went into the house of a leper, in order to cleanse him. Leper implies, not one who is a leper, but who has been leprous; he was a leper before he received the Lord, but after he received Him, and the jar of perfume was broken in his house, the leprosy vanished. He retains his former identity, however, in order to manifest the power of the Savior. Similar is the case of the apostles who keep their former names to proclaim the power of the One who called them and made of them what they are. In the same way, Matthew, the publican, becomes an apostle and, after his entrance into the apostolate, continues to be called a publican, not because he is one, but because from being one, he became an apostle. He retains his previous title, moreover, that the power of the Savior may be evident. Similarly, Simon the

6 Mark 14.3.
7 Cf. Cant. 1.2, 3.
8 Cf. Ps. 75.2.
9 Mark 14.3.

leper is called by his old name to show forth that he has been cured by the Lord.[10]

'There came a woman with an alabaster jar of ointment.'[11] The Pharisees, the Scribes, and the priests are in the temple and they have no ointment. This woman is outside the temple and carries with her a jar of ointment containing nard, genuine nard, from which she has prepared the ointment; hence, you are called genuine [nard], or the faithful. The Church, gathered together from the Gentiles, is offering the Savior her gifts, the faith of believers.[12] She has broken the alabaster jar that all may receive its perfume; she has broken the alabaster jar that was kept sealed in Judea. 'She broke the alabaster jar.' Just as the grain of wheat, unless it falls into the ground and dies, does not bring forth any fruit,[13] so, also, unless the alabaster jar be broken, we cannot spread its fragrance.

'She poured it on his head.'[14] This woman, who broke the alabaster jar and poured the perfume on His head, is not the same woman of whom it says in another Gospel[15] that she washed the Lord's feet. That woman, like a prostitute and sinner, clings to His feet; this one, like a saint, holds His head. The one, like a prostitute, washes the feet of the Savior with her tears and dries them with her hair. She seems, indeed, to be washing the Savior's feet with her tears, but actually she is washing away her own sins.[16] The priests and Pharisees do not give the Savior a kiss; she kisses His feet. You, likewise, who are going to receive baptism, since we are all sinful, and 'there is no one without sin even if he lived but a single day,'[17] 'and with his angels he can find fault,'[18]

10 Cf. *Commentary on Matthew* 26.6, PL 26.198(211).
11 Mark 14.3.
12 Cf. *Commentary on Matthew* 26.7, PL 26.199(212).
13 Cf. John 12.24.
14 Mark 14.3.
15 Cf. Luke 7.37-50; cf. *Against Jovinian* 2.29, PL 23.340(370).
16 Cf. *Commentary on Matthew* 26.7, PL 26.199(212).
17 Cf. Job. 14.4, 5, LXX.
18 Cf. Job 4.18.

first, hold fast to the feet of the Savior, wash them with your tears, dry them with your hair. When you have done that, then, you will reach His head. When you descend into the life-giving font with the Savior, then, you must learn how the ointment comes upon the head of the Savior. If the head of every man is Christ,[19] your head must be anointed, and after baptism you are anointed.

'There were some who were indignant among themselves,'[20] not all, but some. To this day, the Jews are indignant when we anoint Jesus' head. Then, too, in another place,[21] it says that Judas the betrayer was indignant; in him, the Jews are represented.[22] Right down to this day, Judas is indignant because the Church anoints Jesus' head. What does he say? 'To what purpose has this waste of ointment been made?'[23] To him, it seems to be wasting the ointment because the jar is broken, but, for us, it was a great good because the perfume spread throughout the world. Why are you indignant, Judas, because the alabaster jar is broken? God, who made you and all the nations, is bedewed with that precious perfume. You wanted to keep the perfume sealed up so that it would not reach others. With truth is it said of you in another text: 'You have the key of knowledge, you have not entered yourselves, and those who were entering you have hindered.'[24] You have the alabaster jar; rather, you had it in the temple and kept it sealed. A woman came along and took it into Bethany; in the house of a leper, she anoints Jesus' head. What do they who are indignant say? 'It might have been sold for three hundred denarii,'[25] for He who was anointed with this perfume was crucified. We read in Genesis[26] that

19 Cf. 1 Cor. 11.3.
20 Mark 14.4.
21 Cf. John 12.4.
22 Cf. Homily 35 on Ps. 108, p. 259.
23 Mark 14.4.
24 Cf. Luke 11.52.
25 Cf. Mark 14.5.
26 Cf. Gen. 6.15.

the ark that Noe built was three hundred cubits long, fifty cubits wide, and thirty cubits high. Notice the mystical significance of the numbers. In the number fifty, penance is symbolized because the fiftieth psalm of King David is the prayer of his repentance.[27] Three hundred contains the symbol of the crucifixion. The letter T is the sign for three hundred, whence Ezechiel says: 'Mark THAV on the foreheads of those who moan; and do not kill any marked with THAV.'[28] No one marked with the sign of the cross on his forehead can be struck by the devil; he is not able to efface this sign, only sin can.

We have spoken of the ark, of the number fifty, of the number three hundred. Let us comment on the number thirty because the ark was thirty cubits high and finished above in one cubit.[29] First, we repent in the number fifty; then, through penance, we arrive at the mystery of the cross; we reach the mystery of the cross through the perfect Word that is Christ. As a matter of fact, when Jesus was baptized, according to Luke: 'He was thirty years of age.'[30] These same thirty cubits were finished off one cubit above. Fifty, and three hundred, and thirty were finished above into one cubit, that is, into one faith of God. Why have we said all this? Because it says here in the Gospel: 'It might have been sold for three hundred denarii.' Afterwards, the Lord Savior was sold for thirty pieces of silver. It is not surprising that a jar of nard might have been sold for three hundred denarii, for He was sold for thirty! It is written in Leviticus and in Exodus[31] that the priests did not begin their duties until they were thirty years old. Before they were thirty, it was not permitted them to enter the temple of God, as the perfect age for beasts of burden and brute animals is the third year. It says in

27 Cf. *Commentary on Isaia* 3.3, PL 24.59(49).
28 Cf. Ezech. 9.4, 6; cf. *Commentary on Ezechiel* 9.4, 6, PL 25.88(95-96).
29 Cf. Gen. 6.15, 16.
30 Cf. Luke 3.23.
31 Cf. Num. 4.3.

Genesis,[32] when Abraham performed the 'dichotomḗmata' [divisions into two], that he used a heifer, a she-goat, and a lamb, of three years each, in order to show that that was the perfect age for brute animals; in like manner, among men the perfect age is thirty. Could not our Lord have received baptism at twenty-five? At twenty-six? At twenty-eight? Yes, but He waited for the perfect age of man in order to give us an example. It is written, also, in the beginning of the Book of Ezechiel: 'In the thirtieth year, while I was among the exiles.'[33] We have mentioned all this in order to unfold the mystical meanings of the numbers that contain thirty. The Jews are indignant, aliens to faith are indignant, because that jar of ointment was broken, but our Lord, on the contrary, says: 'Let her be. Why do you trouble her? She has done me a good turn.'[34]

Because of that woman's good work, we have made these few comments on the Gospel, and, most opportunely, has the fourteenth psalm been read.[35] It is now time to discuss it.

32 Cf. Gen. 15.9-11.
33 Cf. Ezech. 1.1; cf. *Commentary on Ezechiel* 1.1, PL 25.17(4); *on Aggai* 2.17-19, PL 25.1411(767).
34 Mark 14.6.
35 Cf. Homily 5 on Ps. 14, p. 38.

VARIOUS HOMILIES

(85-96)

HOMILY 85

ON THE GOSPEL OF MATTHEW 18.7-9

'WOE TO THE WORLD because of scandals! For it must needs be that scandals come, but woe to the man through whom scandal does come!' This seems, indeed, to refer especially to Judas,[1] for it must needs be that the Lord Jesus suffer; if He had not suffered, the human race could not be saved. That the Lord's Passion, moreover, would be a scandal, the apostle, also, attests when he says that His cross is a stumbling-block to the Jews, and to the Gentiles foolishness![2] You see, then, that the Passion of the Lord had to be the scandal of the cross; nevertheless, woe to that man through whom scandal does come! It was both necessary and expedient that Jesus suffer, but woe to Judas through whom this gain has come to us!

'Woe to the world because of scandals!' He calls this earth the world: 'tòn perígeion tópon légei.' We must not, therefore, take world in the sense of heaven and earth, but world, here, as this earth. That is how our Lord meant it in: 'My kingdom is not of this world;[3] if I were of the world, the world would love me';[4] also, when He says to the apostles: 'You are not of the world.'[5] Similarly in many passages, world signifies this earth. Woe, then, to the world, to this earthly place, because of scandals!

1 Cf. Homily 35 on Ps. 108, p. 266.
2 Cf. 1 Cor. 1.23.
3 John 18.36.
4 Cf. John 15.18, 19.
5 John 15.19.

'It must needs be that scandals come,' not that scandals, as such, are a necessity, but it is necessary for this world that scandals come. Do not miss the subtlety. If it must needs be that scandals come, is he blameworthy through whom the scandal comes?[6] But we say, scandal does not come except in a world that is earth-bound. Do you want to avoid scandal? Then, do not be of earth, worldly. That is why I say scandal belongs to the earth; it cannot avoid it. Do not bear the likeness of the earthy, but the stamp of the heavenly[7] and you shall not be an occasion of scandal.

'Woe to the man through whom scandal does come'—a generalized statement. He then becomes specific (Kaì katakermatízei aùtó): 'If thy hand or thy foot is an occasion of sin to thee, cut it off and cast it from thee! It is better for thee to enter life lame, than, having two hands or two feet, to be cast into the everlasting fire.'[8] If your hand or your foot is an occasion of sin to you: since He is speaking to the apostles, and upon them He has established the Church, whatever He says to them, He is saying to the Church, for it has only one body, but many members. The apostle expresses this same concept in his letter to the Corinthians where he treats of spiritual gifts:[9] there are prophets, teachers, priests, miracle-workers, and those possessing other powers. It is there that he says: 'Can the eye say to the hand, "I do not need thy help"; nor again the hand to the feet, "I have no need of you"?'[10] He says this by way of example, but the passage is much too long to reproduce. The point he makes, however, is that from many members is formed the one body of the Church. The Church has real eyes: manifestly its churchmen and teachers who see in Holy Writ the mysteries of God, and to them applies the Scriptural appellation of 'seer.'[11] It is correct, then, to call these seers the eyes of

6 Cf. *Commentary on Matthew* 18.7, PL 26.134(138).
7 Cf. 1 Cor. 15.49.
8 Cf. Matt. 18.8.
9 Cf. 1 Cor. 12.
10 Cf. 1 Cor. 12.21.
11 Cf. 1 Kings 9.9.

the Church. It also has hands, effective (praktikoús) men who, of course, are not eyes, but hands. Do they know the mysteries of Holy Writ? No, but they are powerful in works. The Church has feet. Those who are feet are not those who see, nor those who work, but those who make official journeys of all kinds; the foot runs that the hand may find the work that it is to do. The eye does not scorn the hand, nor does the hand scorn the foot, nor do these three scorn the belly as if it were idle and unemployed. Often, it happens that the apparently less honorable members are actually the more useful; hence, the apostle also says: 'Our less honorable members have more abundant honor.'[12] Why do I say all this? Because the Church, the body of the Lord, is adorned and formed of many members. If, therefore, it should happen that the eye of the Church is a stumbling-block to you, the hand a scandal to you, the foot an occasion of sin, it is better for you to be without that faculty and go with the rest of them into the kingdom of heaven; better to have a blind eye and a lame foot than to go into everlasting hell-fire. A bishop has wandered from the truth; a priest has fallen into sin; a deacon has transgressed. Do not say that he is greater in rank, but let the eye be plucked out, the hand cut off, the foot amputated, that the rest of the members may be saved.[13]

We have been following a more lofty form of exegesis. We ought to know, however, that another interpretation is possible. If your eye or your hand or your foot is a source of sin, if any of your dear ones—father, mother, brother, son, and the rest of your relatives—are a scandal to you, cut them away from you; better to reign without a mother than to perish with a mother. This applies very specially to monks, for it applies very specially to the apostles, and it is the monk's vocation to pattern his life on theirs. Do you want to be My disciple, O monk; nay, rather, do you want to be a disciple

---

12 Cf. 1 Cor. 12.23.
13 Cf. Letter 51.4, PL 22.520(245); 125.7, PL 22.1076(936).

of My disciples? Do what Peter and James and John did. . . . They had an eye that was a stumbling-block: their father and the boat and the net. Jesus says to them: 'Come, follow me.'[14] Paternal authority was their stumbling-block, a bad eye; the eye is torn out, and they follow Jesus. Let no one say, therefore: I have a mother, I have a father, a brother, a son, a wife; I have all the other dear ones to whom I am bound by ties of affection. Monks are the imitators of the apostles, but we cannot make them our models unless we do what they did. No monk, then, should ever say: I have a father, a mother. I shall answer: You have Jesus, why do you seek the dead? He who has Jesus has father, mother, children, every kind of relative. Why do you go looking for the dead? Follow the living: 'leave the dead to bury the dead.'[15] One of the disciples says to the Lord: 'Lord, let me first go and bury my father.'[16] He did not mean, Let me go to be with my father, but let me have an hour's time. What is the Lord's answer to him? In an hour, you may perish; look out, lest while you are intending to bury the dead, you die yourself. A father who is dead does not exact duty from a son.

I say to you, monk, why do you ask for your father, your mother? Either she is a Christian or she is not; either she is a saint or she is a sinner; she is one or the other; it cannot be otherwise. If she is a saint, she rejoices that you are serving the Lord; if she is a sinner, leave her, she is dead. I shall now direct a question to you, O Christian mother. 'Your son serves Christ in the monastery; he serves his Commander. He has been branded with the seal of his King. He has a shield of fasting, a helmet of faith; his sword is the word of God; he has armor, the garment of Jesus that he received in baptism. Thus is he armed, ready for battle. He must go out into the battlefield and meet the enemy. Will you say to him, Leave your arms and come into my chamber? The same proposal is

14 Matt. 4.19, 20.
15 Cf. Matt. 8.22.
16 Matt. 8.21; cf. Letter 38.5, PL 22.465(176).

made to you, O monk, as to Adam: 'Before you is life, before you is death, choose whichever you wish.'[17] You have two fathers, a spiritual and a natural; you cannot love them both. If you love the Father of the spirit, you scorn the father of the flesh; 'you cannot serve two masters.'[18] 'He who loves father or mother more than me, is not worthy of me.'[19] If you wish to follow your carnal father, leave your spiritual Father. You are evading the issue without reason, my monk, when you say, 'What if I love my father or my mother, am I not thereby serving the Lord? Is it not written in the Law and in the Gospel: "Honor thy father and thy mother,"[20] and "Let him who curses father or mother be put to death"?[21] Are we, therefore, to serve God so as not to honor our parents?' I say to you in reply, honor your parents insofar as they do not hinder your service[22] to the Lord, your General. To whom be glory forever and ever. Amen.

17 Cf. Sir. (Ecclus.) 15.17.
18 Cf. Matt. 6.24.
19 Matt. 10.37; cf. Letter 14.3, PL 22.549(30).
20 Matt. 15.4; Exod. 20.12; cf. Letter 54.3, PL 22.551(283); 123.6, PL 22.1049(904).
21 Matt. 15.4; Exod. 21.17.
22 Cf. *Against John of Jerusalem* 8, PL 23.378(415).

HOMILY 86

ON THE GOSPEL OF LUKE 16.19-31[1]

The Rich Man and Lazarus

'THERE WAS A CERTAIN RICH MAN.' When the Lord had declared: 'No servant can serve two masters; you cannot serve God and mammon,'[2] and the greedy Pharisees had rebuked Him, He set before them an example, or rather, a truth, in the form of an example and parable. Strictly speaking, it is not really a parable when the names of the characters are given. A parable poses an example, but suppresses identification. Where Abraham is mentioned by name, and Lazarus, the prophets, and Moses, there Lazarus is genuine; if Abraham is a true person, so also is Lazarus. We have read who Abraham was; we have not read of Lazarus, but He who made Lazarus, also made Abraham. If he speaks of Abraham as a real person, then we understand Lazarus, also, as a living reality, for fiction is not congruous with the actual.

'There was a certain rich man.' Just think of the kindness of the Lord! Lazarus, the beggar, is called by his name because he was a saint, but the man who is rich and proud is not deemed worthy of a name. 'There was a certain rich man.' I say, 'certain,' because he has passed like a shadow. 'There was a certain rich man who used to clothe himself in purple and fine linen.' Ashes, dust, and earth, he covered up with purple and silk. 'Who used to clothe himself in purple and

1 After the beginning of Lent, following the recitation of Ps. 103.
2 Cf. Luke 16.13.

fine linen, and who feasted every day in splendid fashion.' As his garments, so his food; and with us, likewise; as our food, so our garments.

'There was a certain poor man, named Lazarus.' The meaning of Lazarus' name is 'boēthoúmenos,' one who has been helped; he is not a helper, but one who has been helped. He was a poor man and, in his poverty, the Lord came to his assistance. 'Who lay at his gate, covered with sores.' The rich man, in purple splendor, is not accused of being avaricious, nor of carrying off the property of another, nor of committing adultery, nor, in fact, of any wrongdoing; the evil alone of which he is guilty is pride. Most wretched of men, you see a member of your own body lying there outside at your gate, and have you no compassion? If the precepts of God mean nothing to you, at least take pity on your own plight, and be in fear lest you become such as he. Why do you save what is superfluous to your pleasures? Give in alms to your own member what you waste. I am not telling you to throw away your wealth. What you throw out, the crumbs from your table, offer as alms.

'Who lay at his gate.' He was lying at the gate in order to draw attention to the cruelty paid to his body and to prevent the rich man from saying, I did not notice him; he was in a corner; I could not see him; no one announced him to me. He lay at the gate; you saw him every time you went out and every time you came in. When your throngs of servants and clients were attending you, he lay there full of ulcers. If your eyes disdained to look upon putrid flesh, did not your ears, at least, hear his plea? 'Who lay at his gate, covered with sores.' He did not have just one sore, his whole body was sores, so that the magnitude of his suffering might arouse your utmost compassion. 'Who lay at his gate, covered with sores, and longing to be filled with the crumbs that fell from the rich man's table.' There is some relief to sickness if one has resources, but if you add poverty to extreme weakness the infirmity is doubled. Sickness is always fastidious and cannot take anything indelicate; it is nauseated by it. How much real suffering that causes! In the midst of so many wounds, he does not, however, think of the pain of his afflictions, but of the pangs of hunger. 'Longing to be filled with the crumbs that fell from the rich man's table.' In a certain way, he is saying to the rich man: The crumbs from your table are enough for me; what you brush off the table, give in alms; draw profit from your losses. 'Even the dogs would come and lick his sores.' What no man deigned to bathe and touch, gentle beasts lick.

'It came to pass that the poor man died and was borne away by the angels into Abraham's bosom; but the rich man also died and was buried; and in hell lifting up his eyes. . . .'[3] We have heard what each has suffered on earth; let us consider how they fare in the nether world. The temporal has passed and is over; what follows is for all eternity. Both are dead; the one is met by angels, the other with torments; the one is borne away on the shoulders of angels, the other goes to his punishment; the one, Abraham receives into his bosom of happiness; the other, hell devours. Lazarus 'was borne away by the angels.' Great sufferings are suddenly exchanged for delights. He is carried by angels and borne away without even the effort of walking. He is carried after his great trials because he was exhausted. 'Was borne away by the angels.' One angel was not enough to carry the pauper, but many came to form a chorus of jubilation. 'Was borne away by angels.' Every angel rejoices to touch so precious a burden. With pleasure, they bear such burdens in order to conduct men into the kingdom of heaven. He was escorted and carried into the bosom of Abraham, not to the side of Abraham, but into the bosom of Abraham, that Abraham might caress him, revivify him; that he might hold him in his bosom and,

3 Cf. Luke 16.22, 23.

like a tender and compassionate father, warm him back to life again.

'The rich man also died and was buried,' earth has returned to its earth. 'In hell lifting up his eyes.' Note the import and appropriateness of each word. 'In hell lifting up his eyes.' Lazarus was above; he was below; he lifted up his eyes to behold Lazarus, not to despise him. 'Lifting up his eyes, being in torments.' His whole being was in anguish; his eyes alone were free, free to gaze upon the happiness of the other man. He was allowed the liberty of his eyes to be tortured the more because he does not enjoy what the other has. The riches of others are torments to those who are in poverty. 'Lifting up his eyes, being in torments.' The one many angels carry away; the other is held fixed in never-ending torments. Being in torments: the Gospel did not say in torment, but in torments, for such are the rewards of covetous wealth. He saw Abraham afar off; he looked up at him only to increase his torture. 'Lazarus in his bosom.' Abraham's bosom was the poor man's Paradise. 'Abraham afar off and Lazarus in his bosom.' Someone may say to me: Is Paradise in the nether world? I say this, that Abraham's bosom is true Paradise, but I also grant that the bosom of a holy man is Paradise.

'He cried out and said,' (excruciating pain increases the volume of the voice) ' "Father Abraham have pity on me." ' 'Father Abraham.' Even though I am in the grip of torments, nevertheless, I call upon my father. Just as that son who squandered all his possessions calls his father,[4] even so I call you father, despite my punishments. By nature, I call you father, even though I have lost you as father through sin. Have pity on me. 'In the nether world who gives you thanks?'[5] Vain is your repentance in a place where there is no room for repentance. Torments, not the disposition of your soul, force you to repent. 'Have pity on me.' A saint, indeed, is Abra-

4 Cf. Luke 15.18, 19.

5 Ps. 6.6.

ham, holy and blessed, and all of us are in haste to enter his bosom, but I am not so sure that it is possible for anyone in hell or in heaven to feel pity. The Creator pities His creature; one Physician came to restore the dead, for the others could not.

'Send Lazarus to dip the tip of his finger in water.' 'Send Lazarus.' You are mistaken, miserable man; Abraham cannot send, but he can receive. 'To dip the tip of his finger in water.' Recall your lifetime, rich man; you did not condescend to see Lazarus and now you are longing for the tip of his finger. 'Send Lazarus.' You should have done that for him while he lived.[6] 'To dip the tip of his finger in water.' See the conscience of the sinner; he does not dare ask for the whole finger. 'Cool my tongue, for I am tormented in this flame.' Cool my tongue, for it has uttered many a proud word. Where there is sin, there is also the penalty for sin. 'To cool my tongue, for I am tormented in this flame.' How evil the tongue can be, James has told us in his Letter: 'The tongue also is a little member, but it boasts mightily.'[7] The more it has sinned, the more it is tortured. You long for water, who formerly were so fastidious at the mere sight of smeary and spattered dishes.

'Abraham said to him, "Son, remember that thou in thy lifetime hast received good things." ' Be sure you know what he means: good things to you; but they are not good. You have received what you thought were good, but you cannot have been a lord upon earth and reign here too. It is not possible to have wealth both on earth and in hell.[8] 'Lazarus in like manner evil things.' If ever we are sick, if we are beggars, if we are wasting away in sickness, if we are perishing from the cold, if there is no hospitality for us, let us be glad and rejoice; let us receive evil things in our lifetime. When the

6 Cf. Letter 48.21, PL 22.510-511(234).
7 James 3.5.
8 Cf. Letter 108.6, PL 22.881(694).

crushing weight of infirmity and sickness bears down upon us, let us think of Lazarus. 'Besides all that, between us and you a great gulf is fixed.' It cannot be bridged, removed, or levelled. We can see it, but cannot cross it. We see what we have escaped; you see what you have lost; our joy and happiness multiply your torments; your torments augment our happiness.

'He said, "Then, father, I beseech thee."' The miserable creature does not cease to call him father. 'Then, father, I beseech thee.' You should have called him father in former times, for he was your true father. Did you acknowledge your father, you who despised your brother? 'To send him to my father's house.' Notice the perversity; not even in pain does he speak truth. You see what he says: 'Then, father, I beseech thee.' Your father, then, is Abraham; how can you say, therefore, send him to my father's house? You have not forgotten your father; you have not forgotten that he who was your father has destroyed you. Because he was your father, you have five brothers. You have five brothers: sight, smell, taste, hearing, touch. These are the brothers to whom formerly you were enslaved; they were your brothers. Since they were the brothers you loved, you could not love your brother, Lazarus. Naturally, you could not love him as brother, because you loved them. Those brothers have no love for poverty. Your sight, your sense of smell, your taste, your sense of touch, was your brother. These brothers of yours loved wealth; they had no eye for poverty. 'I have five brothers, that he may testify to them.' They are the brothers who sent you into these torments; they cannot be saved unless they die. 'Lest they too come into this place of torments.' Why do you want to save those brothers who have no love for poverty? It must needs be that brothers dwell with their brother.

'Abraham said to him, "They have Moses and the Prophets, let them hearken to them."' Why do you ask that Lazarus go? 'They have Moses and the Prophets.' Besides, Moses and the prophets went about in goatskins,[9] wandering in their caves and in holes in the ground; they were poor men just like Lazarus, and they suffered calamities and endured hunger. Why do you ask me to send Lazarus? They have Lazarus in Moses and the prophets. Moses was Lazarus; he was a poor man; he was naked. He esteemed the poverty of Christ greater riches than the treasures of Pharao.[10] They also have the prophets. They have Jeremia who is thrown into a cistern of mud[11] and who fed upon the bread of tribulation. They have all the prophets; let them hearken to them. Every day Moses and the prophets are preaching against your five brothers; let them teach them; let them instruct them. Let them summon the eye; and what do they say to it? Do not look upon the carnal, but discern the spiritual. 'What we have seen with our eyes,' says the apostle, 'what we have heard, what our hands have handled: of the Word of God.'[12] He instructs the ear, too, the sense of smell, of taste. All the prophets and all the saints teach these brothers.

'He answered, "No, father Abraham, but if someone from the dead goes to them, they will repent." ' Here, a dogma is being revealed without our realizing it. One thing is said, another is foreshadowed. He knows that these brothers of his cannot be saved unless someone rises from the dead. The Jews, indeed, hearken only to Moses and the prophets, and no one has come back to them from the dead, therefore, our Savior has such brothers. 'If someone from the dead goes to them, they will repent.' 'If someone from the dead goes.' I do not know who will go, for I who am fixed in punishment do not deserve to know Him who will rise from the dead. This I do know, however. Whoever rises from the dead and teaches can save these brothers. He has saved ears, for He

9 Cf. Heb. 11.37, 38.
10 Cf. Heb. 11.26.
11 Cf. Jer. 38.6, 9.
12 Cf. 1 John 1.1.

says: 'He who has ears to hear, let him hear';[13] and eyes, for He says: 'The lamp of the body is your eye.'[14] In His name, the apostle says: 'We are the fragrance of Christ';[15] and the psalmist: 'Taste and see how good the Lord is.'[16] He saves, also, the sense of touch, for, in a way, John is speaking of all these brothers when he says: 'What we have seen, what we have heard, what our hands have handled.'[17] To these brothers, the Resurrection of the Lord brought salvation.

These brothers were in us, also, before our Lord rose from the dead. My eyes used to look upon evil; they led me in pursuit of a prostitute. I simply could not look at a beautiful woman without her beauty setting me aflame. Formerly, my ear was a snare, for I used to delight in popular songs and to listen gladly to shameful tales. Perfumes were my pleasure, not, indeed, good fragrance, but evil, for they were destroying my soul. Neither land nor sea was able to satisfy my palate. With every kind of delicacy, my slaves catered to me as an epicure. My sense of touch held me captive; I was seduced in the embrace of women. Do you see how these brothers, before the Resurrection of Christ, were leading me into death? He died and I lived; He died and these brothers rose from the dead; rather, they died in order that they might live; they died in the flesh that they might live in the Spirit. Now, my eye looks upon Christ; my ear hears only Him; my taste relishes Him alone; my sense of smell detects Him; my touch embraces Him.

'He said to him, "If they do not hearken to Moses and the Prophets."' Mark how our Lord instructs the soul by His own word and by recalling Scripture. When we had said, moreover, that these brothers could not be saved unless someone rose from the dead, we had, by no means, given place to

13 Matt. 11.15.
14 Cf. Matt. 6.22.
15 2 Cor. 2.15.
16 Ps. 33.9.
17 Cf. 1 John 1.1.

Marcion and to Mani, who tear down the Old Testament. They maintain that the soul cannot be saved except through, and only through, the Gospel; they do away completely with the Old Testament. Abraham, on the other hand, does not do away with Him who is going to rise from the dead, for he does not say, let them hearken to Moses and the prophets; why do you wait for Him who is going to rise from the dead? If he had said that, he would have destroyed the Gospel. What does he say? 'If they do not hearken to Moses and the Prophets, they will not believe even if someone rises from the dead.' 'If you believed Moses you would believe me also, for he wrote of me.'[18] See now what Abraham means? You do well, indeed, to wait for Him who will rise from the dead, but Moses and the prophets proclaim that He is the One who is going to rise from the dead. It is Christ, in fact, who speaks in them; if you hearken to them, you will hearken, also, to Him.

There is so much more to be said. The psalm that has been read, the one-hundred-third, is mystical, especially so where it says: 'With Leviathan, which you formed to make sport of it';[19] and: 'The highest of them is the home of the stork.'[20] The whole psalm is replete with mystical meaning, and but a day, not an hour, is scarcely long enough to do it justice.[21] Since, however, it is already Lent, we shall, if the Lord grants an opportunity, attempt at another time to unveil the mysteries hidden in it. For the present, let it suffice to hear about Lazarus, or rather, to hear that he was the rich man. May the torments of the rich man be a restraint upon us and the example of the poor man an incentive to us. The Christian soul, the soul of the monk, the soul of him who naked follows the naked Christ, when it looks with envy upon a rich man, or when it itself revels in wealth and display, may it call to mind

18 John 5.46.
19 Ps. 103.26.
20 Cf. Ps. 103.17.
21 Cf. Homily 11 on Ps. 77, p. 84.

Dives; may it ponder well his voice as he cries out and begs for the touch of Lazarus' finger.

While we are still thinking about Lazarus, let us consider something we had all but forgotten to mention, for someone may, by this question, introduce a false doctrine: Is this scene presented to us as taking place before the last judgment or after? One answer might be, after the judgment because the one is suffering punishment and the other is enjoying consolation. What, then, is the meaning of: 'They have Moses and the Prophets'? On the other hand, if Christ Himself is the one speaking and He is teaching before the Resurrection which, according to our interpretation, is in expectation, then, the scene is taking place before the Resurrection, and, reasonably, is before the last judgment. I shall give an example to bring out the truth. Imagine that a man has been caught in the act of robbery and is sent to a very dark prison; he has been put into prison and is in torments while actually waiting for sentence. He, surely, is subject to some kind of punishment, and comes to realize what he is going to suffer in the future. Even though he has not yet received final condemnation, and the day of the trial, or judgment, has not yet come; nevertheless, from the imprisonment, from the darkness, filth, hunger, creaking of chains, groaning of the fettered, weeping of those who are with him, he understands fully what kind of penalty will be his. If the prelude to punishment is so painful, what will the punishment itself be like? If he has not yet come to trial, and his penalty is not yet meted out, yet he longs for cool water, what will he suffer after judgment!

It must also be taken into account that Abraham was in the nether world. Christ had not yet risen from the dead to lead him into Paradise, for, before Christ died, no one had ascended into heaven, not even the thief. That flaming, flashing sword[22] was keeping Paradise safe; no one could open the gates which Christ had closed. The thief was the first to enter

22 Cf. Gen. 3.24; Letter 39.4(3a), PL 22.469(181); 60.3, PL 22.591(333).

with Christ; his great faith merited the greatest of rewards. His faith in the kingdom was not attendant upon seeing Christ; he did not see Him in His radiant glory nor behold Him looking down from heaven; he did not see the angels administering to Him. Certainly, to put it plainly, he did not see Christ walking about in freedom, but on a gibbet, drinking vinegar, crowned with thorns; he saw Him fixed to the cross and heard Him beseeching help: 'My God, my God, why have you forsaken me?'[23] Under such circumstances, he believed, O fickle, fallen state of man! The apostles had followed Him, and they had run away; this criminal on the cross acknowledged the Lord. O Peter, O John, you who had boldly asserted: 'Even if I should have to die with thee, I will not desert thee!'[24] You make a promise and you do not keep it; behold another who is condemned for homicide fulfills the promise that he had not made! You have been excluded from your place; a thief has shut you out and is the first to enter Paradise with Christ.

We have disgressed on the thief, but we have not forgotten the theme of our discussion, for when speaking of Paradise, we had said that no one would go there before the coming of Christ.[25] Let us return, therefore, to that proposition. The thief's crown must not lead us astray; let it rather incite us to win the crown. Abraham was not yet in Paradise because Christ had not yet entered with the thief. Christ came, and He suffered, and many bodies of the saints arose from their graves and were seen in the holy city.[26] The cross of Christ is the key to Paradise, the cross of Christ opened it. Has He not said to you: 'The kingdom of heaven has been enduring violent assault, and the violent have been seizing it by force'?[27] Does not the One on the cross cause the violence? There is

23 Ps. 21.2.
24 Matt. 26.35.
25 Cf. Homily 76 (II) on Mark 1.13-31, p. 134.
26 Cf. Matt. 27.52, 53.
27 Matt. 11.12; cf. Letter 60.3, PL 22.591 (333).

nothing between; the cross and, at once, Paradise. The greatest of pains produces the greatest of rewards.

So much for what we have been saying. Let us pray the Lord that we may imitate the thief and this Lazarus, the beggar; if there is persecution, the thief; if peace, Lazarus. If we become martyrs, straightway we are in Paradise; if we endure the pains of poverty, instantly we are in Abraham's bosom. Blood has its own abode and so has peace. Poverty, too, has its martyrdom; need well borne is martyrdom—but need suffered for the sake of Christ and not from necessity. How many beggars there are who long to be rich men and, therefore, commit crime! Poverty of itself does not render one blessed, but poverty for the sake of Christ. Faith does not fear hunger. The lover of Christ has no fear of hunger; he who has Christ, with Him possesses all riches. A certain merchant, a very wise man, sold all his material possessions, all his pearls,[28] and purchased for himself a single pearl, the most precious of all. He, certainly, had pearls, and they were very beautiful and precious pearls. He had Moses, Isaia, Jeremia, the holy prophets, but, in comparison to Christ he deemed these pearls as dung, wherefore the apostle says: 'But the things that were gain to me, I count them as dung that I may gain Christ,'[29] that I may buy the one pearl. Similarly, one of the prophets says: 'Stand beside the roads, ask the pathway.'[30] It is as if he were saying, sell the pearls and, with the pearls, purchase the one pearl. The prophet did not say, abandon the ways, but stand on the ways, and ask and seek the Way, Christ. To whom be glory forever and ever. Amen.

---

28 Matt. 13.45, 46; cf. 54.11, PL 22.555 (289).
29 Cf. Phil. 3.7, 8.
30 Cf. Jer. 6.16.

HOMILY 87

ON THE GOSPEL OF JOHN 1.1-14

THE GOSPEL SAYS OF JOHN: 'There has been a man, one sent from God.'[1] Consider the vast difference between God and man, for of God it says: 'In the beginning was the Word, and the Word was with God; and the Word was God.' Notice how an unlettered fisherman made use of a new word in its proper signification of God: 'In the beginning was the Word'—as we have already quoted; we have no time to repeat the entire passage. He says of man: 'There has been a man sent from God.' Mark the 'has been.' Of the Son of God, he says 'was,' of man, 'has been.'[2] In referring to God, John says: 'In the beginning was the Word'; in referring to the Son of God he says, 'the Word'; of man, 'There has been a man.' Because he is a man, he has been sent from God. 'Whose name was John.' In his name, one senses grace, for the name 'John' means the grace of the Lord. IO means the Lord, ANNA means grace. Whose name was *'Ioannes.'* Truly, he merits the name he bears (pherő́númos).[3] Why 'pherő́númos'? Because he is true to his name; he has received a very great grace; hence, in the desert, he searches into the reason and nature of things and keeps himself for the coming of Christ. Because he was to announce Christ, from day to day, he is fed in the desert; there, from day to day, he grows. He has no desire to converse with men; in the wilder-

1 Cf. John 1.6.

2 Cf. Homily 75 (I) on Mark 1.1-12, p. 123.

3 Cf. Letter 47.2, PL 22.492 (210); beginning of *Commentary on Abdia* 1.1, PL 25.1099(363).

ness, he communes with the angels. John had always known that Christ would come. Not only had he known Him from infancy, but when he was in the womb of his mother, he had recognized Christ and had already greeted Him. It is written, in fact: 'The babe in the womb leapt for joy.'[4] Just think, as he was being formed in his mother's womb, he perceived the advent of the Lord!

Realize your nobility, monks! John is the first one of our calling.[5] He is a monk. Right after his birth, he lives in the wilderness; he is reared in the wilderness; there, he waits for Christ. Meditate on the difference. When John was born and lived in the wilderness, how much wealth was stored away in the Temple that we now see in ruins, how much gold, silver; what crowds worshiped in it. Do you want to know how vast was the throng of worshipers? Josephus, the Jewish historian, gives an account of the number at the time when Jerusalem was captured by Vespasian and Titus. He says that eight-hundred-one-thousand[6] were captured in a single day. Grasp what that means. When that many have been captured, how many inhabitants must there have been altogether; how many died; how many did hunger kill; how many the sword? He also records the quantity of gold there was, the silver, precious gems, silk; the numerous priests, scribes, and various other officials.[7] On the other hand, see how Christ esteems humility. Christ, the Son of God, is not recognized in the Temple, but He is proclaimed in the desert. The humble Christ loves the humble. Why do I lay such stress on this? To teach you that John the Baptist set the example for our way of life. Blessed are they who imitate John, than whom there has not been a greater among those born of women![8] He was waiting

4 Cf. Luke 1.41; cf. Letter 107.3, PL 22.870(680).
5 Cf. Letter 22.36, PL 22.421(121).
6 Cf. *De Bello Iudaico* 6.9.3; where according to Josephus' statistics, 97,000!
7 Cf. *De Bello Iudaico* 5.5.
8 Cf. Matt. 11.11; cf. *Against the Luciferians* 7, PL 23.170 (178).

for Christ; he knew that He was to come; he did not deem it fitting for his eyes to look upon anyone else.[9]

'All things were made through him, and without him was made nothing that has been made.' Many read this inaccurately because they add without any punctuation, 'that which has been made in him was life.' The correct statement: 'All things were made through him, and without him was made nothing that has been made,' meaning that that which has been made without Him has not been made. The Holy Spirit has not been made; hence, the Holy Spirit is not through Him. Admittedly, the Holy Spirit, who has made all things, has not been made by the Lord. 'By the word of the Lord the heavens were made; by the Spirit of his mouth all their host.'[10] You perceive that there are two who create. I dismiss the Father, for there is no doubt about Him, although three persons are plainly indicated in this versicle. When Scripture says: 'By the word of the Lord the heavens were made,' it speaks of the 'Lógos,' i.e., it speaks of the Word, and the Lord, Father and Son; two persons are mentioned. 'By the Word of the Lord the heavens were made,' in other words, by the Son of the Father, the heavens were made, 'and by the Spirit of his mouth all their host.' There is clear demonstration in this versicle that the Father, the Son, and the Holy Spirit are the creators of all things. 'All things were made through him.' Now, if all things were made through Him, is the Father, on that account, excluded from creation, or Holy Spirit, and has the Son alone worked? Because the evangelist had said: 'All things were made through him,' lest he take away creation from the Holy Spirit and the Father, he added: 'And without him was made nothing that has been made.' When he says: 'without him was made nothing,' he reveals that another has made, but has made nothing without Him.

---

9 Cf. Homily 75 (I) on Mark 1.1-12, pp. 124-125.
10 Cf. Ps. 32.6.

In fine, what does wisdom say in Proverbs? 'When he established the heavens I was there.'[11]

'The life was the light of men. And the light shines in the darkness; and the darkness grasped it not.' In general, of course, it is said of God the Creator that He is ever in the midst of His creatures; nevertheless, the creature does not recognize its Creator. In particular, however, this text refers to the Lord Savior, and says that the Word who was God, and was in God, was also in the world to shine in the darkness of the Jews; and the Jews, who are the darkness, did not grasp the Light.

'There has been a man, one sent from God.' We shall comment briefly on each word. 'There has been a man sent from God.' Notice the precision of idiom. What does it say about God? Of the Son of God? 'In the beginning was the Word.' Was. He who was has no beginning; He who was has ever been. Of John, however, although he is a saint and the precursor, it does not say, he was, for he did not exist before he was conceived; he was not before he became the forerunner nor before he was conceived in a womb. Let heresy listen to this. He is not sent who was, but he who was not is sent and becomes the precursor. What is the meaning of: 'There has been a man sent from God'? Notice the propriety of the words. 'In the beginning was the Word, and the Word was with God; and the Word was God. He was in the beginning with God.' We have read secular literature, we have studied Plato and the other philosophers. Our fisherman has found what the philosopher failed to detect.[12] If he had said, In the beginning was God the Son, he would seem to have excluded the Father, or even to be making two gods; and it would have been no gain for us from the Gentiles if we had abandoned many gods to believe in two gods. See, then, how prudently, how gradually, the evangelist moves along? He does not say,

11 Prov. 8.27.
12 Cf. Letter 53.4, PL 22.543 (273).

in the beginning was God, lest it seem that god and god created, that two gods had been associated, but he calls the Son, the Word. While he is saying that the Word Itself is in the Father, he is also saying that the Son is God, so that there is no misunderstanding that God is one. By the same process of reasoning through which we affirm the Son to be God and affirm, moreover, one God in the Father and in the Son, so in the Father and in the Son and in the Holy Spirit, there is indeed, a trinity, but one divine nature.

'There has been a man, one sent from God.' John has been, who before was not; he has been made, who before was not; a man has been, not the Word. A man, therefore, has been because he was a man. The Word has not been, but always was. 'There has been a man sent from God.' 'In the beginning was the Word'; the Word is not sent. 'A man has been sent from God.' Whatever, therefore, the man says, it is the One who sent him who is heard. 'He who receives you, receives me,'[13] the honor of the sender is recognized and acknowledged in him who is sent. 'There has been a man sent from God.' Where we say 'sent,' the Hebrews say, one sent forth; in Greek, 'apóstolos'; in Hebrew SILOAS.[14] You see, therefore, that this John, the prophet, is not only a prophet, but also an apostle. Isaia is sent; he was an apostle. 'Here I am, send me!'[15] 'Sent from God.' Well said, 'sent,' for the Lord says in the Gospel: 'All who have come before me are thieves and robbers.'[16] He did not say, all who have been sent are thieves and robbers, but those who have come on their own. Whom does He mean by all those who have come before Me? 'Those who say, "Thus says the Lord!"[17] whereas the Lord has not sent them'; they who have come on their own authority and have not been sent are the thieves and

13 Matt. 10.40; cf. Letter 75.4, PL 22.688 (455); 109.1, PL 22.907 (726).
14 Cf. *Commentary on Galatians* 1.1, PL 26.335-336(374).
15 Cf. Isa. 6.8.
16 Cf. John 10.8.
17 Cf. Ezech. 13.6.

robbers. But this man has been sent from God. 'Whose name was John,' and whose name corresponds to his calling. The name, '*Ioannes,*' is interpreted as the grace of the Lord, for IO means Lord, and ANNA, grace; hence, John is called the grace of the Lord. His mission as messenger, he receives from the Lord. 'This man came as a witness, to bear witness concerning the light.' There is much to be said, but time prevents.

'The Word was made flesh, and dwelt among us.' The Word was made flesh, but how He was made flesh, we do not know. The doctrine I have from God; the science of it, I do not have. I know that the Word was made flesh; how it was done, I do not know. Are you surprised that I do not know? No creature knows. It is a mystery which has been hidden for ages and generations, but now is clearly shown in our time.[18] Someone may object: If it has been revealed, why do you say that you do not know? That it has been brought to pass has been revealed, but how it was brought to pass is hidden. Isaia even says: 'Who can describe his generation?'[19] What had Isaia meant, then, by saying: 'The virgin shall be with child and bear a son'?[20] He is telling us what has happened; but when he says: 'Who can describe his generation,' he is revealing to us the fact that He has been born, but how He has been born, we do not know. Holy Mary, blessed Mary, mother and virgin, virgin before giving birth, virgin after giving birth! I, for my part, marvel how a virgin is born of a virgin, and how, after the birth of a virgin, the mother is a virgin.

Would you like to know how He is born of a virgin and, after His nativity, the mother is still a virgin? 'The doors were closed and Jesus entered.'[21] There is no question about that. He who entered through the closed doors was not a

18 Cf. Col. 1.26.
19 Cf. Isa. 53.8, LXX; cf. *Against John of Jerusalem* 10, PL 23.380(417).
20 Isa. 7.14.
21 Cf. John 20.19, 26; cf. Letter 48.21, PL 22.510 (233).

ghost nor a spirit; He was a real man with a real body. Furthermore, what does He say? 'Feel me and see; for a spirit does not have flesh and bones, as you see I have.'[22] He had flesh and bones, and the doors were closed. How do flesh and bones enter through closed doors? The doors are closed and He enters, whom we do not see entering. Whence has He entered? Everything is closed up; there is no place through which He may enter. Nevertheless, He who has entered is within and how He entered is not evident. You do not know how His entrance was accomplished, and you attribute it to the power of God. Attribute to the power of God, then, that He was born of a virgin, and the virgin herself after bringing forth was a virgin still.

We read in Ezechiel in regard to the building of the Temple: 'The east gate facing the east is to remain closed; it is not to be opened for anyone to enter by it except only the chief priest.'[23] The gate is closed and no one enters by it but the chief priest alone. The Savior's tomb had been hewn out in the hardest kind of rock,[24] and it is written that in it no one had ever yet been laid,[25] for it was a new tomb. What has taken place historically is very clear; the sepulchre was hewn out of rock (we must give the literal interpretation first), very hard rock; He was laid in a new tomb, and a great stone was rolled to the entrance; and a military guard was stationed there to prevent any possibility of stealing Him away. Now all this precaution took place that the power of God would be all the more manifest when He arose from the dead. If the tomb had been in the ground, they could say, 'They have dug a tunnel and have stolen Him away.' If a stone of ordinary size had been placed as a seal, they could say, 'It was a small stone and they carried Him away while

22 Luke 24.39.
23 Cf. Ezech. 44.1-3; cf. *Commentary on Ezechiel* 44.1-3, PL 25.430 (538); Letter 48.21, PL 22.510 (233).
24 Cf. Matt. 27.60.
25 Cf. Luke 23.53.

we were sleeping.' As a matter of fact, what is written in the Gospel? 'The next day the scribes, the Pharisees, and the chief priests went in a body to Pilate, saying, "Sir, that deceiver used to say that he would rise again. Lest, therefore, his disciples may come and steal him away and say, 'He has risen from the dead'; and the last imposture be worse than the first, give us guards to guard his sepulchre lest they take him away by stealth." Pilate said to them, "You have a guard; go, guard it as well as you know how." '[26] The extreme caution of the scribes and the enemy has rendered service to our faith.[27] Look out, Pharisees; watch out; God cannot be shut in; God cannot be confined in a sepulchre. He who made heaven and earth, in the palm of whose hand rest heaven and earth, who poises the universe on three of His fingers—the Hebrew expression for this is translated by the Greek 'en trisốmati'[28]—He who, as I was saying, balances the universe, cannot be contained in a single sepulchre.

Then, too, when the women, Mary Magdalene and Mary the mother of James and Joseph [*sic.*], pious and well-meaning women, to be sure, but mistaken,[29] were looking for God in the tomb, He accepted, indeed, their good desire, but the angel who rolled back the stone made known to them their error. He was sitting upon the stone, and what was it he made them understand? This stone upon which I am sitting, I, who am servant of Him who really is, is not able to confine my Lord since He would then be restrained by His own slave. That stone could not shut in Jesus. The angel says to the women who had come to seek Him: 'Are you seeking Jesus? He is not here.'[30] Where is He, in heaven? He is beyond the heavens. On earth? He is beyond earth. Wherever He wills, there He is; wherever He is, He is there whole and entire.

26 Cf. Matt. 27.62-65.
27 Cf. *Commentary on Matthew* 27.64, PL 26.224 (240).
28 Cf. Isa. 40.12; cf. *Commentary on Isaia* 40.12, PL 24.406 (487).
29 Cf. Homily 44 on Ps. 131, p. 330; 1 on Ps. 1, p. 3.
30 Cf. Matt. 28.5, 6.

Wherever He is and wherever you are, you who are seeking Him are in Him whom you seek.

Listen to what the angel says to the women: 'Why do you seek the living one among the dead?'[31] Why do you seek the Lord in a tomb? You seek Jesus; you seek the Lord; why do you keep looking for Him? Certainly, if you knew that He is living, you would heed the words: 'In the midst of you there has stood one whom you do not know';[32] and: 'The kingdom of God is within you.'[33] What does the angel say to these women? Do you seek Jesus in the tomb? Believe that He has risen, and ponder well that He whom you seek is within you.

When Mary Magdalene had seen the Lord and thought that He was the gardener . . . she thought that He was the gardener; she was mistaken, indeed, in her vision, but the very error had its prototype. Truly, indeed, was Jesus the gardener of His Paradise, of His trees of Paradise. 'She thought that he was the gardener,'[34] and wanted to fall at His feet. What does the Lord say to her? 'Do not touch me, for I have not yet ascended to my Father.'[35] Do not touch Me; you do not deserve to touch Me whom you looked for in a grave. Do not touch Me whom you only suppose, but do not believe, has arisen. Do not touch Me, for to you I have not yet ascended to My Father. When you believe that I have ascended to My Father, then, it will be your privilege to touch Me; with the help of Christ our Lord, who liveth and reigneth forever. Amen.

---

31 Luke 24.5; cf. Letter 39.5, PL 22.472(185).
32 John 1.26.
33 Luke 17.21.
34 Cf. John 20.15.
35 John 20.17; cf. Letter 59.4, PL 22.588(329).

HOMILY 88

ON THE NATIVITY OF THE LORD[1]

'She laid him in a manger, because there was no room for them in the inn.'[2] His mother laid Him in a manger.[3] Joseph did not dare to touch Him, for he knew He had not been begotten of him. In wonderment, he rejoiced at a son, but he did not dare to touch the Son. 'She laid him in a manger.' Why in a manger? That the prophecy of Isaia, the prophet, might be fulfilled: 'An ox knows its owner, and an ass, its master's manger.'[4] In another place, it is written: 'Man and beast you save, O Lord.'[5] If you are man, eat the Bread; if you are a beast, come to the manger.

'Because there was no room for them in the inn.' Rightly said: 'There was no room for them in the inn,' for Jewish unbelief had overflowed into everything. He found no room in the Holy of Holies that shone with gold, precious stones,[6] pure silk, and silver. He is not born in the midst of gold and riches, but in the midst of dung, in a stable (wherever there is a stable, there is also dung) where our sins were more filthy than the dung. He is born on a dunghill in order to lift up those who come from it; 'from the dunghill he lifts up the poor.'[7] He is born on a dunghill, where Job, too, sat and afterwards was crowned.

1 Delivered on 25 December in the presence of the Bishop.
2 Luke 2.7.
3 Cf. *Against Helvidius* 8, PL 23.201 (254).
4 Isa. 1.3.
5 Ps. 35.7.
6 Cf. Letter 46.11, PL 22.490 (207).
7 Ps. 112.7.

'There was no room for them in the inn.' The poor should derive great comfort from this. Joseph and Mary, the mother of the Lord, had no servant boy, no maid servant. From Nazareth in Galilee, they come all alone; they own no draught-animal; they are their own masters and servants. Here is a new thought. They go to the wayside inn, not into the city, for poverty is too timid to venture among the rich. Note the extent of their poverty. They go to a wayside inn. Holy Writ did not say that the inn was on the road, but on a wayside off the road, not on it, but beyond it; not on the way of the Law, but on the by-way of the Gospel, on the by-road. There was no other place unoccupied for the birth of the Savior except a manger, a manger to which were tethered cattle and asses. O, if only I were permitted to look upon that manger in which the Lord lay! Now, as an honor to Christ, we have taken away the manger of clay and have replaced it with crib of silver,[8] but more precious to me is the one that has been removed. Silver and gold are proper to heathendom; Christian faith is worthy of the manger that is made of clay. He who was born in that manger cared nothing for gold and silver. I do not find fault with those who made the change in the cause of honor (nor do I look with disfavor upon those in the Temple who made vessels of gold), but I wonder at the Lord, the Creator of the universe, who is born, not surrounded by gold and silver, but by mud and clay.

'There were shepherds in the same district keeping watch.'[9] They will not find Christ unless they keep watch, as it is the shepherd's duty. Christ is not found except by the vigilant. That is why the bride says: 'I was sleeping, but my heart kept vigil.'[10] 'Indeed he neither slumbers nor sleeps, the guardian of Israel.'[11] There were shepherds in the same district. Herod was there; the high priests, the Pharisees were there; while

8 Cf. Letter 147.4, PL 22.1199(1089).
9 Cf. Luke 2.8.
10 Cant. 5.2.
11 Ps. 120.4.

they were sleeping, Christ is found in a lonely grotto. 'Shepherds keeping watch over their flock by night.' They were guarding their flock lest the wolf attack while they slept. They were keeping careful watch; the threat to the flock from the treachery of beasts was reason enough. They were keeping watch, as it were, over the flock of the Lord, but they could not safeguard it; hence, they besought the Lord to come and save it. 'Behold, an angel of the Lord stood by them.'[12] They who were so vigilant deserved to have an angel come to them. 'The glory of God shone round about them, and they feared exceedingly.' Human fear is unable to gaze upon a sublime and majestic vision. Because they were so thoroughly terrified, the angel speaks and, like a healing salve applied to wounds, restores their confidence. 'Do not be afraid,'[13] for you cannot grasp what I am saying if you are paralyzed by fear. 'There has been born to you today in the town of David a Savior, who is Christ the Lord.'[14] These are weighty words. While they were so astonished: 'Suddenly there was with the angel a multitude of the heavenly host praising God and saying.'[15] As one angel had announced the nativity of the Lord, and lest only one seem to bear witness, the entire host resounds in one song of praise: 'Glory to God in the highest, and peace on earth among men of good will.'[16]

If sins, according to the heretics, are a daily occurrence in heaven,[17] how can there be glory in heaven, and why is peace prayed for on earth? Notice what the Gospel says. In heaven, where there is no discord, glory rules; on earth, where every day is warfare, peace prevails.[18] On earth peace. Peace among whom? Among men. Why are the Gentiles without peace; why, too, the Jews? That is exactly the reason for the quali-

12 Luke 2.9.
13 Luke 2.10.
14 Luke 2.11.
15 Luke 2.13.
16 Luke 2.14.
17 Cf. *Commentary on Matthew* 6.10, PL 26.44(34).
18 Cf. Letter 75.1, PL 22.686(452).

fication: Peace among men of good will, among those who acknowledge the birth of Christ.

'The shepherds said to one another, "Let us go over to Bethlehem." '[19] Let us leave the deserted Temple and go over to Bethlehem. 'And see the word which was made.'[20] Truly alert, they did not say, Let us see the child, let us find out what is being announced; but: 'Let us see the word that has been made.' 'In the beginning was the Word.'[21] 'And the Word was made flesh.'[22] The Word that has always been, let us see how it was made for us. 'And see this word which was made, which the Lord has made, and has made known to us.'[23] This same Word made itself, inasmuch as this same Word is the Lord. Let us see, therefore, in what way this same Word, the Lord Himself, has made Himself and has made His flesh known to us. Because we could not see Him as long as He was the Word, let us see His flesh because it is flesh; let us see how the Word was made flesh. 'So they went with haste.'[24] The ardent longing of their souls gave wings to their feet; they could not keep pace with their yearning to see Him: 'So they went with haste.' Because they ran so eagerly, they find Him whom they sought.

Let us see what they find. 'Mary and Joseph.' If she were truly wife, it would be improper to say, they found the wife and the husband; but the Gospel named the woman first, then the man. What does Holy Writ say? 'They found Mary and Joseph': they found Mary, the mother, and Joseph, the guardian. 'And the babe lying in the manger. And when they had seen, they understood concerning the word, what had been told them concerning this child. But Mary kept in mind all these words, pondering them in her heart.'[25] What does

19 Cf. Luke 2.15.
20 *Ibid.*
21 John 1.1; cf. Letter 108.10, PL 22.884(698).
22 John 1.14.
23 Cf. Luke 2.15.
24 Luke 2.16.
25 Cf. Luke 2.16-19.

pondering mean? It must have meant weighing carefully in her heart, meditating within herself, and, in her heart, comparing notes. A certain exegete explains, 'pondering in her heart' thus: She was a holy woman, had read the Sacred Scriptures, knew the prophets, and was recalling that the angel Gabriel had said to her the same things that the prophets had foretold. She was pondering in her heart whether the prophets anticipated the words: 'The Holy Spirit shall come upon thee and the power of the Most High shall overshadow thee; and therefore the Holy One to be born shall be called the Son of God.'[26] Gabriel had said that; Isaia had foretold: 'The virgin shall be with child, and bear a son.'[27] She had read the latter; she had heard the former. She looked upon the child lying before her; she saw in the manger the child crying; she saw there the Son of God, her Son, her one and only Son; she looked upon Him, and in her musing, she compared what she had heard with what she had read and with what she herself perceived.

Since she was pondering in her heart, let us, likewise, meditate in our hearts that on this day Christ is born. There are some who think that He was born on Epiphany.[28] We do not censure the opinion of others, but follow the conclusions of our own study. 'Let everyone be convinced in his own mind and perhaps the Lord will reveal to each one.'[29] Both they who say the Lord is born then, and we who say He is born today, worship one Lord, acknowledge one Babe. Let us review a few facts, however, not to reprove others by our reasoning, but to confirm our own position. We are not airing our own opinion, but supporting tradition. The common consent of the world is contrary to the thinking of this province. Perhaps someone may object: 'Christ was born here; are they who are far away better informed than those who are close by?

26 Luke 1.35.
27 Isa. 7.14.
28 Cf. *Commentary on Ezechiel* 1.3, PL 25.18(6).
29 Cf. Rom. 14.5; Phil. 3.15; cf. Letter 144.1, PL 22.1183(1069).

Who told you?' They who are of this province, of course, the apostles, Peter and Paul, and the rest of them. You have rejected tradition; we have accepted it; Peter who was here with John, who lived here with James, taught us also in the West. The apostles are both your teachers and ours.

Here is another fact. The Jews, at that time, were ruling in Judea. Furthermore, the Acts of the Apostles relates: 'There broke out on that day a great persecution and those who believed were scattered abroad.'[30] They went into Cyprus and into Antioch, and the dispersed Jews penetrated the whole world. Since, therefore, the Jews were in power for forty-two years after the Ascension of the Lord, everywhere else there was peace; here, alone, there was war. Tradition could, then, be preserved more easily in the West than in Judea where there was discord. After forty-two years, the armies of Vespasian and Titus arrived; Jerusalem was overthrown and destroyed; all the Jews and Christians were driven out, every one of them. Until the time of Hadrian, Jerusalem remained a wilderness; there was not one Jew nor one Christian left in this entire province. Then Hadrian came and, because another revolution of the Jews broke out in Galilee, he laid waste what had remained of the city. He further proclaimed by law that no Jew was permitted to approach Jerusalem, and brought new settlers into the city from different provinces. I might mention that Hadrian's name was Aelius Hadrian,[31] and that, after he had destroyed Jerusalem, he called the restored city Aelia.

Why am I saying all this? Because they say to us: This is where the apostles lived; this is where the tradition has been established. Now, we say that Christ was born today; on Epiphany, He was reborn. You who maintain He was born on Epiphany prove for us generation and regeneration. When did He receive baptism, unless you face the consequence that on the same day He was born and reborn? Even nature is in

30 Cf. Acts 8.1.
31 Cf. Letter 108.9, PL 22.883(697).

agreement with our claim, for the world itself bears witness to our statement. Up to this day, darkness increases; from this day on, it decreases; light increases, darkness decreases; the day waxes, error wanes; truth advances. For us today, the Sun of Justice is born. In conclusion, consider another point. Between the Lord and John the Baptist, there are six months. If you study the nativity of John in relation to Christ's, you will see that they are six months apart.

Since we have touched on many things and have heard the Babe crying in the manger and have adored Him there, let us continue our adoration of Him today. Let us pick Him up in our arms and adore Him as the Son of God. Mighty God who for so long a time thundered in heaven and did not redeem man, cries and as a babe redeems him.[32] Why do I say all this? Because pride never brings salvation, but humility does. As long as the Son of God was in heaven, He was not adored; He descends to earth and is adored. He had beneath Him the sun, the moon, the angels, and He was not adored; on earth, He is born perfect man, a whole man, to heal the whole world. Whatever of man's nature He did not assume, He could not save; if He assumed only the body and not the soul, He did not save the soul. Did He, then, save what is of less value and not redeem that which is of greater? If, nevertheless, they admit that He saved the soul that He assumed, then consider that, just as the soul is superior to the body, reason is similarly the ruling faculty of the soul itself. If Christ did not redeem human rationality, He did not save the soul either which is less. You reply that He did not take upon Himself a human mind, in order that His heart might be free from human vices, evil thoughts, and desires. Do you mean, therefore, that if He could not control what He made, I should deem myself unworthy if I cannot conquer what He should have conquered?[33]

---

32 Cf. Letter 82.1, PL 22.736(513).
33 Cf. Homily 35 on Ps. 108, pp. 268-269; cf. Letter 98.6-8, PL 22.797-798(590).

We have forgotten our resolution and said more than we intended; the mind planned to do one thing, the tongue in its zeal slipped ahead. Let us be ready now to give our attention to the Bishop and take earnestly to heart what he has to say on what I have left out. Let us bless the Lord, to whom be glory forever and ever. Amen.

HOMILY 89

FOR EPIPHANY

On the Gospel Text of the Lord's Baptism and on Psalm 28

THE FEAST OF THE EPIPHANY is called by its Greek name, 'epipháneia,' which is the Greek expression for our concept of appearance, or manifestation. This, therefore, is the title given to our Lord and Savior's manifestation on earth. Even though He had been born of Mary and had already completed thirty years of His life, nevertheless, He was unknown to the world. His identity was revealed at the time when He came to the Jordan to be baptized by John the Baptist, and the voice of the Father was heard thundering from heaven:[1] 'This is my beloved Son, in whom I am well pleased.'[2] The Father had proclaimed Him by His voice from the heavens, and the Holy Spirit, settling upon His head in the form of a dove,[3] ordained to make Him known by that revelation, lest the people mistake anyone else for the Son of God. What is more sublime than His humility, more noble than His belittlement? He is baptized by His servant and He is named Son by God. Along with publicans, prostitutes, and sinners, He came for baptism, and He is holier than the one who baptizes. He is purified by John in the flesh, but He purifies John in the spirit. The waters that had been wont to cleanse others are now purified[4] by the cleansing of our Lord.

1 Cf. Ps. 28.3.
2 Matt. 3.17.
3 Cf. Matt. 3.16.
4 Cf. Letter 69.6, PL 22.660(420).

The Jordan river that dried up[5] when Josue led the Israelites into the Land of Promise, now longed to gather together all its waters into one place, if it could, to bathe the body of the Lord.

Notice, brethren, how this Gospel lesson has been foreshadowed in the twenty-eighth psalm: 'The voice of the Lord is over the waters.'[6] In fact, the Son of God said to John: 'Let it be so now, for so it becomes us to fulfill all justice.'[7] The psalm continues: 'The God of glory thunders'[8] when the Father gave testimony to the Son, saying: 'This is my beloved Son, in whom I am well pleased.'[9]

'The voice of the Lord breaks the cedars,'[10] for Christ is baptized, and the demons, that formerly had been arrogant and lofty, crash down in a heap of destruction. 'The Lord breaks them like the cedars of Lebanon, and dashes them headlong like a calf,'[11] tossing in the air the fragments of trees and scattering the pieces far and wide.

On the other hand, what does the psalm have to say of the Savior? 'As the beloved son of unicorns.'[12] Our beloved Lord and Savior is the Son of the unicorns, the Son of the cross, of whom Habacuc sings: 'Rays shine forth from beside him, where his power is concealed.'[13] After this beloved Son was crucified, then, was fulfilled the prophecy of the psalm: 'The voice of the Lord strikes fiery flames';[14] for when Christ had been baptized and the entire universe had been purified in His cleansing, the fire of hell was extinguished.

'The voice of the Lord shakes the desert.'[15] The desert was

---

5 Cf. Jos. 3.17; cf. Letter 108.12, PL 22.888(702).
6 Ps. 28.3.
7 Matt. 3.15.
8 Ps. 28.3.
9 Matt. 3.17.
10 Ps. 28.5.
11 Cf. Ps. 28.5, 6.
12 Cf. Ps. 28.6.
13 Hab. 3.4; cf. Letter 53.8, PL 22.547(278).
14 Ps. 28.7.
15 Ps. 28.8.

the Church that, at first, had no children. By the preaching of Christ, this wilderness 'was shaken,'[16] and 'came to labor and gave birth, and there was born in a single day an entire nation.'[17] She, who before was called the 'wilderness of Cades,' the desert of holiness—inasmuch as she had been barren of virtues—begins 'to bring forth stags'[18] and send out in throngs her holy men who kill the serpents on earth, contemptuous of their poisons. While they are running throughout the world proclaiming the gospel of Christ, 'in his temple all say "Glory" ' to God![19]

The psalm continues: 'The Lord is enthroned above the flood.'[20] Let us bring the whole world into our meditation; let us reflect upon the nations of barbarians; let us survey mentally the Roman Empire; everywhere they believe in Christ; everywhere they are baptized in our Lord. So it comes to pass that there is not just one immersion, but, so to speak, a deluge of baptisms.

Therefore, dearly beloved brethren, since: 'the feast of Tabernacles has come to a close'[21]—for that is the title of our psalm—since the Church is made of living stones: 'Let us bring to the Lord the children of God, let us bring to the Lord the offspring of rams'[22]—of the apostles and of the faithful—and let us imitate our Savior who is Himself called Shepherd and Lamb and Ram; who was immolated for us in Egypt;[23] who was caught by the horns in the bush[24] for the sake of Isaac; and let us say: 'The Lord is my shepherd; I shall not want. In verdant pastures he gives me repose; beside

16 Cf. Ps. 28.8.
17 Cf. Isa. 66.7, 8; cf. Letter 69.6, PL 22.660(420).
18 Cf. Ps. 28.9.
19 *Ibid.*
20 Ps. 28.10.
21 Cf. Ps. 28.
22 Cf. Ps. 28.1.
23 Cf. Exod. 12.6.
24 Cf. Gen. 22.13.

restful waters he leads me,'[25] to whom are the glory and the dominion forever.[26]

25 Ps. 22.1, 2.
26 Cf. 1 Peter 4.11.

HOMILY 90

ON LENT

First Sunday in Lent

JUST AS A SOLDIER NEVER CEASES to train for battle and prepares in sham warfare for the real wounds that are to come, every Christian must exercise self-restraint at all times, but especially when the enemy is near at hand with his well-trained hosts marshalled against us. It is always necessary for God's servants to fast, but it is even more imperative when we are preparing for the sacrifice of the Lamb, for the sacrament of Baptism, for the Body and Blood of Christ. As soon as the devil is aware that his sheep are determined to withdraw from his flock, he rages in madness, and in fury gathers all his forces against them, reckoning that whatever is saved for Christ is lost to him; whatever is given life for the Church is dead to his synagogue.

Consequently, dearly beloved brethren, since we are making our preparation for the Sacrament of the Lord by a fast of forty days, let us fast for our sins as many days as the Lord fasted for our evil deeds. After our Lord's baptism, the devil tempted Him. He did not know that He was the Son of God and, for that reason, was off his guard. In the sequel, he questions the Lord, tempting Him: 'If thou art the Son of God, command that these stones become loaves of bread,'[1] and: 'If thou art the Son of God, throw thyself down.'[2] Because he

1 Matt. 4.3; cf. Letter 130.10, PL 22.1116(987).
2 Matt. 4.6.

knows that we want to become children of God, he plots to take us by surprise, and, like a slimy serpent, coils himself about our feet to keep us from mounting to heaven. If with vile cunning he has dared to tempt the Lord, how much more boldly will he presume to deceive us? If he, a broken vessel, has fought against the Son of God and his own potter,[3] how much more daring will he be in attacking us who are by nature inferior to him? 'If the just man scarcely will be saved, where will the impious and the sinner appear?'[4] Not that our Lord could be deceived by the devil, but He who took upon Himself the nature of a slave[5] wished to give Himself as an example[6] in all things so that no one might trust in his own sanctity, since even He is tempted whom no temptation is able to overcome.

Our motive in going over all this, dearly beloved brethren, is that we may be on our guard, for fear that, after coming out from Egypt and hastening through the desert for forty days—for forty years, as it were—to reach the Land of Promise, we should long for the fleshpots of Egypt[7] and be bitten to death by the serpents.[8] We have left Egypt; what have we to do with the food of Egypt? We who have Bread from heaven, why do we go in search of earthly foods? We who have left Pharao, let us call upon the help of the Lord so that the Egyptian king may be drowned in the baptism of those who believe. Let his horses and their riders perish there;[9] let the raging army of the adversary be destroyed. Let us not murmur against the Lord lest we be struck down by Him.

Let us not talk about our priests. Let us abstain from vices rather than from food—although too much food excites concupiscence. If when Aaron and Mariam spoke against Moses,

3 Cf. Rom. 9.21, 22; Apoc. 2.28; cf. Letter 133.9, PL 22.1157(1037).
4 1 Peter 4.18.
5 Cf. Phil. 2.7, 8.
6 Cf. 1 Peter 2.21-25; cf. Letter 130.10, PL 22.1115(986).
7 Cf. Exod. 16.3.
8 Cf. Num. 21.6.
9 Cf. Exod. 15.1; Deut. 11.4.

they instantly experienced the punishment of God, coming in defense of His servant,[10] how much more will anyone of you be punished by divine judgment if, with viperous lips, he slanders his Bishop. Priests also must take care lest they be insincere, lest they doubt the power of God. If Aaron and Moses (who seemed to waver at the waters of Contradiction)[11] did not deserve to enter the Promised Land, does it not stand to reason that we, bent under the burden of sin, shall be far less able to cross the river Jordan and reach Galgal, the place of circumcision,[12] if we shall cause one of these little ones to sin?[13] Since, then, the fertility of the flock is proportionate to the labor of the shepherd and the abundance of the harvest to the zeal of the farmer in preparing the Lord's granaries, let us strain every effort to be made worthy of the coming of the Pasch and the flesh of the Lamb, Christ Jesus. Amen.

10 Cf. Num. 12.1-9.
11 Cf. Num. 20.8-13; 20.24; 27.14.
12 Cf. Deut. 11.30, 31.
13 Cf. Luke 17.2.

HOMILY 91

ON THE EXODUS

The Vigil of Easter

TODAY, THE PEOPLE OF ISRAEL, truly man-seeing-God[1] (that is the meaning of Israel), receive the command to depart from Egypt. Today, the Lamb of God that takes away the sins of the world is slain for the salvation of all. Today, the doorposts of the houses, our foreheads are being painted with His blood. Today, the Egyptians are destroyed, and God's people are liberated from the slavery of Pharao. Today, the first-born of the Egyptians are struck down, and not only the children of the Israelites, but even brute beasts are saved. To men, indeed, and to beasts of burden alike the Lord brings salvation.[2] Let us prepare ourselves for the sacrifice of the Lamb, and obtain the victim, not when the light is faint and the moon is a crescent, not when it begins to wax or wane, but on the fourteenth day, when the light of the moon is most perfect and full,[3] when its rays are undimmed and its circumference filled out. Nor let us be under the impression that this yearling lamb can be eaten anywhere. The precept bids us to partake of it in one house only, lest we think that the Lamb may be immolated outside the Church. From this, it is evident that the Jews and heretics, and all assemblies of perverted doctrine, because they do

1 Cf. Homily 42 on Ps. 127, p. 324.
2 Cf. Ps. 35.7.
3 Cf. Homily 5 on Ps. 14, p. 38.

not eat the Lamb in the Church, do not eat the flesh of the Lamb, but the flesh of the dragon, which, as the psalmist tells us, was given as food to the Ethiopians.[4] Just as in the flood no one was saved who was not in the Ark of Noe, and in the fall of Jericho, only the house of the harlot Rahab[5]—which signifies the faithful Church of the Gentiles—was spared; so is it true that, in the sacrifice of the Lamb, the Lamb is slain only when it is sacrificed in the one house.

'The lamb,' the Lord says, 'must be without blemish. You may take it from either the sheep or the goats.'[6] In another place of Holy Writ, it is prescribed that if anyone is unable to keep the Passover in the first month, he is to do so in the second.[7] According to the regulation above, anyone who is unable to sacrifice a lamb may substitute a kid. In the house of the Church, moreover, Christ is offered in a two-fold manner: if we are just, we eat of the flesh of the lamb; if we are sinners and do penance, for us, a goat is slain. This does not mean that Christ is from the goats that stand, as He has taught, on His left hand; but that Christ becomes a lamb or a goat in conformity with individual and personal merit.

Why is this lamb offered up in the evening and not during the day? The reason is plain enough, for our Lord and Savior suffered His Passion at the close of the ages; whence, John says in his letter: 'Dear children, it is the last hour.'[8] Since, moreover, it is the last hour, it is the beginning of night, for day has come to an end. It must be understood, however, that as long as we are in this world, as long as we abide in Egypt, we are not in a clear light, but in a dark mist. Although the Church shines as the moon[9] in the nighttime, nevertheless, we cannot dwell in the full splendor of the true Sun.

4 Cf. Ps. 73.14.
5 Cf. Jos. 6.25; cf. Letter 22.38, PL 22.422(123).
6 Cf. Exod. 12.5.
7 Cf. Num. 9.10, 11.
8 1 John 2.18.
9 Cf. Homily 30 on Ps. 103, pp. 226-227.

'In one household they shall eat its roasted flesh with unleavened bread and bitter herbs. It shall not be eaten raw or boiled, but roasted whole.'[10] We are bid not to eat bread with the old leaven of malice and wickedness.[11] The Lord warns His disciples in the Gospel against this, saying: 'Beware of the leaven of the Pharisees,'[12] and a little later He interprets it as their perverted teaching.[13] If we, therefore, want to be strangers to the teachings of this generation and live our lives detached from the ways of the world, let us submit to persecutions and tribulations, and, following the apostle, eat the unleavened bread of sincerity and truth. Do you really grasp what I am saying, O auditor? Speak the truth; be sincere; show favoritism to no one, not to the rich nor the powerful. No matter how influential or noble a sinner may be, rebuke him, and then you are eating in bitterness the unleavened bread of sincerity and truth. In this same mood, the apostle also says: 'I have become your enemy, because I tell you the truth';[14] and a certain poet, expressing a proverb of the pagan world, writes: 'Indulgence makes friends, truthfulness enemies.'[15] Now, as to the directive that we should not eat the flesh of the lamb raw nor boiled, we are to understand that we should not interpret Holy Writ—which is truly the flesh of the Lamb[16]—merely in an historical sense as the Jews do, and digest its meat raw. Nor, on the other hand, should we interpret it as do the heretics, who with their allegories and nebulous explanations turn it into perverted dogma, tear out its very sinews, extract the life-blood of its truth, and smother it with figurative obscurities. Rather, let us understand Holy Writ, historically, yes, just as it is written; however, let us fire

10 Cf. Exod. 12.8, 9.
11 Cf. 1 Cor. 5.8.
12 Matt. 16.6.
13 Cf. Matt. 16.12.
14 Cf. Gal. 4.16; cf. *Against the Pelagians* 1.26, PL 23.543(723).
15 Terence, *'Andria'* 1.1.41; cf. *Commentary on Galatians* 4.16, PL 26.409(462).
16 Cf. Homily 55 on Ps. 145, p. 396; 57 on Ps. 147, p. 410.

it well in the flame of the Holy Spirit and unfold with spiritual discernment whatever in it seems incongruous or obscure when taken literally.

'You shall eat it with its head and shanks and inner organs.'[17] To me, the head seems to be that of the Lamb, written of in St. John's Gospel: 'In the beginning was the Word, and the Word was with God; and the Word was God He was in the beginning with God';[18] the shanks represent the human nature that He deigned to assume for our salvation. Another interpretation, however, is also possible. The head may be taken to signify spiritual understanding; the shanks, historical narrative; the inner organs are whatever lies hidden within the letter, whatever is not perceived on the surface, but is brought to light by exegetes only after they have well considered it in painstaking investigation. What was considered vile and unseemly may, as a result, be found vital. What, for example, can be more improper in Holy Writ than that Osee should be commanded to take a harlot for wife; Juda lie with Thamar, his daughter-in-law; David defile Bersabee with adultery; Selom,[19] the son of Juda, waste his seed on the ground lest he beget children?[20] If these things are to be taken literally, are they not to be condemned and laughed to scorn by the heathens and certain unbelievers, as if they were the dunghill of Scripture? If you should shake them out and examine them, however, if you should cleanse and refine them in the fire of the Holy Spirit, they turn into nourishment for the soul, and that which was thought contemptible is discovered to be a divine mystery.

'None of it must be kept beyond the next morning; whatever is left over in the morning shall be burned up.'[21] We are not to save any of the flesh of the lamb for the future world;

17 Cf. Exod. 12.9.
18 John 1.1, 2.
19 Onan; cf. Gen. 38.8-10; cf. Letter 123.13, PL 22.1054(909); *Against Jovinian* 1.20, PL 23.249(269).
20 Cf. Homily 80 on the Gospel of Mark 9.1-7, p. 165.
21 Exod. 12.10.

we are to eat as much as we can here. If there are strong things in it, such as the Church's dogma on the Trinity, the Resurrection, the soul, the angels, and other matters of this kind, we should not argue about them and cling to opinions based on distorted interpretations and pound them to pieces; but state them exactly as the strong doctrine that they are. If anything, moreover, should escape us merely because we are human, and if we should not be able to eat of the flesh of the lamb, we must know that in the future world the doctrine of the Holy Spirit will be made known to us, and we shall feed upon it.

'This is how you are to eat it: with your loins girt, sandals on your feet and your staff in hand, you shall eat like those who are in flight. It is the Passover of the Lord God.'[22] Up to this point, we have been told what meats we are to eat of the lamb; now, the manner in which we are to eat it is prescribed. 'With your loins girt,' Scripture says, and to the apostles Christ gives the command: 'Let your loins be girt about and your lamps burning.'[23] John, too, wears a leathern girdle about his loins;[24] and there was nothing soft or effeminate in Elias, but every bit of him was hard and virile[25] (he certainly was a shaggy man); he, too, is described as having worn a girdle of leather about his loins.[26] If we intend, therefore, to eat the flesh of the lamb, we must mortify our loins, the works of the flesh, and destroy in ourselves what Job said of the devil: 'Behold the strength in his loins, and his vigor in the sinews of his belly.'[27] We must not permit the flesh to lust against the spirit,[28] but, with the spirit, mortify the deeds of the flesh and, thus purified, enjoy the flesh of the lamb.

That you may understand, moreover, why anyone who

22 Exod. 12.11.
23 Luke 12.35; cf. Letter 22.11, PL 22.401(96).
24 Cf. Mark 1.6.
25 Cf. Homily 42 on Ps. 127, p. 320.
26 Cf. 4 Kings 1.8; cf. Letter 130.4, PL 22.1108(978).
27 Job 40.16; cf. Letter 22.10, PL 22.400(95); 130.10, PL 22.1116(987).
28 Cf. Gal. 5.17.

renders his wife her due is not free to give himself to prayer[29] nor eat of the flesh of the lamb, remember that Moses receives the command that for three days he is to purify the people who were about to approach Mount Horeb;[30] and that when David had come to Achimelech, the priest asks him if his young men are clean, and he answers that they have been clean from yesterday and the day before.[31] If, indeed, the bread of proposition could not be eaten by those who had had contact with their wives, how much more the Bread that comes down from heaven cannot be touched and violated by those who shortly before have clung to them in conjugal embraces! We do not say this to condemn marriage, but to prove that we must not be defiled from works of the flesh when we are about to eat the flesh of the Lamb.

In regard to the following words: 'With sandals on your feet and your staff in hand,' the command is that, as long as we are treading our way through the desert of this world, we must be shod with the sandals of peace, lest somewhere in the wilderness a scorpion or a snake steal upon us, lest the serpent should lie in wait for our heel.[32] If, perchance, the serpent should rise up against us, we should have a staff in our hands and smite the snake and exclaim: 'Your rod and your staff give me courage.'[33] Now, grasp the mystical meaning of Holy Writ. As long as we are walking through the wilderness, it is necessary that we wear sandals to cover and protect our feet, but when we shall have entered the Land of Promise, we shall hear with Jesus, the son of Nave: 'Remove your sandals from your feet, for the place upon which you are standing is holy.'[34] When, therefore, we enter into the kingdom of heaven, we shall have no need of sandals nor for protection

29 Cf. 1 Cor. 7.3-7.
30 Cf. Exod. 19.15; cf. Letter 48.15, PL 22.505-506(227).
31 Cf. 1 Kings 24.4, 5; cf. *Against Jovinian* 1.20, PL 23.249(269).
32 Cf. *Commentary on Isaia* 20, PL 24.260(301).
33 Cf. Ps. 22.4.
34 Jos. 5.15; cf. *Against Jovinian* 1.21, PL 23.250-251(271).

against this world, but—to give you a new thought—we shall follow the Lamb that has been slain for us. It is of us that John says: 'These are they who were not defiled with women; for they are virgins. These follow the Lamb wherever he goes.'[35]

35 Apoc. 14.4; cf. *Against Jovinian* 1.40, PL 23.281(305); Letter 48.10, PL 22.500(220).

HOMILY 92

ON PSALM 41(42)

To the Neophytes

I HAVE GONE THROUGH THE ENTIRE PSALTER with considerable care and nowhere do I find that the sons of Core have sung anything sad.[1] There is always the note of joy and happiness in their songs, always scorn for the worldly and the passing, ardent longing for the heavenly and the eternal. Their spirit is, therefore, in keeping with the significance of their name for which the Latin is *calvities,* or 'baldness.' Because our Lord was crucified and buried in the place called Calvary, those who believe in His cross and Resurrection are sons of Core, the sons of Calvary. Upon this Calvary, our Lord, the true Eliseus, as He ascends into the kingdom of heaven after the Resurrection, is scorned by the Jews, but bears devour His mockers.[2] Brief, but this is sufficient for the title; now let us turn back to the opening words of the psalm.

'As the hind longs for the running waters, so my soul longs for you, O God.' It is the hind's nature to have no fear of snakes. Actually, with the breath of their nostrils, they draw them out of their holes[3] in order to kill and maul them to pieces. If the poison from the snakes begins to burn within them, however, although it cannot kill them, it fills them with

1 Cf. Homily 16 on Ps. 83, p. 118; 17 on Ps. 84, p. 127.
2 Cf. 4 Kings 2.23, 24.
3 Cf. Homily 51 on Ps. 140, p. 372; 30 on Ps. 103, p. 226.

a burning thirst. Then it is that they long for the cool pure waters of the brook to quench the fire of the parching poison. Now just as the deer—and we as well—long for the running waters, so even do our young deer, who, in withdrawing from Egypt and from the world, have put Pharao to death in their own waters and have destroyed in baptism his entire army. After slaying the devil, their hearts ardently long for the running waters of the Church, the Father, the Son, and the Holy Spirit. In Jeremia, there is witness to the Father as fountain: 'They have forsaken me, the source of living waters; they have dug themselves cisterns, broken cisterns, that hold no water.'[4] In another place in Scripture, we read appropriately of the Son: 'They have forsaken the fountain of wisdom';[5] and of the Holy Spirit, in turn: 'He who drinks of the water that I will give him, the water shall become in him a fountain of water, springing up unto life everlasting.'[6] The evangelist explains, at once, that the Savior said this of the Holy Spirit.[7] From the testimony of these texts, it is established beyond doubt that the three fountains of the Church constitute the mystery of the Trinity.

These are the waters for which the soul of the believer longs, the waters for which the soul of the baptized yearns, when he cries: 'Athirst is my soul for God, the living fountain.'[8] No faint desire has his been to see God, but, totally consumed with the vehemence of his thirst, he has yearned with all the ardor of his being. The neophytes, before they received baptism, were wont to complain to one another: 'When shall I go and behold the face of God?'[9] Behold, their petition has been fulfilled! They have come and they have stood in the presence of God; they have come before the altar

4 Jer. 2.13; cf. Letter 108.22, PL 22.898(715).
5 Cf. Bar. 3.12.
6 Cf. John 4.13, 14; John 7.38, 39.
7 Cf. John 7.39.
8 Cf. Ps. 41.3.
9 Ps. 41.3.

and have beheld the mystery of the Savior.[10] No one deserves to gaze upon this sight except those who, from the depths of their heart and conscience, cry out in mournful contrition: 'My tears have been my bread day and night.'[11] During the whole time of Lent, they have been free for prayer and fasting, they have slept in sackcloth and ashes, seeking future life in the confession of their sins. Because they have poured forth tears in sorrow and lament, it is said to them: 'Those that sow in tears shall reap rejoicing';[12] 'Blessed are they who mourn, for they shall be comforted.'[13]

When the devil continued to taunt them spitefully with: 'Where is your God?'[14] they speak up boldly now that they have received the Body of Christ and have been reborn in the life-giving waters,[15] and repeat: 'I shall go over into the place of the wonderful tabernacle, even to the house of God.'[16] The house of God is the Church, the wonderful tabernacle, for in it abide cries of joy and thanksgiving and all the sounds of festival. Indeed, the angels in heaven and all the hosts rejoice because now our brethren have merited to receive faith and to attain life everlasting. If over one sinner doing penance, and over one sickly lamb that the shepherd has carried back on his shoulders, the angels are glad and rejoice, how much more will the whole kingdom of heaven exult at the sight of so many brethren cleansed and reborn in life-giving waters, purified from the ancient stain of sin and made ready for their heavenly dwelling?

You, who now have put on Christ, and who, under our guidance, by the word of God are lifted out of the abysmal waters of this world like so many tiny fish, meditate as follows. In

---

10 Cf. Homily 36 on Ps. 109, pp. 274-275; 55 on Ps. 145, p. 396; 57 on Ps. 147, p. 410.
11 Cf. Ps. 41.4.
12 Ps. 125.5; cf. Letter 122.1, PL 22.1040(892).
13 Matt. 5.5.
14 Ps. 41.4.
15 Cf. Homily 84 on Mark 13.32, 33; 14.3-6, p. 190.
16 Cf. Ps. 41.5.

us, the nature of things has been changed. Fish that have been taken out of the sea die, but the apostles have fished for us and have drawn us out of the sea of this world that, from dead, we might become alive. As long as we were in the world, our eyes were fixed upon the abyss, our life was spent in the mire. After we were snatched from the billows, we began to see the sun, to look up at the true light and, troubled in the presence of so much joy, we say to our soul: 'Hope in God! For I shall again be thanking him, in the presence of my savior and my God.'[17] 'So will I remember you from the land of the Jordan and of Hermon, from the modest hill. Deep calls upon deep.'[18] From the land of the Jordan—that is, from the river in which our Lord was baptized, and from Hermon—from the malediction of this world (for Hermon means anathema),[19] and from the little hill of this world (for even the saintliest of men, while he is abiding in this world, is not on a grand and lofty mountain, but a common lowly hill), let us call upon the Lord, probe the depths of His sacred writings, and be guided in our interpretation by other testimonies from Holy Writ. Whatever we cannot fathom in the deep recesses of the Old Testament, we shall penetrate and explain from the depth of the New Testament in the roar of God's cataracts—His prophets and apostles. All the breakers of the Lord, and His billows, and the swiftly flowing stream that gladdens the city of God,[20] have passed over us.

17 Ps. 41.6.
18 Cf. Ps. 41.7, 8.
19 Cf. Homily 45 on Ps. 132, p. 339.
20 Cf. Ps. 45.5.

HOMILY 93

ON EASTER SUNDAY

I HAVE NOT THE POWER to bring forth in words what I conceive in my mind, nor does my tongue give full expression to the joy that is in my heart. It is not my travail only, this longing to share with you my inmost feelings, but you, too, are suffering with me, for the joy of your souls is greater than words can convey. To me, it seems that this day is brighter beyond all other days. A brighter sun has begun to shine upon the world. The stars, too, and all the elements rejoice, and those that had withdrawn their proper light during the Lord's Passion and had fled, refusing to look upon their Creator crucified, now fulfill their appointed duty and are in attendance upon Him, the Victor, as He rises from the dead in the brilliance of their glow (if one may so speak). Heaven believes; earth believes; and the great net that has been cast for the whole world has not been able to contain the Jews.

'This is the day the Lord has made; let us be glad and rejoice in it.'[1] Just as the Virgin Mary, the Mother of the Lord, holds the first place among all women,[2] even so, this day is the mother of days among all days. I am going to tell you something new,[3] supported, moreover, by the words of Holy Writ: this day is both one from seven and one beyond seven. This is the day that is called the octave and is the reason why

1 Ps. 117.24.
2 Cf. *Commentary on Sophonia,* Prologue, PL 25.1337(671-672).
3 Cf. Homily 13 on Ps. 80, p. 101; 18 on Ps. 86, p. 144; 23 on Ps. 95, p. 187; 45 on Ps. 132, p. 336.

certain psalms are entitled, 'for the octave.' This is the day on which the synagogue comes to an end and the Church is born. This is the day in the number of which eight souls were preserved in the Ark of Noe,[4] and: 'Its counterpart, the Church,' says Peter, 'now saves you.'[5] This is the day of which Ecclesiastes admonishes: 'Make seven or eight portions.'[6] These are the eight steps by which, in Ezechiel, we ascend the temple of God. This is the eighth day the mystical meaning of which, with the faith of all nations in Christ, inspired the opening words of the eighth psalm: 'O Lord, our Lord, how glorious is your name over all the earth!'[7]

Why do I repeat symbol after symbol without end, even though I do not have the day that it would require if I wanted to expound upon all the mysteries enshrined in this feast? This much I shall say, that the solemnity of this day has replaced altogether the obligation of the Sabbath, according to the ancient tradition of the Jewish people. They performed no servile work on the Sabbath; on the Lord's day, the day of the Resurrection, we perform no servile work, for we are not slaves to vice and sin. 'Everyone who commits sin is a slave of sin.'[8] They did not leave their homes nor do we leave the house of Christ, for we are in the Church. They did not enkindle a fire on the day of the Sabbath; we, on the contrary, enkindle within ourselves the fire of the Holy Spirit, and burn out all the disease of sin. The Lord says of this fire: 'I have come to cast fire upon the earth, and what will I but that it be kindled?'[9] It is the Lord's yearning desire that it glow within us and that, according to the apostle,[10] we be fervent in the Holy Spirit so that the charity of Christ may not grow cold in us. On the Sabbath day, the Jews do not make a

4 Cf. Gen. 7.14; cf. *Against the Luciferians* 22, PL 23.185(195).
5 Cf. 1 Peter 3.21; cf. *Against Jovinian* 1.17, PL 23.247(267).
6 Eccles. 11.2.
7 Ps. 8.2.
8 John 8.34.
9 Luke 12.49.
10 Cf. Rom. 12.11.

journey, for they have lost Him who said: 'I am the way';[11] but we say: 'Happy are they whose way is blameless, who walk in the law of the Lord,'[12] and again: 'The way of truth I have chosen';[13] 'Make me understand the way of your precepts.'[14] They crowned the Lord with thorns; but we, as precious stones, shall become the crown of our Lord. A diadem adorns the head of the emperor of this world; we are set upon the head of our King so that the Head may adorn us. They have rejected Christ, but accept the Antichrist;[15] we have recognized and acknowledged the humble Son of God, that afterwards we may have the triumphal Savior. In the end, our he-goat will be immolated before the altar of the Lord; their buck, the Antichrist, spit upon and cursed, will be cast into the wilderness. Our thief enters Paradise with the Lord; their thief, a homicide and blasphemer, dies in his sin. For them, Barabbas is released; for us, Christ is slain.

For these many reasons, let us sing together in one harmonious voice: 'This is the day the Lord has made; let us be glad and rejoice in it.'[16] Today, Christ, with the thief, has removed the flaming sword[17] and reopened the gate of Paradise that no one has been able to storm. Today, He has said to the angels: 'Open to me the gates of justice; I will enter them and give thanks to the Lord.'[18] Once this gate has been opened, it is never again closed to those who believe. From the time that our Lord suffered His Passion down to the present day, this gate has been closed and been opened; closed to sinners and unbelievers, opened to the just and to believers. Through this gate, Peter entered, and Paul, and all the saints and martyrs; through this gate daily the souls of the

11 John 14.6.
12 Ps. 118.1.
13 Ps. 118.30.
14 Ps. 118.27.
15 Cf. *Commentary on Isaia* 23.18, PL 24.205(232).
16 Ps. 117.24.
17 Cf. Gen. 3.24; cf. Homily 86 on Luke 16.19-31, p. 209; cf. Letter 39.3(a), PL 22.469(181); 60.3, PL 22.591(333).
18 Ps. 117.19.

just enter from every part of the world. There are two gates: the gate of Paradise and the gate of the Church. Through the gate of the one, we enter the gate of the other. We must conduct our lives in such a way that we may never be driven out of this house and cast forth to be devoured by beasts, as the prophet cries out in dread: 'Deliver not up to beasts, the soul that trusts in thee.'[19] Behold, our Lord is standing at the gate of Paradise; He is saying to us who are gathered here together in His house: 'This is the gate of the Lord, enter it ye just.'[20] Every saint enters by this gate, no matter how much the devil tries to prevent him, no matter how much the devil accuses him (since he is 'the accuser of our brethren,'[21] he is the revengeful enemy). The one-hundred-twenty-sixth psalm says: The faithful servant 'shall not be put to shame when he contends with enemies at the gate.'[22]

19 Cf. Ps. 73.19.
20 Cf. Ps. 117.20.
21 Apoc. 12.10.
22 Cf. Ps. 126.5.

HOMILY 94

ON EASTER SUNDAY

THE ENTIRE PSALTER SINGS in prophecy of our Lord since, indeed, it is He who 'has the key of David, he who opens and no one shuts, and who shuts and no one opens';[1] but especially does the psalm that has just been read, the one-hundred-seventeenth, herald the mystery of His Resurrection. As our Lord ascends to the Father in triumph, He issues commands to the angels saying: 'Open to me the gates of justice; I will enter them and give thanks to the Lord.'[2] These are the gates of which in the twenty-third psalm the angels were speaking while they were preparing for the entrance of the Lord: 'Lift up, O gates, your lintels; reach up, you ancient portals, that the king of glory may come in!'[3] Aptly are the gates commanded to lift up high and raise aloft their portals, since, in accordance with the dispensation and mystery of the flesh, and in conformity with the victory of the cross, He reenters heaven mightier than He had come down upon earth.

'This gate is the Lord's; the just shall enter it.'[4] Through this gate,[5] Peter has entered, and Paul, and all the apostles and martyrs, and today the saints continue to go in; through this gate, the thief was the first to pass with the Lord. Have faith, therefore, and be hopeful for your own entrance. The psalm does not say that the apostles and martyrs, but that

1 Apoc. 3.7.
2 Ps. 117.19.
3 Ps. 23.7, 9.
4 Ps. 117.20.
5 Cf. Homily 93 on Easter Sunday, p. 249.

'the just shall enter it.' Any man who lives in justice and has merited to be among the Lord's loving servants shall enter through this gate, for the Lord does not seek the blood of those who bear witness to Him, but the faith through which they shed it. If our faith is strong enough for martyrdom, then, it is credited to us.

O truly unhappy Jews, O truly wretched and pitiable Jews, who failed to realize that the stone, which Isaia promised would be laid in the foundations of Sion[6] and would unite both people, was the Lord Savior, the Son of God! That is the stone you rejected when you were building the congregation of the Lord and were the custodians of the sacred rites of His Temple. Rejected by you, He has become the cornerstone; and the first Church, gathered from among the Jews and the believers from the nations, He has united into one flock and into one divine mystery. 'By the Lord has this been done; it is wonderful in our eyes.'[7] It is wonderful that we who, before the Passion of the Lord were without covenant and without law, should be adopted into the sonship of God, and that while the former loincloth was disintegrating and falling away,[8] God should weave for Himself another, prepare for Himself another people.[9] You have the Scriptures, and we, the understanding of the Scriptures; you read the Books, we believe in Him of whom the Books are written; you cling to the pages, we to the meaning in the pages; you fold together the skins of dead animals, we possess the life-giving Spirit. What can be more wonderful than a mystery of this kind? What is more blessed than this day on which the Lord has died for the Jews and has come back to life for us; this day on which the synagogue has set and the Church has risen; this day on which He has raised us up with Himself into His heavenly kingdom to live and dwell, and fulfilled what He promised in

6 Cf. Isa. 28.16.
7 Ps. 117.23.
8 Cf. Jer. 13.7-12.
9 Cf. Homily 26 on Ps. 98, p. 205.

the Gospel: 'And I, if I be lifted up from the earth, will draw all things to myself.'[10]

Truly: 'This is the day the Lord has made; let us be glad and rejoice in it.'[11] The Lord has made all days, of course; but other days may belong as well to the Jews, and the heretics, too; they may even belong to the heathens. The Lord's day, however, the day of the Resurrection, the day of Christians, is our day. It is called the Lord's day because on this day the Lord ascended to the Father as Victor; but when the heathens call it the day of the sun, we are most happy to acknowledge their title, for today has risen: 'the sun of justice with its healing wings.'[12] Does the sun really have wings? Let the Jews answer,[13] and those who, like them, accept only a literal interpretation of Holy Writ. We say: Whoever has been under the wings of this Sun who has said in the Gospel: 'How often would I have gathered thy children together, as a hen gathers her young under her wings, but thou wouldst not!'[14] shall be safe from the devil-hawk, safe under the great wings of that mighty eagle in Ezechiel,[15] and all the wounds of his sins shall be healed.

To prove, moreover, that this psalm is actually written of the Lord, the boys who, in the Gospel, raised aloft their branches as the Savior entered Jerusalem and kept on crying: 'Hosanna in the highest! Blessed is he who comes in the name of the Lord! Hosanna in the highest!'[16] borrowed[17] these versicles from Psalm 117. Hosanna, moreover, is the Hebrew for: 'O Lord, grant salvation!'[18] The Jews, therefore, im-

---

10 John 12.32.
11 Ps. 117.24.
12 Cf. Mal. 3.20; cf. *Against Jovinian* 2.25, PL 23.336(365).
13 Cf. Homily 13 on Ps. 80, p. 100; 25 on Ps. 97, pp. 201-202; 57 on Ps. 147, p. 408.
14 Matt. 23.37.
15 Cf. Ezech. 17.3, 7.
16 Cf. Mark 11.9, 10.
17 Cf. *Commentary on Matthew* 23.39, PL 26.182(192); *Commentarioli on ps.* 117.25.
18 Ps. 117.25.

patient beyond endurance, tried to silence these children to whom the Lord referred in Isaia: 'Look at me and the children whom the Lord has given me.'[19] Since the seniors and the elders of the Jews are silent, and the Pharisees, too, in the gnawing of envious malice, children cry out and acclaim Christ. Even if they had been silent, the very stones would have shouted—the Gentiles of whom it is written in the Gospel: 'The Lord is able out of these stones to raise up children to Abraham.'[20] These stones typify us who were hard of heart at one time, but now believe in Christ Jesus and have been adopted among the children of Abraham, the children of God Almighty. To whom be glory forever and ever. Amen.

19 Isa. 8.18.
20 Cf. Matt. 3.9.

HOMILY 95

ON OBEDIENCE

NOTHING IS SO PLEASING TO GOD as obedience. Ham was cursed, and down through the ages his curse continues: 'Seed of Chanaan and not of Juda,'[1] because he did not obey his father. On the other hand, Sem, who did obey his father, retained his blessing for all generations. I tell you, therefore, that it is not for sons to judge their fathers. No one goes to a teacher to instruct him; you have come to me in order that I might teach you your letters. If I should write for you and say: You write now, just as I do, surely, you would have to imitate the one whom you have chosen for your teacher. Is somebody or other a man of skill? Straightway, the pupil rushes over to the more skillful teacher. Why do I say all this? That we may render obedience to our fathers. Those who do not obey their fathers, do not obey God, for the Lord says: 'He who rejects you, rejects me.'[2] He who rejects the apostles, rejects Christ; he who rejects his father, rejects Christ who is in him.

I say this because, for us who are here, obedience is the highest and the only virtue. If you should fast day and night and pray without ceasing; if you should go about in sackcloth and ashes; and if you should do nothing else except what is prescribed in the rule, and look upon yourself as a wise man, yet refuse obedience to your Abbot, you have lost all your virtues. One act of obedience is more meritorious than all

1 Cf. Dan. 13.56.
2 Luke 10.16.

other virtuous acts put together. Fasting or continence, unless you are diligently on guard, provoke pride in you, and pride is the enemy of God. There is nothing so detestable to Him. The man who does not obey is not motivated from holiness, but from pride, for it goes without saying that he who does not obey thinks himself better than the one to whom he refuses submission.

Candidly, I say to you, God hates all sin without exception: lying, perjury, theft, robbery, adultery, fornication; and if anyone should be caught in any of these acts, he would not be able to raise his eyes, and we would look upon him as one accursed. Yet, the proud man commits a far worse sin than adultery, and still we continue to converse with him. The fornicator may say, My flesh overcame me; youth was too much for me. I am not advocating that you yield to such a sin, for God hates that as well as any other; but, in comparing evils, I maintain that whatever other wrong a man may commit, theft, for example, he can always find an excuse for it. What excuse does he give? I committed the theft because I was in need, I was dying from hunger, I was sick. What can the proud man say? Realize how evil pride is from the very fact that there is no excuse for it. Other vices harm only those who commit them; pride inflicts far more injury upon everyone. I am saying all this lest you consider pride a trifling sin. What, in fact, does the apostle say? 'Lest he incur the condemnation passed on the devil.'[3] The man who is puffed up with his own importance falls into the judgment of the devil. On the strength of Holy Writ, therefore, I declare: 'When God is dealing with the arrogant he is stern, but to the humble he shows kindness,'[4] so that we may shun all sin, most of all pride. There is this about pride: to itself, it always passes for wisdom. If any one of the brethren should advise a proud man: 'Brother, you must not act that way,' he thinks it be-

3 Cf. 1 Tim. 3.6; cf. Letter 76.1, PL 22.689(455).
4 Cf. Prov. 3.34, 35.

neath his dignity to listen because he considers himself a much wiser man. What does he say in his heart? 'I think I know better; do I not have to follow my own conscience? Do you think you are wiser that I?' Granted, he does not say all this in so many words; nevertheless, because he rejects the advice of his brother, he says it in his heart.

I maintain, therefore, that for a proud man to be virtuous is a contradiction; rather, he does not possess virtue, but merely its semblance. How can a man who clings to that which is contrary to God, at the same time, possess that which makes him His friend? There can be pride even in the monastery. When we fast, we think we are noble; we pray for our sins and take pride in so doing. A monk fasts for his sins and does penance; then puffs right up with pride. Is that why you fast, why you pray, why you observe rules, in order to work against God? If a monk is proud, it would be much better for him to get married. I say frankly and boldly, that it would be better for the proud man to have all the other vices (and I say this in a comparison of evils), for then he would be driven to repentance and would not despise everyone else. If, moreover, after committing sin he should do penance, certainly, he would be deserving of God's merciful compassion. The man who is proud, however, possesses in his pride the source of all other evils, and he does not do penance, for he thinks that he is in God's favor. Pride is contrary to God because it does not submit to Him; hence, the proud man considers himself just. He does not repent of his evil deeds, but glories in his sham good works.

My motive in stressing all this is to put you on your guard, that you may know yourselves and take the pitfalls of others as a warning. Our very purpose in coming to the monastery, in giving up the freedom of the world, is to accept the servitude of Christ. In the second place, I want to say a few words for the benefit of the brethren who make it a practice to dwell away from the monastery, lest their example breed inevitable pride. You have lived in the monastery; are you now satisfied to dwell ten miles away? You must not disdain the community of holy brethren. Do not think it beneath you to come into the city to the brethren. If you felt impelled to go out and see women, and found it necessary to go into the public square, rightly, you would not go. But you do not go where holy brethren gather? O you who live in the wilderness, either you are better than the brethren in the monastery, or you are worse; if you are better, come, that you may give them the good example of your life; if worse, come, that you may learn what you do not know. Pride is engendered when anyone boasts that he dwells by himself in the desert and plumes himself because he does not deign to see or visit the brethren.

I am saying this deliberately in the presence of the holy brother who is actually doing this, so that you may know that he is doing the very thing that I am condemning. Finally, there are many saintly abbots, fathers in the true sense, who are charged with the guidance of saintly souls. When they see any young men go into the desert and not return to the monastery, yielding to pride, they hasten to exert pressure and prevail upon them, not to hurt them in any way, but to destroy their pride. I say this, therefore, so that they who are living away in solitude and come to the monastery to visit the brethren may not be reproved as recalcitrant by those who live there, but approved for being humble. Let no one say of you: See, there he comes, the one who dwells in the desert because he cannot bear restraint; but instead: He comes with the intention of edifying; not of tearing down, but of putting an end to pride. See the kind of life he leads? He lives in the desert, yes, but without that honor and esteem that is the due of hermits.

Omnipotent God, grant that, by the prayers of thy saints, we, too, may be faithful to all that we have said. Magnanimity does not consist in words, but in deeds.[5] If I am saying some-

5 Cf. Homily 58 on Ps. 148, p. 419.

thing that I am unable to do myself, I say it that he who is able may do it. 'He who has ears to hear, let him hear,'[6] in Christ Jesus our Lord.

6 Matt. 11.15.

HOMILY 96

ON THE PERSECUTION OF CHRISTIANS

Time and again, we have averred that Christians always suffer[1] persecution. This world is in the power of the evil one.[2] Our adversary, the devil, rules in the world, and do we think that we shall escape persecution? Besides, what is there that is not a source of persecution to the Christian? Everything that is of the world holds endless torment for him. Is it any wonder that others persecute us if we have determined to serve Christ? Even our parents do. Everyone who does not share our beliefs, harasses and hates us. Should we be surprised if we are the object of universal malevolence? Our own body constantly afflicts us. Even if I eat ever so little, but my miserable body becomes robust, its very vigor cruelly tempts my soul. Wherever I turn, there is persecution. If I look at a woman, my eye tortures me; it craves for the destruction of my soul. If I look at riches, at gold, at silver, at possessions, whatever I see and covet, that is an attack on my soul.

Let us not imagine that the shedding of blood is the only form of martyrdom;[3] there is martyrdom in everything. Passion persecutes youth; passion wants to pour out the blood of the soul. When your soul is in peril, gathering, as it were, all its forces for the contest, then, Jesus stands at the right side of the Father and fights for His young warrior. Be assured, moreover, if there is martyrdom in time of peace, there

1 Cf. Homily 34 on Ps. 107, p. 253.
2 Cf. 1 John 5.19.
3 Cf. Letter 108.31, PL 22.905(723).

is also betrayal. Let no one say, there is no martyrdom. There is martyrdom and there is betrayal. If I, who today seem to be a monk, should abandon my state of life, I have rejected Christ. If in times of peace, I deny Him, what would I do in time of trial? I am not being tortured nor set on fire, yet I deny Christ. If I were being stretched on the rack, were burning at the stake, what would I do? The traitor under persecution is pardonable; his stripes plead in his behalf.[4] What is his plea? I wanted to fight; my flesh failed me in the death struggle; it was not my soul that yielded, but my body; my mind intended one thing; my body was forced to utter another. Yet, he really has no excuse, for there is no force that ought to overthrow the love of Christ. What does Christ say to you? You were burning in flames; you were suspended on the wooden rack; you were tortured for Me; and do you say, 'I was not able to endure the torments'? How, then, did Peter endure? Paul? The rest of the martyrs? They had bodies just as you have. O Monk, you who shirk fasting, do you think you would not shun fire?

Therefore, I repeat, there will always be martyrs; there will always be deserters. What does the apostle have to say in respect to widows who marry again? They 'are to be condemned because they have broken their first troth.'[5] He declares: 'O widow, before you promised Me that you would remain a widow, you had the power to wed. But from the moment that you avowed to devote your life to Me, you began to be Mine; if it is your desire to remarry, you are rejecting Me. It is the same with you, O Monk. Before you promised yourself to Me, you had the power to do whatever you wanted. Your own voice bound you to Me. Did I, then, compel you? Did I in any way coerce you? Were you not free? It was within your power to make the promise. You made it and you

4 Cf. *Commentary on Galatians* 1.6, 7, PL 26.343(381); *on Isaia* 22.2, PL 24.268(311).

5 1 Tim. 5.12; cf. Letter 123.3, PL 22.1048(901).

became Mine. I do not intend to give up what is My own; you do not have the liberty to release yourself from your promise. Yours it was to promise; it is not yours to release yourself. If you break your word, you are not in the same relation to Me as you were before. You were free; you were, indeed, of My household, though not in My presence;[6] you were not of My ministers; you were, nevertheless, of My family. You were not a servant, but a member of the family; you were not with Me, but you were Mine. If you have begun now to wage war against Me, if you withdraw your promise, I no longer consider you a member of the household, but a fugitive.' Now, why am I saying all this? Because it was in our power to pledge our service to God; it is not in our power to release ourselves. Did you promise? You have the reward. Did you break your promise? You pay the penalty. Either course is yours through your own will and conscience. We have said it once, and now, again, we repeat: Did you promise? You enjoy the reward. Did you refuse? You suffer the penalty. It is not mine to determine, the decision is yours; choose which you will. You have before you the road to death and the road to life; the choice is yours.

I am saying all this to you, lest any one of you harbor the illusion that he has legitimate reason to question: They who have wives, who live in cities, who are in military service, they who engage in business—in fact, the whole world is in danger, and do monks only have to struggle to be saved?[7] There is no parity between our state and theirs. They realize their own weakness and do not promise to do what they know they cannot do. They are Christians, certainly; but there is the Christian layman, the Christian businessman, the Christian soldier. Cornelius was a centurion, and he was saved. I, who am a monk, who have ceased to be a layman and have become a monk, either am saved as a monk, or I am not saved at all.

6 Cf. Homily 46 on Ps. 133, p. 343.
7 Cf. Homily 54 on Ps. 143, p. 389; Letter 58.4, 5, PL 22.582(322); 125.17, PL 22.1082(944); 9, PL 22.1077(938).

There is no middle course. If I wish to abandon the life of the monk and live out in the world, the Lord will not consider me a secular, but a renegade. It is not granted us, therefore, to abandon the way of life we have undertaken.

Someone may ask, 'What shall I do if I have sinned? And what am I going to do in this state of life, neither a secular nor a monk?' Does anyone expect to amend a sin by committing a greater sin? If you have sinned, and are established in this mode of life, do penance as a monk—not as a layman, but as a monk. Somebody may say, 'I have fled my master lest he kill me; I always have to run away.' If you really repent that you ran away, you must return to your master, God. No one should say, I am sorry because I fled, but I always have to escape. Whether we are saints or sinners, it is not permitted us to change the manner of life that we have voluntarily taken upon ourselves. If you are a saint, you are a happy monk; if you are a sinner, you are a wretched monk, but still a monk. You cannot change your state of life, even though you have lost its merit. I say this for all, and what I say to you, I say just as much for myself, lest anyone think that he has the authority to change the plan of life he has chosen by profession.

I am going to tell you something novel; by way of comparison, not prescription. Suppose that two monks have fallen, each has committed sin. One of them has admitted without any reserve that he is a layman; for example, he has married and said, I cannot endure the life, I cannot persevere as a monk. The other realizes his sin, but tells it to no one. He grieves, however, over what he has done; day and night, he entreats the Lord to have mercy upon him. I do not say that he has done well, for he has sinned; yet, in comparison to the man whose wickedness is public, he is a holy man. Why do I say that? Not, certainly, to encourage sinners and promote sinning, but I maintain that even the man who has sinned has not the right to change the state of life that he has undertaken by a voluntary promise. The Lord, however, has the power to set you and me completely free from the devil and all his entanglements.

INDICES

GENERAL INDEX

INDEX OF HOLY SCRIPTURE

(BOOKS OF THE OLD TESTAMENT)

(BOOKS OF THE NEW TESTAMENT)

THE FATHERS OF THE CHURCH SERIES

(A series of approximately 100 volumes when completed)

VOL. 1: THE APOSTOLIC FATHERS (1947)

LETTER OF ST. CLEMENT OF ROME TO THE CORINTHIANS (trans. by Glimm)
THE SO-CALLED SECOND LETTER (trans. by Glimm)
LETTERS OF ST. IGNATIUS OF ANTIOCH (trans. by Walsh)
LETTER OF ST. POLYCARP TO THE PHILIPPIANS (trans. by Glimm)
MARTYRDOM OF ST. POLYCARP (trans. by Glimm)
DIDACHE (trans. by Glimm)
LETTER OF BARNABAS (trans. by Glimm)
SHEPHERD OF HERMAS (1st printing only; trans. by Marique)
LETTER TO DIOGNETUS (trans. by Walsh)
FRAGMENTS OF PAPIAS (1st printing only; trans. by Marique)

VOL. 2: ST. AUGUSTINE (1947)

CHRISTIAN INSTRUCTION (trans. by Gavigan)
ADMONITION AND GRACE (trans. by Murray)
THE CHRISTIAN COMBAT (trans. by Russell)
FAITH, HOPE, AND CHARITY (trans. by Peebles)

VOL. 3: SALVIAN, THE PRESBYTER (1947)

GOVERNANCE OF GOD (trans. by O'Sullivan)
LETTERS (trans. by O'Sullivan)
FOUR BOOKS OF TIMOTHY TO THE CHURCH (trans. by O'Sullivan)

VOL. 4: ST. AUGUSTINE (1947)

IMMORTALITY OF THE SOUL (trans. by Schopp)
MAGNITUDE OF THE SOUL (trans. by McMahon)
ON MUSIC (trans. by Taliaferro)

ADVANTAGE OF BELIEVING (trans. by Sr. Luanne Meagher)

ON FAITH IN THINGS UNSEEN (trans. by Deferrari and Sr. Mary Francis McDonald)

VOL. 5: ST. AUGUSTINE (1948)

THE HAPPY LIFE (trans. by Schopp)

ANSWER TO SKEPTICS (trans. by Kavanagh)

DIVINE PROVIDENCE AND THE PROBLEM OF EVIL (trans. by Russell)

SOLILOQUIES (trans. by Gilligan)

VOL. 6: ST. JUSTIN MARTYR (1948)

FIRST AND SECOND APOLOGY (trans. by Falls)

DIALOGUE WITH TRYPHO (trans. by Falls)

EXHORTATION AND DISCOURSE TO THE GREEKS (trans. by Falls)

THE MONARCHY (trans. by Falls)

VOL. 7: NICETA OF REMESIANA (1949)

WRITINGS (trans. by Walsh and Monohan)

SULPICIUS SEVERUS

WRITINGS (trans. by Peebles)

VINCENT OF LERINS

COMMONITORIES (trans. by Morris)

PROSPER OF AQUITANE

GRACE AND FREE WILL (trans. by O'Donnell)

VOL. 8: ST. AUGUSTINE (1950)

CITY OF GOD, Bks. I-VII (trans. by Walsh, Zema; introduction by Gilson)

VOL. 9: ST. BASIL (1950)

ASCETICAL WORKS (trans. by Sr. M. Monica Wagner)

VOL. 10: TERTULLIAN (1950)

APOLOGETICAL WORKS (vol. 1), (trans. by Arbesmann, Sr. Emily Joseph Daly, Quain)

MINUCIUS FELIX

OCTAVIUS (trans. by Arbesmann)

VOL. 11: ST. AUGUSTINE (1951)

COMMENTARY ON THE LORD'S SERMON ON THE MOUNT WITH SEVENTEEN RELATED SERMONS (trans. by Kavanagh)

VOL. 12: ST. AUGUSTINE (1951)

LETTERS 1-82 (vol. 1), (trans. by Sr. Wilfrid Parsons)

VOL. 13: ST. BASIL (1951)

LETTERS 1-185 (vol. 1), (trans. by Deferrari and Sr. Agnes Clare Way)

VOL. 14: ST. AUGUSTINE (1952)

CITY OF GOD, Bks. VIII-XVI (trans. by Walsh and Mtr. Grace Monahan)

VOL. 15: EARLY CHRISTIAN BIOGRAPHIES (1952)

LIFE OF ST. CYPRIAN BY PONTIUS (trans. by Deferrari and Sr. Mary Magdeleine Mueller)

LIFE OF ST. AMBROSE, BISHOP OF MILAN, BY PAULINUS (trans. by Lacy)

LIFE OF ST. AUGUSTINE BY POSSIDIUS (trans. by Deferrari and Sr. Mary Magdeleine Mueller)

LIFE OF ST. ANTHONY BY ST. ATHANASIUS (trans. by Sr. Mary Emily Keenan)

LIFE OF ST. PAUL, THE FIRST HERMIT; LIFE OF ST. HILARION; LIFE OF MALCHUS, THE CAPTIVE MONK (trans. by Sr. Marie Liguori Ewald)

LIFE OF EPIPHANIUS BY ENNODIUS (trans. by Sr. Genevieve Marie Cook)

A SERMON ON THE LIFE OF ST. HONORATUS BY ST. HILARY (trans. by Deferrari)

VOL. 16: ST. AUGUSTINE (1952)—Treatises on Various Subjects:

THE CHRISTIAN LIFE, LYING, THE WORK OF MONKS, THE USEFULNESS OF FASTING (trans. by Sr. M. Sarah Muldowney)

AGAINST LYING (trans. by Jaffee)

CONTINENCE (trans. by Sr. Mary Francis McDonald)

PATIENCE (trans. by Sr. Luanne Meagher)

THE EXCELLENCE OF WIDOWHOOD (trans. by Sr. M. Clement Eagan)

THE EIGHT QUESTIONS OF DULCITIUS (trans. by Mary DeFerrari)

VOL. 17: ST. PETER CHRYSOLOGUS (1953)

SELECTED SERMONS (trans. by Ganss)

ST. VALERIAN

HOMILIES (trans. by Ganss)

VOL. 18: ST. AUGUSTINE (1953)
LETTERS 83-130 (vol. 2), (trans. by Sr. Wilfrid Parsons)

VOL. 19: EUSEBIUS PAMPHILI (1953)
ECCLESIASTICAL HISTORY, Bks. 1-5 (trans. by Deferrari)

VOL. 20: ST. AUGUSTINE (1953)
LETTERS 131-164 (vol. 3), (trans. by Sr. Wilfrid Parsons)

VOL. 21: ST. AUGUSTINE (1953)
CONFESSIONS (trans. by Bourke)

VOL. 22: ST. GREGORY OF NAZIANZEN and ST. AMBROSE (1953)
FUNERAL ORATIONS (trans. by McCauley, Sullivan, McGuire, Deferrari)

VOL. 23: CLEMENT OF ALEXANDRIA (1954)
CHRIST, THE EDUCATOR (trans. by Wood)

VOL. 24: ST. AUGUSTINE (1954)
CITY OF GOD, Bks. XVII-XXII (trans. by Walsh and Honan)

VOL. 25: ST. HILARY OF POITIERS (1954)
THE TRINITY (trans. by McKenna)

VOL. 26: ST. AMBROSE (1954)
LETTERS 1-91 (trans. by Sr. M. Melchior Beyenka)

VOL. 27: ST. AUGUSTINE (1955)—Treatises on Marriage and Other Subjects:
THE GOOD OF MARRIAGE (trans. by Wilcox)
ADULTEROUS MARRIAGES (trans. by Huegelmeyer)
HOLY VIRGINITY (trans. by McQuade)
FAITH AND WORKS, THE CREED, IN ANSWER TO THE JEWS (trans. by Sr. Marie Liguori Ewald)
FAITH AND THE CREED (trans. by Russell)
THE CARE TO BE TAKEN FOR THE DEAD (trans. by Lacy)
THE DIVINATION OF DEMONS (trans. by Brown)

VOL. 28: ST. BASIL (1955)
LETTERS 186-368 (vol. 2), (trans. by Sr. Agnes Clare Way)

VOL. 29: EUSEBIUS PAMPHILI (1955)
ECCLESIASTICAL HISTORY, Bks. 6-10 (trans. by Deferrari)

VOL. 30: ST. AUGUSTINE (1955)
LETTERS 165-203 (vol. 4), (trans. by Sr. Wilfrid Parsons)

VOL. 31: ST. CAESARIUS OF ARLES (1956)
SERMONS 1-80 (vol. 1), (trans. by Sr. Mary Magdeleine Mueller)

VOL. 32: ST. AUGUSTINE (1956)
LETTERS 204-270 (vol. 5), (trans. by Sr. Wilfrid Parsons)

VOL. 33: ST. JOHN CHRYSOSTOM (1957)
HOMILIES 1-47 (vol. 1), (trans. by Sr. Thomas Aquinas Goggin)

VOL. 34: ST. LEO THE GREAT (1957)
LETTERS (trans. by Hunt)

VOL. 35: ST. AUGUSTINE (1957)
AGAINST JULIAN (trans. by Schumacher)

VOL. 36: ST. CYPRIAN (1958)
TREATISES (trans. by Deferrari, Sr. Angela Elizabeth Keenan, Mahoney, Sr. George Edward Conway)

VOL. 37: ST. JOHN OF DAMASCUS (1958)
FOUNT OF KNOWLEDGE, ON HERESIES, THE ORTHODOX FAITH (trans. by Chase)

VOL. 38: ST. AUGUSTINE (1959)
SERMONS ON THE LITURGICAL SEASONS (trans. by Sr. M. Sarah Muldowney)

VOL. 39: ST. GREGORY THE GREAT (1959)
DIALOGUES (trans. by Zimmerman)

VOL. 40: TERTULLIAN (1959)
DISCIPLINARY, MORAL, AND ASCETICAL WORKS (trans. by Arbesmann, Quain, Sr. Emily Joseph Daly)

VOL. 41: ST. JOHN CHRYSOSTOM (1960)
HOMILIES 48-88 (vol. 2), (trans. by Sr. Thomas Aquinas Goggin)

VOL. 42: ST. AMBROSE (1961)
HEXAMERON, PARADISE, AND CAIN AND ABEL (trans. by Savage)

VOL. 43: PRUDENTIUS (1962)
POEMS (vol. 1), (trans. by Sr. M. Clement Eagan)

VOL. 44: ST. AMBROSE (1963)
THEOLOGICAL AND DOGMATIC WORKS (trans. by Deferrari)

VOL. 45: ST. AUGUSTINE (1963)
THE TRINITY (trans. by McKenna)

VOL. 46: ST. BASIL (1963)
EXEGETIC HOMILIES (trans. by Sr. Agnes Clare Way)

VOL. 47: ST. CAESARIUS OF ARLES (1964)
SERMONS 81-186 (vol. 2), (trans. by Sr. Mary Magdeleine Mueller)

VOL. 48: ST. JEROME (1964)
HOMILIES 1-59 (vol. 1), (trans. by Sr. Marie Liguori Ewald)

VOL. 49: LACTANTIUS (1964)
THE DIVINE INSTITUTES, Bks. I-VII (trans. by Sr. Mary Francis McDonald)

VOL. 50: OROSIUS (1964)
SEVEN BOOKS AGAINST THE PAGANS (trans. by Deferrari)

VOL. 51: ST. CYPRIAN (1965)
LETTERS (trans. by Sr. Rose Bernard Donna)

VOL. 52: PRUDENTIUS (1965)
POEMS (vol. 2), (trans. by Sr. M. Clement Eagan)

VOL. 53: ST. JEROME (1965)
DOGMATIC AND POLEMICAL WORKS (trans. by John N. Hritzu)

VOL. 54: LACTANTIUS (1965)
THE MINOR WORKS (trans. by Sr. Mary Francis McDonald)

VOL. 55: EUGIPPIUS (1965)
LIFE OF ST. SEVERIN (trans. by Bieler)

VOL. 56: ST. AUGUSTINE (1966)
THE CATHOLIC AND MANICHAEAN WAYS OF LIFE (trans. by Donald A. and Idella J. Gallagher)

VOL. 57: ST. JEROME (1966)
HOMILIES 60-96 (vol. 2), (trans. by Sr. Marie Liguori Ewald)